PERFORMANCE ANXIETY

A Workbook for Actors, Singers, Dancers, and Anyone Else who Performs in Public

ERIC MAISEL, Ph.D.

For Ann, as always

Senior Editor: Mark Glubke
Project Editors: Mark Wood and Ross Plotkin
Cover Design: Steve Cooley
Interior Design: Sivan Earnest
Production Manager: Hector Campbell

Copyright © 1997, 2005 by Eric Maisel, Ph.D.

First published in 2005 by Back Stage Books,
an imprint of Watson-Guptill Publications,
a division of VNU Business Media, Inc.
770 Broadway, New York, NY 10003
www.wgpub.com

The Cataloging-in-Publication data for this title is on file with the Library of Congress

Library of Congress Control Number: 2005931773

ISBN: 0-8230-8836-7 (Paperback)

This book is a revision of a title originally published by Watson-Guptill in New York in 1997 under the title *Fearless Presenting*.

Manufactured in the United States of America

First printing 2005

1 2 3 4 5 6 7 8 9 / 11 10 09 08 07 06 05

CONTENTS

PREFACE TO THE SECOND EDITION

I'm very pleased that you've found your way to this revised, updated, and expanded version of *Fearless Presenting*, renamed *The Performance Anxiety Workbook*. In this edition I've elaborated on techniques that will help you reduce and manage your experience of performance anxiety.

I've been working with creative and performing artists for more than two decades as a psychotherapist and creativity coach. I've worked with countless clients who suffer from stage fright, in all the arts disciplines; I've employed the strategies described in this book with clients and with study subjects suffering from performance anxiety; and I've shared my techniques in a variety of other settings.

Most recently I've participated as a charter member of the mental health panel involved in the nationally based Health Promotion in Schools of Music project. I'm keenly aware of the prevalence of performance anxiety as a problem and the need for sensible guidance in this area. I hope that this revised edition provides you with all the tools you need to reduce—and even eliminate—your stage fright.

I will be making the following point throughout the book but I want to make it here at the outset. Performance anxiety is the kind of problem that rears its ugly head in both straightforward and subtle ways. It can be as much a problem for a painter or a writer as for an actor or a musician. Whenever we put ourselves on the line and perform, whether in public or in the privacy of our own studio, anxiety is likely to be provoked. The performance can be just about anything: the making of a painting, the cooking of a meal for company, approaching the boss for a raise, or, yes, singing the lead in *Carmen*. So get ready for a wide-ranging discussion.

The following passage describes the journey we're obliged to make if we're to reduce our performance anxiety. The speaker is the Buddha.

"There was a man who, having taken a bath, stepped upon a wet rope, and he thought it was a snake. Horror overcame him, and he shook from fear, anticipating in his mind all the agonies caused by its venomous bite. What a relief does this man experience when he sees that it is no snake. The cause of his fright lies in his error, his ignorance, his illusion. If the true nature of the rope is recognized, his tranquility of mind will come back to him; he will feel relieved; he will be joyful and happy."

Let me begin on that optimistic note. Like the man who sees that the snake is only a rope, may you see through the shadowy threats that currently provoke performance anxiety in you. Then, one day soon, you will begin to perform joyfully and happily.

PART ONE:
Performance-Anxiety Challenges

Chapter One

RECOGNIZING PERFORMANCE ANXIETY

Welcome! For the first half of this book we're going to explore the territory of performance anxiety and get to know it intimately in all of its shapes and disguises. It'll be many pages before we get to solutions. If you want to get to solutions faster than that, please turn directly to the second half of the book. In Chapter 9, I discuss how you can handle past and future criticism, a key element in ridding yourself of the experience of performance anxiety. In Chapter 10, you'll learn detachment training, which allows you to put performances in their correct perspective. In Chapter 11, I'll introduce you to ten-second centering, a special calming tactic. In Chapter 12, I describe how you can use the Sleep Thinking Program I've developed as an additional tool. Chapters 13 and 14 outline an array of strategies you can use to manage your performance anxiety. Chapters 15 and 16 provide a long-term anxiety-management program. If you want to start with solutions, by all means dive right into the second half of the book. If you can hold off, however, I think you'll find the first half useful and rewarding. Let's get going!

HIDDEN PERFORMANCE ANXIETY

As a psychotherapist and creativity coach who works with people in the arts, I see countless clients struggling with performance anxiety, a problem they themselves often don't recognize. This may seem surprising at first glance, and in the beginning it surprised me, too. Now, two decades later, I'm convinced that the typical view of performance anxiety is far too limited. Many people suffer from it without knowing they do, and many more life situations elicit performance anxiety than we generally realize.

For every actress who is keenly aware of her anxiety before an audition, there are dozens more who flounder as they attempt to select an audition piece and who do not recognize their floundering as a special case of performance anxiety. They don't identify as symptoms of performance anxiety the feelings they're experiencing—agitation in the bookshop as they face a row of monologue books, queasy feelings of indecisiveness, fear that they'll choose a too-popular monologue or a too old-fashioned one, even a powerful desire to flee the store. Embedded in such moments is the painful anxiety that can arise in anticipation of performing.

These "hidden" cases of performance anxiety abound. A dancer may assert that she never experiences performance anxiety, but it turns out that she can't ask her teacher to recommend her to a local dance company director nor can she ask a prominent choreographer whom she knows for a special audition chance. The dancer can certainly produce reasons why it's best not to ask for the recommendation or the audition chance, but when these reasons are explored they turn out to be rationalizations masking performance anxiety. She may argue that she's not ready to audition, that her body isn't really in shape, that the choreographer will be annoyed, and so on. But her arguments do not stand up even to mild scrutiny. Something else is going on—and that something else is performance anxiety.

As I grew more attuned to the hidden signs of performance anxiety, I began to see that creative artists in all the disciplines—painters, poets, screenwriters, composers—were bothered, and sometimes even plagued, by this problem. The painter who couldn't recontact a gallery owner who'd expressed interest in him, the poet who couldn't pick up the phone and ask for a few days to turn in her writers' colony residency application, the playwright who sabotaged himself at dinner with his agent by announcing that their conversation bored him, all were victims of this hidden anxiety.

It dawned on me that many instances of creative blockage were better conceptualized as instances of performance anxiety. This point was driven home to me in the course of a conversation with the publisher of one of my books. He was describing himself as a frustrated writer—a writer manqué. I remarked that I was working on a book about anxiety that addressed the problems people face when they have to present themselves or their creative products. I suggested that many writing blocks were in fact cases of performance anxiety. Without needing me to elaborate further, he replied that that was true in his own case; he'd simply never realized it before. Creative blockage and performance anxiety felt different in the body, he continued, and it was the latter he experienced when he attempted to write.

When we begin to understand that a painter may be viewing the act of painting as a certain kind of performance, we better understand why he may come to the blank canvas with a preformed idea, which is quite different from coming with a willingness to encounter the canvas without knowing what will appear. This is analogous to the difference between giving a speech for which one can prepare and tackling the question-and-answer period after the speech, which for many public speakers is the more frightening part; or the difference between a theatrical performance for which one can rehearse and an improvised performance.

- *Do you have the sense that performance anxiety may be affecting you in "hidden" ways?*

_____

_____

- *Playing detective, can you identify some of these hidden instances of performance anxiety in your life?*

_____

_____

_____

_____

_____

[I suggest that you keep a special notebook or journal in which you answer or expand upon these questions and the other questions I'll be presenting. You may also use the blank pages in the back of this workbook.]

THE TERRITORY OF PERFORMANCE ANXIETY

The territory that interests us is a large one. It includes the performance anxiety we associate with musical, theatrical, and dance performances. It also includes business situations, cases of creative blockage, and many other presentation situations. It's a territory that includes the performers named below (see box), but also tens of millions of people, professional and amateur performers and nonperformers alike. Indeed, when the general public is surveyed about their fears and phobias, invariably heading the list, before a fear of flying or a fear of snakes or any other simple or complex phobia, is a fear of public speaking.

Our territory includes people whose experience of performance anxiety ranges anywhere from mild to severe. It also includes a great number of people who regularly avoid performing, including professionals in whose best interests it is to perform. Because they want to avoid the experience of anxiety, they make it their business to avoid performance situations. It's especially for them that the issue of performance anxiety remains a hidden one.

IN THE SPOTLIGHT
Getting up in front of an audience and having the spotlight turned our way is apparently one of our greatest fears—even for those who have an exhibitionist streak in them. Consider these names from the performing arts who have wrestled with stage fright.

Richard Burton	Gertrude Lawrence	Estelle Parsons
Maria Callas	Frederic March	Luciano Pavarotti
Enrico Caruso	Anna Moffo	Maureen Stapleton
Pablo Casals	Laurence Olivier	Carly Simon
Franco Corelli		

Some performances are easy to avoid, others very difficult. It's easy not to telephone a literary agent or a talent agent. It's much more difficult to cancel your Carnegie Hall recital. It's easy not to attend a writers' conference where you might have to engage editors in one-on-one conversation. It's much harder to refuse to return your editor's call if you are under contract. Thus our territory includes both the performance anxiety you feel before making a presentation and the performance anxiety you would feel if you faced making the presentation you're avoiding.

- *Do you tend to avoid performing because of performance anxiety?*

_____

_____

- *Do you avoid it only sometimes or do you avoid it as a rule?*

_____

_____

If you avoid performance situations, you won't experience performance anxiety. So, paradoxically, it follows that some of the severest cases of performance anxiety produce no symptoms at all. That is, people simply don't write their novel, don't practice their instrument, don't audition for roles, don't date, don't state their opinions at work. They may look calm and confident but only because their anxiety has been eliminated through avoidance. They resemble the person with a fear of flying who is perfectly calm on the ground and can even talk about flying with insight and enthusiasm, knowing that he or she will never, ever board a plane.

Even someone like an actor whose life revolves around performing may avoid performing. An actor may read about a particular audition, experience anticipatory anxiety (without realizing that he's growing anxious), and decide not to audition, rationalizing away his avoidance by saying, "Oh, I don't think I'm right for that role," "I'm sure that part's pre-cast," or "That director's never liked me." This is another classic instance where the sufferer has no idea that anxiety is *the* issue.

It bears repeating that few people realize the extent to which performance anxiety operates in all areas of their life, including their creative life. Not only are they regularly unaware of how it prevents them from approaching talent agents, literary agents, editors, supervisors, directors, producers, and gallery owners, but they may be equally unaware of how it prevents them from manifesting their creative potential. Because creating can feel like a performance, and since the creation is eventually going to be offered to the public and evaluated by the public, performance anxiety regularly rears its head.

For example, many artists work more mechanically, with an emphasis on technique, correct ideas, formula, and general safety, than they really want to. They do this because doing otherwise would feel dangerous and produce too many anxious feelings. Thus an actor may be reluctant to get too deeply into a role or a musician may be reluctant to interpret a piece too personally out of fear of losing control, gaining unwanted attention, or provoking criticism. Likewise, safety-minded visual artists may discover that they can't move toward abstraction or realism, even though they feel pulled in that direction; and a safety-minded sales manager may avoid presenting a novel sales strategy out of fear that his idea will look foolish.

- *In the creative work that you do, do you see a connection between performance anxiety and your unwillingness to work deeply or explore new directions?*

_____

_____

_____

_____

INSTANCES OF PERFORMANCE ANXIETY

Let's look at a few thumbnail sketches of people learning how to recognize the presence of performance anxiety in their lives.

- An artist-therapist began to see that her reluctance to show her paintings to gallery owners and even to friends and her reluctance to present art-therapy case material at conferences were related phenomena—related in that she felt performance anxiety in both situations. Slowly she began to recognize the symptoms of that anxiety, especially the shallow breathing that accompanied each episode. She also began to recognize the sorts of internal messages that contributed to the anxiety, especially "It's not good enough" (about her paintings and her presentations) and "I'm not good enough."

- An actress grew aware in therapy that her hypochondria, fear, and general irresolution were anxiety manifestations. She began to notice that free-floating anxiety was also manifesting itself at auditions, in acting classes, in her interactions with directors, and in her unwillingness to audition for certain roles. She especially shied away from roles where the character had to appear "larger than life," as one of the ways her anxiety manifested itself was as chronic shyness and her unwillingness to "strut her stuff."

- A teacher who regularly worked until midnight preparing her lessons and who always came into class overprepared, nevertheless still never *felt* prepared. It turned out that because she treated teaching as a performance for which she needed a perfect script, she never felt free to improvise, relax, or "just let kids discuss things" in her class. Once she realized this, she began to make more modest preparations, to interact more with her students, and to enjoy teaching more.

- A musician procrastinated for many months about selecting the music she wanted to sing in her café act. What was the right mix of ballads and up-tempo tunes? What songs would her accompanist handle best? Would club

DEBILITATING PAROXYSMS

Fred Silver explained in Auditioning for the Musical Theatre: *"There is a vast difference between the mild anticipatory nervousness that is a healthy part of the performance process and that shows that you care enough to want to give it your best shot and the debilitating paroxysms of fear that can immobilize a performer."*

owners who'd expressed an interest in her like her choices? If the set was crafted for just one club, would it be right for other clubs? If it wasn't right for other clubs, did that mean that she needed to put together different sets right from the beginning? And on and on it went. It gradually became clear to her that her many doubts represented not a set of actual problems to be solved but rather her anxiety about performing; and this despite the fact that she never experienced anxiety while onstage. Given the chance to doubt herself beforehand, she freely did so; faced with an audience, she stopped doubting herself and performed with great confidence.

The experience of performing is more than mildly disturbing for a great many people. To take just a pair of examples, in a 1987 survey of 2,212 professional classical musicians, twenty-four percent complained of suffering from significant performance anxiety. In a more recent survey of ninety-four classical musicians, fifteen reported suffering from severe performance anxiety. In informal discussions with performers, as many as eighty or ninety percent complain of suffering from significant performance anxiety.

- A photographer, bold enough to pose subjects outdoors in the nude, nevertheless experienced performance anxiety in her sales clerk job with respect to personnel reviews and even simple conversations with her supervisor. Toward society and its norms she confidently rebelled, but toward her critical supervisor she felt meek and incompetent. In exploring the contours of her Southern upbringing, it became apparent that she had over-learned deference, politeness, and other social niceties and had acquired a keen sense of her family's inferior position in the world. As an artist she had somehow managed to shed that baggage and could act in socially nonconforming ways, but as a department store clerk she could not. At work she was a "good girl" again, anxious to please, worried about appearances, and nervous about being found wanting in her performance.

- A singer expressed puzzlement that she sounded much worse when she performed publicly than when she practiced, and worse yet when she auditioned. She blamed her shortcomings on several factors: starting as a singer later in life than her peers, studying with a teacher who harmed her with his ideas and harshly criticized her, not having enough time to devote to her singing career, and so on. Still, none of her reasons quite explained why her singing deteriorated when she moved from private practice to public performance. When asked to examine concretely the differences between her singing in private and in public, she discovered that she was losing two or three notes at each end of her range when she performed in public. That helped locate the problem in the territory of performance anxiety, where it properly belonged.

- A painter in his late sixties, after forty years of professional painting, still wasn't satisfied that he'd found a distinctive style. He presented as one issue his inability to do an abstract painting. He claimed to love abstract painting and had even shared a studio with one of America's preeminent abstract painters, whose work he revered. But he himself could only produce paintings based on preconceived images. In session I invited him to attempt a quick, abstract sketch, and the failed attempt revealed the depth of his anxiety.

Instead of playing with the crayons as a child might and enjoying himself or unselfconsciously attacking the page as a bold abstract painter might, he drew tentatively and peppered me with questions like "What's the point?" "What are you looking for?" and "Is this what you want?" It became apparent to both of us that improvisation provoked anxiety in him. In no other session did he manifest such evident anxiety, nor did any session disturb him as much as this one.

• A playwright learned over time to identify his ineffective ways of "performing" in art-related business situations. Together we identified four such ways:

1. Often he would disparage himself and his work, so that if asked how his new play was going, he would inevitably reply, "Oh, you know—terribly."

2. Sometimes he would turn himself "inside out" in order to please the other person. For example, he would be all too ready to accept without question the deadline suggested by a theater director on a play commission or his agent's opinion that a character in his latest screenplay "wasn't working."

3. Other times he would act seductively, with men and women alike, and "play little games."

4. Most often he would simply withdraw, as when a well-known director visited his roommate. Instead of "networking," the playwright retired to his room to read the newspaper.

Identifying these interactions as performance situations that provoked anxiety helped him begin to improve the effectiveness of his art business and, more generally, reduce the anxiety in his life.

• A singer-songwriter who also worked as a psychotherapist claimed to experience little anxiety when he performed—the bigger the crowd, the better. But among his presenting issues were periodic panic attacks and other anxiety symptoms. His difficulties made me wonder if performance anxiety might be a hidden issue in his life. As it happened, we both attended a meeting of psychotherapists one morning at which participants had to "check in" and introduce themselves to the group. Mild anxiety is natural in such circumstances, but it was clear that my client was experiencing far more than a few jitters as he stammered his introduction. I resolved to investigate with him the role that performance anxiety was playing in his singing career, a career which was currently stalled.

- A musician, a former professional horn player on the verge of returning to alcohol after ten years of sobriety, understood his susceptibility to bouts of severe performance anxiety. Such bouts had plagued him throughout his career, causing him to dread performing; when he resolved to stop drinking, he also resolved to stop playing professionally. He feared that the anxiety associated with performing would jeopardize his sobriety. Yet performance anxiety still manifested itself in his inability to socialize with his wife's friends or even attend parties with his co-workers. At the time he came to me, he played a synthesizer for his own enjoyment and sometimes considered performing at the annual office Christmas party. Indeed, he missed the limelight and really wanted to perform a certain Russian Orthodox Christmas song that he loved. But his anxiety proved too great an impediment.

He found himself wondering if it might be safe to purchase a horn again and play it just for himself. (He'd crushed his "working" horn in a drunken rage one night.) Over time, we developed the following plan: that he would rent and not buy a horn; that he would think of himself as a "person who played music" and not a "musician"; and that he would return the horn if his anxiety grew too great. In fact, he rented a horn, developed mouth sores, and experienced significant anxiety just handling the instrument. He found that he had to return it almost immediately. This experiment convinced him that he had to avoid horn-playing but also relieved his mind, since wondering about whether or not he could return to horn-playing had become something of an obsession. We continued our work together and, while he could never pick up a horn again, he did eventually play that Christmas song for his office mates, on a portable keyboard.

- *As you consider this discussion, do instances of hidden performance anxiety come to mind?*

_____

_____

_____

_____

THE PERFORMANCE SITUATION

To understand performance anxiety we have to recognize the many situations that can rightly be thought of as performances. Is dating often treated as a performance? Certainly. Are a hundred workplace situations, from presenting at a business meeting to speaking with a new client on the telephone, often viewed by the participants as performances? Indeed they are. Can sculpting in the privacy of his or her studio sometimes be held by a sculptor as a sort of performance? Absolutely. Therefore we need to define performance broadly, to include all sorts of situations, as that's how we experience life.

- *Describe some situations that you hadn't previously thought of as performances that you now understand were performances.*

_____

_____

_____

_____

_____

- *Did you experience performance anxiety before or during those performances?*

_____

_____

_____

_____

What exactly is a performance? A client entering a psychotherapist's office may or may not view the next fifty minutes as a performance. One week, worried that he has nothing to say, he may sweat, feel dizzy on arrival, and display other anxiety symptoms. The following week, feeling unselfconscious and eager to speak, he may experience no symptoms and have no sense that the upcoming hour is a performance. Same client, same therapist, same essential situation—but one week he experiences performance anxiety and the next week he doesn't.

A cool, calm biology teacher who never experiences performance anxiety while speaking about science may stammer and sweat if forced to discuss some personal matter or some unfamiliar subject. A well-known social psychology experiment demonstrated this. A comparison was made of English teachers and science teachers, to determine their rates of "hemming" and "hawing" while lecturing. Presenting their own subject matter, English teachers, having to deal with opinions and imprecise material, were considerably more likely to stumble over their material than were science teachers. But given the same sort of imprecise material to discuss, both groups stumbled at an equal rate and experienced significant anxiety.

A boy who is bouncing a ball off a wall and catching it is not performing. But the second he says to himself, "If I make the next catch, we win the World Series!" he suddenly transforms his innocent game into a performance situation. The perceived importance of his actions—his next throw and catch will win or lose the World Series!—entirely changes the situation.

> ## "DO NOT LEAVE ME ALONE, IAGO"
> *My courage sank and with each succeeding minute it became less possible to resist this horror. I knew with grim certainty that I would not be capable of remaining on stage more than a few minutes. I had to beg my Iago, Frank Finlay, not to completely leave the stage when I had to be left alone for a soliloquy, but to stay in the wings downstage where I could see him. I feared that if I couldn't see him I might not be able to stay there in front of the audience by myself.*
>
> —SIR LAURENCE OLIVIER, *Confessions of an Actor*

True, there is no audience, there's no penalty if he drops the ball, and in an important sense he himself doesn't care, since he can change the rules and still "win the championship" on some subsequent throw. Nothing is really hanging in the balance, and whatever he does he can undo. Still, reality testing notwithstanding, the moment he announces that his next catch will win or lose the World Series, he has created a vivid performance situation whose reality we all understand. Out of nowhere, with a single thought, a performance has been initiated that can and does provoke real anxiety.

Many a child has "choked" in such circumstances. Because of performance anxiety, he fails to make a play he's made a hundred times in a row. This is how we're constructed: we can transform an innocent moment into a performance moment simply by thinking a thought. A man and a woman are chatting easily and then the man thinks, "Should I ask her out now?"—and the situation is suddenly transformed. An employee and her supervisor are chatting casually and then the employee thinks, "I wonder, is this the right moment to ask for those extra days off?"—and, just like that, the situation becomes a completely different one.

- *What makes a performance a performance? How would you define "performance"?*

_____

_____

_____

_____

- *Are you aware of how often ordinary situations shift into performance situations? Can you give some examples?*

_____

_____

_____

_____

_____

_____

- *What changes occur in you when an ordinary situation is suddenly transformed into a performance situation?*

_____

_____

_____

_____

Consider the following. You have an instrument in your hands and an audience in front of you. What exactly are you trying to do? Play the notes, of course, and the right ones at that, at an appropriate tempo, and so on. That's the very least your audience is expecting of you (and even that "very least" is hard to do). But isn't much more expected of you?

Your audience expects you to please them by giving a *performance*. That is, you will "make music," interpret the composition, turn musical phrases into alluring bits of magic, and give the audience enough of your talent, intelligence, technique, wit—without pause and without hesitation—so that they'll be absorbed, mesmerized, transported. You are to excite them when the music calls for excitement and to communicate all the poignancy of the music when poignancy is the message. You must even "perform" your entrances and exits so that everything appears seamless and controlled.

ALONE WITH A THOUSAND STRANGERS
All the other collaborators are in the audience or safely in the wings or in the orchestra pit. The producer, the author or the director may be outside having a drink—or in London. But the actors are alone with a thousand strangers.
—STUART LITTLE and ARTHUR CANTOR, *The Playmakers*

And more besides. Everything that happens while you're onstage is part of this thing, your performance. Occurrences that you cannot be held responsible for, like a plane buzzing low over the concert hall, are nevertheless part of your performance. How many or how few people attend the concert is part of your performance. Water stains on the walls, coughs and sneezes in the audience, and of course your musical choices are all part of the performance. Didn't you choose this late Beethoven quartet, this piano sonata of your own composition, this jazz standard? It seems you will be held responsible for everything.

To be considered successful, the performance must be a special feat, something extraordinary enough to warrant applause at the end, something exemplary—even heroic. Isn't anything less an "unsuccessful" performance?

- *Do you agree that for a performance to rise to the level of "performance" it needs to be special and exemplary?*

_____

_____

- *How good must a performance be for you to judge it a success?*

_____

_____

_____

_____

- *How many mistakes are you allowed per performance?*

_____

_____

_____

_____

• *Is anything less than a perfect performance acceptable to you?*

_____

_____

We'll applaud a young piano student at the end of her mistake-riddled first recital because she is nine years old and a beginner. But if we're to applaud you, you must do exemplary work—dare we say, even perfect work? And aren't these exactly the pressures we put on ourselves when we think about performing? How do we look as we perform? How do we compare to other performers? How do we compare to our previous performances? Aren't all of us sitting in judgment of ourselves and of everyone else, even if we know better, even if we don't want to sit in judgment?

A situation hypnotizes us as soon as we label it a performance situation. As soon as the theater darkens, as soon as the overture commences, as soon as the interview begins, we are arrested. The world closes in around us, whether we are bouncing a ball off a wall or playing in an orchestra at Lincoln Center. In that closed world, we anxiously await our own judgment and the judgment of others.

• *Do you tend to sit in judgment of other performers?*

_____

_____

• *How does judging others affect how you judge your own performances?*

_____

_____

_____

_____

• *What, if any, are some reasonable solutions to this "judgment problem"?*

_____

_____

_____

_____

We've gotten our feet wet now. Let's take a deep breath and look more closely at the following idea: that performance anxiety is both a more frequent and a more hidden problem than most people realize.

Chapter Two

WHAT PERFORMANCE ANXIETY SOUNDS LIKE

We all play tricks on ourselves. We may be afraid of something and not want to admit that we're afraid of that something, so we mask that fear by the "self-talk" we use. Instead of admitting our fear of flying, we tell ourselves "Paris is too cold this time of the year." Instead of turning down a camping trip by admitting our fear of bugs and snakes, we say "I need indoor plumbing." Instead of confessing to our fear of performing, we adopt one or more of the scores of linguistic tricks available to us.

We grow more aware of the presence of performance anxiety by listening carefully and learning to decipher the real message behind the words and phrases we use. For most people, this is a skill that must be cultivated, as we generally don't listen well, especially to what we ourselves are saying. So much of what we say is circumspect and evasive that what is really being said can easily elude us.

Of course, that's our goal—to keep the truth from ourselves. One of the most important "growth edges" for you, if you're to rid yourself of your performance anxiety, is to bravely leave denial behind and face your fears squarely. This means examining what you say. Even if you know that you fear performing, you may still be entirely unaware of how your language works to keep that information hidden from view.

Thinking about it right now, what do you tend to say to yourself before a performance as your anxiety mounts? It almost certainly isn't "I'm experiencing a little performance anxiety and I need to take a deep breath or two." More likely it's something like "My mind's a blank!" "I can't go on!" "I really need the bathroom," or "I'm going to die!" Even though you know "at some level" that it's performance anxiety that you're experiencing, the language you use "moves the discussion" elsewhere—usually to your detriment. Instead of having a little anxiety to deal with, you have your "impossibility of going on" or "imminent death" to face. You've made the situation much worse because of the language you've permitted yourself to use.

AN ACCUMULATION OF MENTAL HABITS

Negative self-talk is nothing more than an accumulation of self-limiting mental habits. You can begin to break these habits by noticing occasions when you engage in unconstructive dialogues with yourself and then countering them, preferably in writing, with more positive, rational statements. It took repetition over many years to internalize your habits of negative self-talk; it will likewise take repetition and practice to learn more constructive and helpful ways of thinking.
— EDMUND BOURNE, *The Anxiety and Phobia Workbook*

Each of the following expressions is likely to point to the presence of performance anxiety. They sound so innocent to the ear that it takes a conscious effort to recognize them as possible warning signs of performance anxiety. I hope you'll take your time and really think through whether you use expressions like the following ones and, if you do, if they signal the presence of "hidden" performance anxiety.

"I'm not ready."

1. I'm not quite ready to ask for a raise.

2. I need another few weeks before my audition piece will be ready.

3. I don't feel ready to sing a Mozart aria.

4. I'm not ready to ask her out yet.

5. It's too early for me to lead a panel discussion.

6. I'm not ready for the sales conference.

As Neil Fiore explains in *The Now Habit*, "procrastination is a mechanism for coping with the anxiety associated with starting or completing any task or decision." It's important to remember that procrastination is an anxiety state. Whenever you say to yourself that you're not ready to perform, you should instantly check in with yourself to see if what you're really saying is that the thought of the performance in question is making you anxious.

- *Do you use phrases like "I'm not ready" when you want to avoid a situation that makes you anxious?*

_____

_____

- Can you distinguish in your own mind when "I'm not ready" is the literal truth and when it reflects your anxious feelings?

_____

_____

- Can you envision doing something even though you're "not ready" to do it?

_____

_____

- In what circumstances would it make sense to go ahead and do something, even though you're "not ready" to do it, and in what circumstances might it be better to wait?

_____

_____

_____

_____

_____

_____

"I don't feel like it."

1. Everybody else at the AA meeting spoke but I just didn't feel like it.

2. I don't feel like working on a new lesson plan right now.

3. I don't feel like fronting the band; Bob's much better at that sort of thing.

4. I don't feel like doing interviews for my new book; the questions interviewers ask are always inane.

5. Yes, there were a few producers at the party, but I didn't really feel like meeting them.

6. I don't feel like auditioning for that.

In polite conversation (including polite conversation with ourselves), we often use euphemisms and accept without argument the euphemisms of others. A euphemism is an inoffensive expression substituted for one that suggests something unpleasant. In each of the above cases, "I don't feel like it" is a euphemism hiding some unpleasant truth, like the fear of fronting the band, going on a book tour, or speaking to producers. If you're convinced that it's in your best interests to speak to producers at parties, but instead find yourself saying, "Oh, I just don't feel like talking to them tonight," alert yourself to the possibility that you're hiding an unpleasant truth from yourself and couching your evasion in one of the euphemisms each of us regularly uses.

• *Do you use the phrase "I don't feel like it" to avoid performance situations?*

_____

_____

• *When you say "I don't feel like it" to yourself, what exactly do you mean?*

_____

_____

_____

_____

• *What strategies might you employ to help yourself do the things you "don't feel" like doing?*

_____

_____

_____

_____

"I don't feel well."

1. The stuffy air in the audition room will make it too hard to breathe.

2. I ate lunch before my recital, and that always gives me stomach pains.

3. I always throw up before I go on the air.

4. I can't believe how tense my shoulders get before a concert.

5. Between my day job and rehearsals at night, I get very sick and run-down.

6. I always get a little dizzy before presenting at a symposium.

Somatic complaints often announce the presence of anxiety. An upset stomach and diarrhea are two everyday symptoms; a more complex example is the syndrome of hypochondriasis, the essential feature of which is a preoccupation with your bodily sensations and the fear that those sensations indicate a serious disease. Coming to understand a little bit about the intricate relationship between your physical complaints and their organic or psychological source is a useful part of the process of learning to manage performance anxiety.

• *Do you tend to feel physically unwell before performances?*

_____

_____

- *Can you distinguish between physical complaints that are symptoms of perform-ance anxiety and those that aren't?*

_____

_____

- *Are you alert to the possibility that somatic complaints might indicate the presence of anxiety?*

_____

_____

- *Does your anxiety tend to manifest itself in physical ways?*

_____

_____

"I can't think straight."

1. I'm finding it harder and harder to concentrate.

2. He asked me how I thought the character might walk, but I just stood there like a dummy.

3. I met with my agent for lunch yesterday, but then I couldn't remember any of the questions I wanted to ask her.

4. I always feel spaced out in marketing meetings.

5. Like any painter, I guess I'm a little crazy.

6. I missed the audition because I couldn't figure out where I'd parked my car.

Anxiety can manifest itself as confusion and as other mental impairments. Mild performance anxiety can produce strange, disturbing thoughts, a sense of inner chaos, memory loss, dissociative feelings, and more. People with severe performance-anxiety problems may even feel as if they're losing their mind. When we say to ourselves that our mind is not working, we should think to look to anxiety as the culprit before we point our finger at some mental shortcoming or disorder.

- *Do you often fear that you're losing your ability to "think straight" before and dur-ing performances?*

_____

_____

- *What characteristic language do you use to signal that problem yourself?*

_____

_____

_____

_____

- *How would you describe the relationship between mental confusion and anxiety?*

_____

_____

_____

_____

- *When you feel you can't "think straight," what do you tend to do?*

_____

_____

_____

_____

"I can't do it."

1. I can't go on tonight.

2. I can't ask such talented musicians to play with me.

3. I can't do my routine in a noisy club.

4. I can't seem to ask my agent to send out my work more often.

5. I couldn't possibly play Hamlet.

6. I know that I won't be able to get the regional managers to pay attention to my Friday presentation.

THROUGH A GLASS DARKLY

Negative thoughts breed negative emotional states. To quote from Corinthians in the New Testament, when we see the world "through a glass darkly," meaning that we always expect the worst, we're going to feel perennially anxious. When our worldview is clouded by fear, we're prone to anxiety. The simple but powerful solution: change the negative thoughts that breed anxiety and you start the process of healing your anxiety.

—JONATHAN DAVIDSON, *The Anxiety Book*

"I can't do it" often means "I might be able to do it but it makes me anxious to think about trying to do it." It may also mean "It's not my preference," "I don't have that skill," or "I can do it but there will be consequences." Whatever it means specifically, it's also likely to signal the presence of anxiety.

Suppose that you're a stand-up comic. Naturally you prefer performing your routine for an attentive, loving audience that sits perfectly still because they're hanging on your every word. Who wouldn't? But sometimes that won't happen. If, out of anxiety, you assert "I can't do my routine in a noisy club," you're limiting yourself and falling into the trap of avoidance. It may not be your preference to perform in a noisy club, but certainly you can do it—unless you mean to let your anxiety stop you from performing.

- *Does your use of the phrase "I can't do it" often mean "It's not my preference" rather than "It's beyond my capabilities"?*

_____

_____

- *Can you distinguish between the "I can't do it" of genuine inability and the I can't do it" of fear and anxiety?*

_____

_____

- *What might you do or say to help yourself do that which you say that you can't do?*

_____

_____

_____

_____

"I don't know what to say."

1. I couldn't talk to my boss's wife at the party—I didn't know what to say.

2. The agent I met last week said to give her a call, but what would I say to her?

3. I have this story about a dinosaur that I've been wanting to write, but I don't know how to begin it.

4. Some people have a knack for saying exactly what they mean, but I always hem and haw and beat around the bush.

5. I wanted to tell the band they weren't taking rehearsals seriously enough, but I didn't know exactly how to put it.

6. I never know what to say when people tell me they love my voice.

Usually we feel equal to speaking even if we aren't perfectly sure what words will come out of our mouth. Normally when the phone rings, we pick it up and answer it without experiencing much anxiety, even though we don't know who is on the other end or what direction the conversation will take. When we greet our mate after work, we find something to say, even though we haven't rehearsed a speech or a story on the commute home. In these and most other situations, we don't need to know what to say beforehand. Therefore, when we assert that we "don't know what to say" in a certain situation, we're announcing that we're experiencing the situation as a performance and feeling anxious about how well we're about to perform.

- *Do you tend to use the phrase "I don't know what to say" to avoid performance situations?*

_____

_____

- *If the issue isn't performance anxiety, what do you actually mean when you assert that you "don't know what to say"?*

_____

_____

_____

_____

- *In what circumstances would preparing "something to say" be a useful thing to do?*

_____

_____

_____

_____

- *How can you help yourself speak (and speak effectively) even though you "don't know what to say"?*

_____

_____

_____

_____

"I can't see the point."

1. I can't see the point of auditioning for that—I'm just not the type.

2. I can't see the point of approaching that gallery owner cold—he'd just show me the door.

3. I can't see the point in publishing my research; it's such a small addition to the field.

4. What good would come from approaching another potential sponsor since they never seem to like my pitch?

5. I can't see the point of trying to call my agent—I never get through to him.

6. I can't see the point trying to get my own band together—I'm a drummer, not an organizer.

If an overweight, out-of-shape couch potato said, "I can't see the point of trying to climb Mt. Everest in the shape I'm in," we'd nod in agreement. If a fit hiker with a love of mountain climbing said the same thing, we wouldn't quite understand. Nor would we understand if a painter said, "I can't see the point of approaching that gallery owner cold—he'd just show me the door." Our reply would likely be, "Well, yes, but maybe he wouldn't. Surely it's worth a try!" Soon we might get to the actual issue: that the thought of presenting herself and her work "cold" to gallery owners is filling this painter with anxiety.

- *Do you find yourself using the phrase "I can't see the point" when a performance that you would prefer to skip looms on the horizon?*

_____

_____

- *When you say that you "can't see the point" in presenting yourself in some way, do you take into account how performance anxiety may be implicated?*

_____

_____

- *When you say you "can't see the point" in doing something, do you tend to forget what your ultimate goals are?*

_____

_____

- *Can you articulate what threats are involved when you conclude that there's "no point" in attempting a given performance?*

_____

_____

_____

_____

"It feels too difficult."

1. It's really hard to interrupt my agent and ask him a question when he goes on and on in that New York way.

2. Memorizing this speech is more than I can handle.

3. This dance is just too difficult to learn!

4. It's impossible to write if you've waited as many years as I have to begin.

5. This sonata is too technically demanding.

6. This is a tough room to lecture in!

We understand what it means to say that it's too difficult to lift up the front end of a Chevy or solve complex algebraic problems in our head. But what does it mean to say that it's too difficult to talk to our literary agent or to audition for a choreographer? Rather than acting as if we understood, we would be better off quizzically shaking our head and asking ourselves, "Is it really too difficult or am I just experiencing some anxiety?"

- *Do you often tell yourself that your upcoming performances are "too difficult" to handle?*

_____

_____

- *What has "too difficult" tended to mean to you in the context of a performance?*

_____

_____

_____

_____

- *Are you good at telling the difference between those situations where a real difficulty exists and those situations where the primary issue is anxiety?*

_____

_____

"What's happening here?"

1. Oh, I didn't know she was one of the auditors!

2. What did the director mean by that look?

3. Am I coming down with a cold?

4. Is that the overture already?

5. Is there a smudge on my forehead?

6. What's that commotion in the audience?

Anxiety often manifests itself as hypervigilance. Because you're anxious, you're acutely aware that the audition room is on the warm side, that the director hasn't said hello to you, and that everyone is more casually dressed than you are. Anxiety can also manifest itself as a heightened startle response, causing you to flush or break out in a sweat if a chair scrapes loudly or someone nearby moves quickly. Rather than recognize that anxiety is the culprit, we jump to the conclusion that something really *is* going on, which doubles our experience of anxiety.

- *When you're anxious, are you also hypervigilant?*

_____

_____

- *Do you tend to be overly aware of what's going on around you before and during performances?*

_____

_____

- *Do you tend to be overly aware of your own physiological processes before and during performances?*

_____

_____

- *Do you tend to be overly aware of your own mental processes before and during performances?*

_____

_____

- *Do you recognize that your hypervigilance and heightened startle response at such times are anxiety symptoms?*

_____

_____

"I do better with . . ."

1. I perform better if I don't eat for two hours beforehand.

2. I do better the second week of a show than the first.

3. I do better when just the casting director's watching me, rather than a roomful of auditors.

4. Our quartet always give a better performance when the audience really understands the music.

5. I'm sure I'd give a better speech if the room were better ventilated.

6. It's better for me to practice when my roommates are out and it's quiet.

"I do better with . . ." is one of many phrases we use when we long for things to be perfect and unconsciously believe that our anxiety would magically disappear if only things were perfect. Since the problem is usually our hidden anxiety and not the actual circumstances of the performance, there is no way the situation can ever be made perfect. Even if everything were corrected—if the room were better ventilated, if the audience really understood the music, if we auditioned for one person rather than several—we would still find some problem to obsess about, since the issue is our anxiety and not externalities.

- *When you feel anxious, do you find yourself wishing that "things were better"?*

  _____

  _____

- *Are you good at distinguishing between those times when a problem is significant and some action should be taken and those times when the problem is more your "anxiety talking"?*

  _____

  _____

- *If the problem is significant but no change is possible, what can you do to reduce your experience of anxiety and make the best of the situation?*

  _____

  _____

  _____

  _____

  _____

- *Do you hold that conditions need to be perfect in order for you to perform well?*

  _____

  _____

"Yes, but . . ."

1. Yes, I should get ready for the conference, but there's lots of time left.

2. Yes, I know I should practice at least three hours every morning, but I have friends visiting this week and next week I've got to do my taxes.

3. Yes, I probably should enter that competition, but the best musicians from around the world will be competing.

4. Yes, I should invite my agent to the play, but she came to see me just three months ago and I don't want to be too pushy.

5. Yes, it's probably my turn to chair a meeting, but John likes doing that and does such a fine job of it.

6. Yes, I'm probably ready to do a little music teaching, but aren't there too many teachers out there already?

"Yes, but . . ." is a special and important sort of "No!" As Eric Berne explained in *What Do You Say After You Say Hello?*: "The most important single word in script language is the particle 'but,' which means, 'According to my script, I don't have permission to do that.'" In the context of performing, every "Yes, but . . ." should be examined to see if it is in fact a case of "Yes, it's in my best interests to give that performance, but the thought of it is making me too anxious."

- *Do you tend to use "Yes, but . . ." constructions to avoid situations that provoke anxiety?*

  _____

  _____

- *Are you aware that when you utter the "Yes" in a "Yes, but . . ." sentence you do not mean "Yes" at all?*

  _____

  _____

- *What is attractive about this way of avoiding a situation? Is it that you get to say "Yes," sparing yourself guilt, while at the same time really saying "No," sparing yourself anxiety?*

  _____

  _____

  _____

  _____

- *Can you begin to say either "Yes" or "No" more directly and begin to eliminate the defensive "Yes, but . . ." from your vocabulary?*

  _____

  _____

Performance anxiety is not the issue every single time you use one of these phrases. But whenever you do use one of these phrases, and many others like them, you should be alert to the possibility that something worth investigating is lurking right beneath the surface.

PAUSING TO RESPOND

We're far enough along in our discussion that I'd like you to take a few minutes to answer the following questions. You'll be better able to answer them later on, but it'll pay real dividends to produce some "baseline" responses now.

- *Before starting this book, what were your thoughts about performance anxiety? Did you consider it a significant problem in your life? A modest one? No particular problem?*

  _____

  _____

  _____

_____
_____
_____

• *What are your thoughts now?*

_____
_____
_____
_____
_____

• *What performances—defining the word broadly—do you engage in? Generate a list of these different performances.*

_____
_____
_____
_____
_____
_____

• *Which performance situations seem to provoke the most anxiety in you?*

_____
_____
_____
_____

• *Which performance situations seem to provoke the least anxiety in you?*

_____
_____
_____
_____

• *Can you discern any differences between these two sorts of situations?*

_____
_____
_____

• *Do you experience less anxiety when you are better prepared?*

_____
_____

- *Do you experience less anxiety the less important you consider the performance?*

_____

_____

- *Do you experience less anxiety the easier the performance is technically (the less there is to memorize, the less demanding the material, and so on)?*

_____

_____

- *Do you experience less anxiety the more you understand "what's wanted" from a given performance?*

_____

_____

- *What elements seem to contribute to making a presentation a pressure-filled situation?*

_____

_____

_____

_____

- *What strategies, effective or ineffective, have you employed in the past to manage your performance anxiety? Generate a list of these effective and ineffective strategies.*

_____

_____

_____

_____

_____

_____

- *What one change in your mindset, personality, or pre-performance preparations would make the biggest positive difference in managing your performance anxiety?*

_____

_____

_____

_____

HOW THE MIND DEFINES PERFORMANCE

In the chapters that follow, we'll look more closely at the phenomenon of performance anxiety and its relationship to threat and danger. If a performance didn't seem threatening to us, there would be no reason for us to play the sorts of linguistic tricks on ourselves that I've just described. One of the reasons that performance feels as threatening as it often does is that many of us have inadvertently added an invisible adjective in front of the word performance. We say "performance," but we mean "important performance." Our mind has turned all performances, even the least significant ones, into "important performances," without our having any idea that that's what we've done.

TALKING STRAIGHT ABOUT ANXIETY

Most people try to wall themselves off from their anxiety. They're anxious but can't admit it to themselves. But the wall they erect does very little to prevent them from experiencing the anxiety. The anxiety leaks through. Sometimes they experience it directly, as phobias, panic attacks, and other anxiety events. More often they experience it as indecisiveness, procrastination, fatigue, depression, addictions, or insomnia. The wall they erect between themselves and their anxiety doesn't serve the intended purpose of helping them lead a happy, productive life. Instead it produces a multitude of ailments and keeps them from knowing what's really going on.

Talk to yourself straight. Let yourself know when you're feeling anxious. What's wanted is less dodging and greater awareness.

Because it's hard to know which are the truly important performances in life, it's easy for us to begin to unconsciously designate all performances as important ones, just to be "on the safe side." The transformation begins in childhood as we begin to associate every performance moment with an "important event," even if that moment consists only of answering a question in French class or going up to the blackboard to do a math problem. And how much more anxiety we feel if that event is something like a recital or a school play!

Our own vital signs at such moments seem like proof positive that getting that math answer right is a very big deal. If the performance is a recital or a school play, then we have additional evidence that the performance is important. Our parents are getting anxious, the household is in something of an uproar as we dress for the event, other family members are going to show up, and so on. The young performer—you—is dressed up and brought to a room filled with expectant others; and without anyone meaning it to happen, you begin to redefine "performance" as a noun with the adjective "important" unconsciously attached.

The problem of unconsciously adding "important" to "performance" might be ameliorated if we had a clear idea of which were the important performances in life and which weren't. Would effectively speaking up for your agenda at a business meeting make a difference in how you're perceived at work and whether you're promoted? Yes, it just might. Would a series of successful speeches, including the ones you deliver at backwater stops on the campaign trail, enhance your chances of election? Yes, they just might. Would success in an audition for even a small part perhaps lead to a breakthrough role later on? Yes, it just might. Therefore it's hard to call your worries irrational as you give a small presentation at work, deliver a speech at a backwater campaign stop, or audition for a minor role. Maybe a performance of this sort *will* turn out to be important—and so the hidden adjective "important" remains firmly attached.

This problem is further exacerbated because we aren't really sure how to prepare ourselves for the variety of performance situations that arise in life. For some situations, like a job interview, we're expected to consciously prepare. But certainly for most we're just supposed to act spontaneously, aren't we? Maybe yes—and maybe no. Theatrical agent Ann Brebner explained in *Setting Free the Actor*, "In my work as a casting director and agent, I was always amazed that people expressed surprise or panic when I said, 'So, tell me something about yourself.' It was the most predictable question in the world. They knew it would be asked, but it was often so intimidating that they seemed to draw a complete blank." An actor should expect to be asked this question. To presume that a spontaneous answer is all that's needed, when you've flubbed the question previously and know that it provokes anxiety in you, verges on self-sabotage.

Consider the following three ways of experiencing a meeting. If you're sitting in a meeting with the assurance that your opinion will not be solicited and you've decided that you won't speak, you take in the meeting one way, with little or no anxiety. If the matter of speaking or not speaking rests entirely with you and you find yourself debating throughout the meeting whether you will or won't voice your opinions, you experience some amount of anxiety, but it can be eliminated as soon as you say to yourself, "No, I don't think I need to speak." However, if you don't know one way or the other whether you'll be required to speak and you have the sense that some real possibility of performing exists, you're likely to attend to the proceedings with an anxiety that can't be fully extinguished. The mere specter of *having* to perform transforms the situation from an unimportant one to an important one—without your even realizing it.

Once we've unconsciously defined all performances as important ones, we can fully expect our anxiety to generalize. That is, not only do we unwittingly connect "important" to "performance," but we begin unconsciously to see performances everywhere. Not only do we feel like we're performing when we talk to gallery owners or collectors, but we begin to feel like we're performing when we're standing in front of a blank canvas and even when we're trying to choose between the raspberries and the strawberries in the market. Everything begins to take on an "important performance" flavor. An actress who can't ask a director she knows to consider her for a part discovers that she also can't make choices while on stage and can't even decide where to take her vacation. Without the painter or the actor intending it to happen, the stakes have been raised everywhere.

- *How do you go about judging which are the important performances in your life and which are the not-so-important ones?*

_____

_____

_____

_____

- *Do you think that you've inadvertently attached the adjective "important" to many—or even all—performance situations?*

_____

_____

- *Do you sense that you demand of yourself a movement from the ordinary to the extraordinary in performance situations?*

_____

_____

This is quite a trick we play on ourselves, transforming so many of our innocent interactions into "important performances." How does it happen that this insidious "upping of the ante" occurs without our noticing it or consciously participating? To answer this important question, we need to turn our attention to the relationship between anxiety and danger.

Chapter Three

ANXIETY AND DANGER

Performance anxiety is, of course, a variety of anxiety. What, then, is anxiety? Is it any or all of the following: fear, dread, stress, panic, nervousness, wariness, uneasiness, apprehension, or worry? Is it primarily a physical condition, primarily sociological, primarily psychological? What do you think?

- *How would you define "anxiety"? How is it different from or the same as words like "fear," "nervousness," "stress," and "worry"?*

_____

_____

_____

_____

"Anxiety" certainly hasn't eluded examination. Thousands of books and articles have been written about it. Its placement as a centerpiece of psychoanalytic theory is one of Sigmund Freud's strongest achievements. Among theories about human nature, human development, and personality, those that ignore the reality and the significance of anxiety are much weaker and less convincing than those that affirm them.

Because the existence of anxiety has been written about so often, and perhaps in reaction to the labeling of the middle decades of the last century as "The Age of Anxiety" (the title of W. H. Auden's 1947 poem), anxiety has recently receded as a concept worth investigating. This has been the case even as such states of anxiety as agoraphobia, multiple personality disorder, obsessive-compulsive disorder, and post-traumatic stress disorder are discussed every day in the popular media. Let's take this opportunity, then, to review our basic understanding of anxiety. From the obser-vations of writers on the subject—featured on the following pages in boxed excerpts from their writings—we can make these points:

- *We rightly fear crossing a tiger's path. But what is it that we fear when we enter a crowded party or get ready to perform at a recital? As Karen Horney explains, the danger is "hidden and subjective." She echoes Freud's thought that the threat that anxiety warns us about may arise as much from within ourselves as from outside ourselves.*

- *We may loudly proclaim that we don't fear calling our literary agent or a gallery owner who might be interested in our paintings, but the fact that we put off that call for months, or even indefinitely, proves that we fear something. As Ernest Becker puts it, anxiety is a reality-tester par excellence.*

- *Why can't musicians, actors, and other performers simply talk themselves through their performance anxiety, calmly and reasonably dismissing it by using* simple, rational arguments? Because anxiety is an intense pressure in the face of perceived danger and, as Harry Stack Sullivan suggests, it is "a sign that something ought to be different at once." The pressure to take some anxiety-binding or anxiety-reducing action at once makes rational thought difficult and sometimes impossible.

ANXIETY THE TEACHER

The flood of anxiety is not the end for man. It is, rather, a "school" that provides man with the ultimate education, the final maturity. It is a better teacher than reality, says Kierkegaard, because reality can be lied about, twisted, and tamed by the tricks of cultural perception and repression. But anxiety cannot be lied about. Once you face up to it, it reveals the truth of your situation, and only by seeing this truth can you open a new possibility for yourself.

—ERNEST BECKER, *The Denial of Death*

• *According to Freud, we try to seek pleasure and avoid unpleasure. Without an awareness of this pleasure principle, it would confuse us to hear a musician say that he plays well, loves music, and is able to give his audience pleasure, but that he gets no personal pleasure from performing. He gets no personal pleasure because his anxiety is causing unpleasure.*

THE UNWANTED EXPERIENCE

Under no conceivable circumstance that has ever occurred to me has anyone sought and valued as desirable the experience of anxiety. No series of "useful" attacks of anxiety in therapy will make it something to be sought after. This is, in a good many ways, rather startling, particularly when one compares anxiety with fear. While fear has many of the same characteristics, it may actually be sought out as an experience occasionally; particularly if the fear is expected or anticipated. For instance, people who ride on roller coasters pay money for being afraid. But no one will ever pay money for anxiety in its own right. No one wants to experience it. Only one other experience—that of loneliness—is in this special class of being totally unwanted. And not only does no one want anxiety, but if it is present, the lessening of it is always desirable. Anxiety is to an incredible degree a sign that something ought to be different at once.

—HARRY STACK SULLIVAN, *The Psychiatric Interview*

• *Silvano Arieti reminds us that our anxiety typically arises from many complex and intertwined sources. Our ambitions, our secret desires, our secret shames, and all aspects of our personality and consciousness are bound up in the concept of anxiety. This very complexity alarms and confounds us and exacerbates those "feelings of incomplete knowledge of the situation" to which D. T. Suzuki refers.*

Charles Frankel suggests that particular episodes of anxiety, like bouts of performance anxiety, may constitute threads in a fabric of a larger, more encompassing anxiety. It is important, therefore, to learn just how encompassing that anxiety is for a given person. In other words, we need to look at performance anxiety within the broader context of how much anxiety a person is experiencing and to what extent a person experiences life as generally threatening.

Christopher McCullough remarks that anxiety is a state of orientation in a specific direction. If the threatening stimulus isn't anywhere on our radar screen—if we are neither consciously nor unconsciously oriented in its direction—then we won't experience anxiety. Additionally, McCullough points out that an anxiety reaction may well have a learned component—that over time we may designate certain situations as threatening that previously we had never felt were threatening.

ANXIETY AND ANTICIPATION

If anxiety's importance has been firmly established, its definition, however, has not been so widely agreed upon. Freud himself changed his early view of this emotion. At first he felt that anxiety is the state of not being gratified. He later abandoned this definition and described anxiety as the emotional response to a situation of danger. To my way of thinking, anxiety is the emotional reaction to the expectation or anticipation of danger. It is the complexity of the cognitive mechanism that distinguishes anxiety from fear.

—SILVANO ARIETI, *The Intrapsychic Self*

Herbert Benson explains that human beings may simply not have the biological resources to maintain "physiologic equanimity" in our contemporary world and that significant anxiety may be the inevitable result. Are people built to perform brilliantly before a thousand people without severely stretching their biological resources and experiencing anxiety? Are they meant to speak charismatically in a business meeting or create breakthrough works of art without experiencing stress? These questions alert us to the possibility that performance anxiety may be a natural reaction to a given set of trying circumstances.

In extreme forms distress is a disabling ailment that may prevent performers from pursuing their careers or may curtail a career already in progress. As the violinist Kato Havas observed about musical performance: "There are few activities in life which can produce tension and anxiety as rapidly and thoroughly as playing a musical instrument in public."

INSECURITY

All forms of anxiety come from the fact that there is somewhere in our consciousness the feeling of incomplete knowledge of the situation. This lack of knowledge leads to a sense of insecurity and then to anxiety, with all its degrees of intensity.

—D. T. SUZUKI, *Zen Buddhism and Psychoanalysis*

- *How would you define being "oriented toward a performance"?*

_____

_____

- *Can you describe how you experience "unpleasure"? Do you have a characteristic reaction or set of symptoms?*

_____

_____

_____

_____

- *When your biological resources are stretched, what tends to happen?*

_____

_____

_____

_____

- *When you feel psychological pressure that demands to be reduced, what do you typically do? Light a cigarette? Have a drink? Physically flee the room? Mentally flee from the thought? Or something else?*

_____

_____

_____

_____

- *If you are unable to reduce that pressure, what happens?*

_____

_____

CLINICAL CATEGORIES OF ANXIETY

It will help us to take a brief look at the ways in which anxiety symptoms constellate into recognizable patterns, or what clinicians call "syndromes." Anxiety complaints appear not only as discrete symptoms—a dry mouth, say, or a queasy stomach—but also come in "packages" that are surprising in two regards. First, it may surprise us to learn which complaints tend to appear together. Second, it may surprise us to learn that certain complaints are symptoms of anxiety.

The psychologist Philip Zimbardo explained in *Psychology and Life*, "When an individual feels chronically threatened by life's hazards and inadequate to the task of coping with them, the ordinary ego defenses we all use are not enough. Gradually such a person may come to rely excessively on one or more neurotic defense patterns." These patterns have in common the search for relief from anxiety. Characterized by an absence of joy in living and by actions aimed at lessening pain rather than constructively solving problems, neurotic defense patterns provide enough temporary relief from anxiety that many individuals cling to them even though they do not solve their basic problems and may even worsen them.

The trauma of war can result in long-term effects which taken together form a pattern that clinicians call post-traumatic stress disorder. In some individuals this syndrome is characterized by nightmares, flashback episodes, irritability, outbursts of anger, and an exaggerated startle response.

Looking at clinical categories of symptoms helps us better understand several points about anxiety, including the following four:

1. Anxiety can manifest itself in a variety of ways: as physical symptoms, psychological symptoms (including disturbances of identity, memory, and consciousness), and/or disturbances of mood. Thus one person before an audition might say, "My palms are sweating," a second might say, "I have a pain in my chest," a third might say, "I don't feel like myself," and a fourth might say, "I feel blue," and each would be reporting his idiosyncratic experience of anxiety.

2. Anxiety in general, and performance anxiety in particular, can significantly disturb a person's thought processes. The anxiety sufferer may have a clear understanding that a bout of "butterflies in the stomach" is symptomatic of anxiety but may not realize that his inability to think clearly or his sense of detachment or unreality is equally symptomatic of his anxiety (and not evidence of stupidity, madness, an attention deficit disorder, or anything *but* the presence of anxiety).

3. Symptoms can and do come in "packages"—in complexes or syndromes—that may reflect something about the source or cause of the anxiety. For instance, recurrent distressing dreams about a traumatic performance from the past, internal efforts to avoid thoughts about that traumatic performance, and irritability or outbursts of anger might all appear together in a package resembling post-traumatic stress disorder.

4. Many of a person's symptoms or complaints, linked to anxiety and the effort to reduce it, may not easily be recognizable as such. Would we look to anxiety as the issue if a pianist complained of hand or finger pain? Yet we might be in the territory of clinical pain disorder. Would we look to anxiety if a model complained that the mole on her neck was costing her work? Yet we might be in the territory of hypervigilant body awareness and body dysmorphic disorder. Would we look to anxiety if a painter complained that she couldn't resume painting until she'd obtained a certain brand of watercolor paper? Yet we might be in the territory of obsessive thinking and even obsessive-compulsive disorder. An understanding and appreciation of clinical categories helps us become better detectives as we sift through our own complaints and the complaints of others.

THE STRESS OF CHANGE

We live in very difficult times, when man is constantly faced with anxieties caused by rapid change. Man simply does not have the biological resources to maintain physiologic equanimity, certainly not without experiencing the effects of so-called stress that may have led to the recent prevalence of the disease hypertension.

—HERBERT BENSON, *The Relaxation Response*

Let's look at one symptom picture scale, compiled by Marilyn Gellis and Rosemary Muat, authors of *The Twelve Steps of Phobics Anonymous*. It includes the symptoms associated with mild, moderate, and severe bouts of performance anxiety, rated on a scale of 1 to 10.

Functional

1. *Butterflies"; a queasy feeling in the stomach; trembling; jitteriness; tension.*

2. *Cold or clammy palms; hot flashes and all-over warmth; profuse sweating.*

3. *Very rapid, strong, racing, pounding, or irregular heartbeat; tremors; muscle tension and aches; fatigue.*

Decreased Functional Ability

4. Jelly legs; weakness in the knees; wobbly, unsteady feelings; shakiness.

5. Immediate desperate and urgent need to escape, avoid, or hide.

6. A lump in the throat; dry mouth; choking; muscle tension.

7. Hyperventilation; tightness in chest; shortness of breath; smothering sensation.

Very Limited Functional Ability or Completely Nonfunctional

8. Feelings of impending doom or death; high pulse rate; difficulty breathing; palpitations.

9. Dizziness; visual distortion; faintness; headache; nausea; numbness; tingling of hands, feet, or other body parts; diarrhea; frequent urination.

Complete Panic

10. Nonfunctional; disorientation; detachment; feelings of unreality; paralysis; fear of dying, going crazy, or losing control. (Frequently people experiencing their first spontaneous "panic attack" rush to emergency rooms, convinced that they are having a heart attack.)

- Where do your experiences of performance anxiety fall on this scale?

_____

_____

_____

_____

- If you experience some symptoms from the various levels on this scale, how would you characterize your experience of performance anxiety on average? Is it relatively mild, moderate, or severe?

_____

_____

- Under what circumstances do the more drastic symptoms tend to occur?

_____

_____

_____

_____

A MENTAL DISORDER?

Our look in the last section at the clinical categories of anxiety may have planted the suspicion that performance anxiety is to be thought of as a mental disorder. This is not the case. There are many good common-sense reasons not to make this connection. Displaying a little nervousness before or during a performance is entirely normal and natural. Such a reaction means, in part, that you're acknowledging the importance of the event and want to do well. It also means that you're alert to the difficulties (or dangers) associated with tasks such as remembering a prodigious amount of material and presenting it with technical acumen and artistry. Nothing disordered there!

Surely we hold the presence of a little nervousness in a performer who is attempting to perform well as healthier than the absence of nerves in an ill-prepared performer who presents poorly and then blames his ineffective showing on the restlessness of his audience or the vagaries of fate. In fact, there are good reasons to be more suspicious of an *absence* of some anxiety in such situations than of its *presence*. Such an absence might mean that the performer has built defenses against the realities of the situation and of his part in the proceedings. His defensive structure shields him from anxiety but may also prevent him from being open to the situation and authentic in his presentation.

Thus, an absence of performance anxiety in a presentation situation does not signify sound mental health any more than a lack of anxiety in a person's day-to-day life does. Indeed, according to one model of personality development, the complete absence of anxiety is a likely sign of a personality disorder. In this model, the normal range of mental health is placed not at one end of a continuum but rather in the middle, producing two directions of mental disturbance.

In one direction we encounter, first, anxiety disorders and, eventually, severe disorders such as obsessive-compulsive disorder and schizophrenia. In the other direction we encounter, first, behavioral disorders and, eventually, personality disorders of the sort found in antisocial and sociopathic people. Individuals in this second direction are marked by their lack of anxiety and, at the extreme end of the continuum, are willing to say and do anything because they do not experience guilt, aren't "in it" with the rest of humanity, and refuse to let others judge them. They have perfectly bound their natural anxiety by becoming the threat rather than the threatened.

We would expect anxiety to have a moderate effect on people in the broad middle or normal range of this model. They are not so divorced from the human race as to constitute a living threat nor so bound up with their worries and fears as to live in perpetual anxiety. Given that the experience of anxiety is normal and even inevitable for this vast majority of people, most people will find themselves facing the task of embracing this natural anxiety and trying to reduce it as much as possible.

PERFORMERS' EXPERIENCES

The experience of "mild" performance anxiety is well known to each of us. At such times we might experience butterflies in the stomach, the need to urinate, or a slight sense of disorientation. We may react with more anxiety before important-seeming or difficult-feeling events, perhaps moving from butterflies to a feeling that approaches nausea, or from slight disorientation to a considerably more "spacey" state.

Each anxious person, whether experiencing his anxiety as "mild," "moderate," or "severe," has his own individual "package" of physical symptoms and distressing thoughts. It's instructive to hear what professional performers have to say about their experience of performance anxiety. The following reports involve performers whose anxiety falls in the range between moderate to severe.

The actress Maureen Stapleton explained about herself:

When I work, the anxiety starts about six-thirty at night. I start to burp. I belch—almost nonstop. I keep burping, right up to the curtain, and then I'm all right. If a truck backfires, I jump. I can hear everything. I get scared that something is going to fall down or that there's going to be an explosion. I'm nervous every night, but opening night is more of a nightmare, there's so much at stake that it just overpowers you.

Among the most common symptoms of performance anxiety are sweaty palms, a dry mouth, increased heart rate, shaky hands, weak knees, shortness of breath, butterflies in the stomach, and an increased need to use the bathroom. As Stephanie Judy explained in *Making Music for the Joy of It*:

It's as if some Bad Fairy visits each person on concert day and bestows the most aggravating symptoms possible: a trembling arm to the strings, a dry mouth to singers, clammy hands to pianists, scant wind to the winds, and a foundering memory to us all.

Psychological symptoms include feelings of confusion, disorientation, powerlessness, and loneliness. A few performers report going briefly deaf or blind. Additional psychological symptoms include the desire to escape or to hide, feelings of impending doom or death, or feelings of unreality. The singer Rosa Ponselle explained, "I actually prayed that a car would run me over so that I wouldn't have to die onstage—a prayer that I was to repeat before every performance for twenty years."

The soprano Anna Moffo recalled, "I've never started a performance without thinking, 'It's only the first act—I'll never live to see the final curtain.'" John Bonham, drummer for the rock band Led Zeppelin, admitted, "I've got terrible bad nerves all the time. I just can't stand sitting around, and I worry about playing badly. Everybody in the band is the same, and each of us has some little thing they do before we go on, like pacing about or lighting a cigarette."

The cellist Pablo Casals wrote in his autobiography *Joys and Sorrows*:

I gave my first real concert in Barcelona when I was fourteen. My father, who had come to Barcelona for the occasion, took me on the tramway. I was terribly nervous. When we got to the concert hall, I said, "Father, I've forgotten the beginning of the piece! I can't remember a note of it! What shall I do?" He calmed me down. That was eighty years ago but I've never conquered that dreadful feeling of nervousness before a performance. It is always an ordeal. Before I go onstage, I have a pain in my chest. I'm tormented.

The actor Paul Lynde confessed, "I have never gotten over being terrified in front of an audience. Oh, I know most performers get the jitters before they go on. My reaction is more like nervous collapse." The actress Estelle Parsons explained, "I get this feeling that I just can't go on. And sometimes I've had to stay in bed all day in order to get to the stage."

Dr. Stephen Aaron in his book *Stage Fright: Its Role in Acting* provided the following examples:

A British actor in his late sixties still becomes so nervous before each performance that he must be dressed and made up by an assistant. First of all, his body is so out of control that he is unable to perform these functions for himself. Second of all, left to his own devices, he often forgets what play he's in and will sometimes appear costumed for another piece in the repertory. An American actress throws up before going on stage; buckets have to be placed by each of her entrance positions. Another actress, who has played many leading roles, says, "Most people are really very frightened. Getting out there on stage is like walking a tightrope. It's like walking on stage naked—naked and looking awful."

THE DYNAMICS OF PERFORMANCE ANXIETY

Our experience of performance anxiety is dynamic, not static. The third night of a performance may provoke intense anxiety, the fourth night no anxiety at all, the fifth night moderate but manageable anxiety, and so on. Today's audition may seem no more important than yesterday's and yet today a severe bout of performance anxiety strikes. Or you experience moderate performance anxiety every time you get on stage and today feel no anxiety at all—absolutely none.

The experience of performance anxiety can also change for an individual over time, the anxiety increasing for one performer and decreasing for another. One significant example of how the experience of performance anxiety changes over time involves performers who stop abusing themselves with alcohol and other drugs and begin to perform "clean and sober."

Before they begin the process of recovery from substance abuse—that is, while they are still using drugs—they are able to bind their anxiety by medicating themselves. As the musician Don Henley explained, "I think the only reason I ever used drugs was to overcome shyness or self-doubt. I didn't use drugs actually to create, but simply to buffer feelings of inadequacy." A performer may be in denial about the dimensions of his drug use and romantically affirm that drugs are a necessary part of the creative life. But as the jazz saxophonist Charlie Parker warned, "Any musician who says he is playing better on tea, the needle, or when he is juiced is a plain straight liar."

Most performers, even those who continue to use drugs, know that their drug use is primarily an anxiety binder. If they take the step of abstaining from drugs and alcohol, they remove this primary anxiety binder from their lives, thus demanding of themselves that they experience anxiety without the buffering effects of chemicals. They know that this pledge will mean that they'll experience more performance anxiety than they did while on drugs. The musician Eric Clapton, for example, explained, "To play sober, to play straight, is like going to the dentist, I suppose. You're very, very nervous until the actual thing is taking place, then you call on some reserve inside of you which is just waiting to be accessed."

Another example of performance anxiety experienced in a recovery program is described by "Henry" in *Stage Fright: Recovery for 12-Step Sharing*:

> *Sharing at meetings is a valuable part of all 12-step programs. Yet, despite the loving, accepting atmosphere, some of us feel too much "stage fright" to share until we've been in the program a long time. Or we share but feel ashamed of what we shared. The task is to get out of denial, to admit that you're afraid, to feel the fear, and to ask for support. Tell someone you're scared to share. Ask for a hug. Begin by admitting you're scared. It's okay to blush, shake, and stutter. It's okay to be nervous. It's okay to risk. It's okay to be a human being.*

At such times the experience of performance anxiety may increase tremendously. With time, practice, growth, and healing, though, it may abate as the performer learns more functional ways of handling the anxiety that remains. He may even simply grow less anxious over time. As Ringo Starr put it, "After I stopped drinking and taking drugs, I realized I wasn't frightened of the dark and I wasn't an insomniac."

ASHAMED OF THE PROBLEM

Performance anxiety is one issue but an equally significant issue is the shame we sometimes feel that we're afflicted with this problem and haven't been able to master it ourselves. You can hear this deep shame in the following report, excerpted from a therapy session conducted in a workshop between therapist John Weakland and an "anxious violinist." Recorded in *The Tactics of Change*, it provides a striking picture of the debilitating effects of performance anxiety and the shame performance anxiety can produce. The "anxious violinist" explained:

> *I am a music teacher and I'm a very, very, very poor performer, to the extent that my hands shake and they sweat when I perform, which they do not do at any other time. When I came back after ten years of not performing, I tried to perform on several occasions and it was as dismal as I remembered it back when I was eighteen, when it made me quit to begin with, because it was so bad. And the rewards I got for performing were so small that I gave it up back then. I'm willing to be a little anxious, willing to be a little nervous, but I'm not—it's too embarrassing—I'm concerned about it being incapacitating, ridiculously incapacitating. I remember that in my second year at the conservatory I had to perform a piece and I forgot a great deal of the piece, my left hand was shaking so much that I couldn't execute a simple scale with any efficiency at all. It was very, very upsetting to me at the time. It was the decisive factor in making me quit.*

In sessions with my clients, I see the same discomfort and embarrassment. Many clients feel self-conscious that they haven't mastered their performance anxiety and believe that they "should" have more answers than they currently possess. Together we investigate the situations that provoke their anxiety and the factors that contribute to their anxiety but, just as important, we sit with the fact that their performance anxiety is real and that it will take work and courage to overcome it.

I commend you, too, on accepting the reality of this problem and bravely looking it in the eye.

- *Does thinking about your performance anxiety make you feel self-conscious or embarrassed?*

_____

_____

- *Does talking about it with another person make you feel even more self-conscious or embarrassed?*

_____

_____

Chapter Four

DEFENDING AGAINST DANGER

Anxiety is a signal of danger. It's at once a biological and psychological signal, alerting us to the fact that something may be up. It's our reaction to the distant whistle of a train—although there may not be a train coming and it may not even be a train whistle that we hear. Anxiety isn't a terribly accurate signal, as very often nothing is up. But most of us hate the experience of anxiety so much that instead of feeling the anxiety when it hits and looking to see whether a train is coming, we try to wall the experience away. We attempt to defend ourselves against the anxiety rather than handle the threat. By doing so, we lose our ability to see what's provoking the anxiety and to eliminate the threat.

I'd like you to understand that a multitude of internal and external triggers cause anxiety and that the best thing to do when anxiety is triggered is to just feel it and see what's being announced. I'd like you to enter into a new relationship with your own anxiety and become something of an "anxiety intuitive." I'd like you to lower the wall of your defenses and see what's going on inside of you. Very few people want to do this because they fear what they'll find. They're worried about what their psychological insides look like. But you don't need to catalog traumas, pin down your faults, or create a long list of woes in order to become smart about anxiety. You don't need to examine your history or the totality of your personality at all. You only need to look at one thing: how you construe and handle threats.

Most therapists believe that you need to know where your anxiety comes from in order to treat it. You don't. All you need to do is see it more clearly. See that bull in the corner? You don't need to know where he came from. But you do need to know that you think he's there, that he looks scary, and that the paralysis you're experiencing is because you're afraid to budge. As long as you claim that there's no bull there, even though you're experiencing his presence, you can't move.

Why am I asking you to look at that bull directly? Because the instant you look at him, he's likely to vanish. What you discover when you normalize anxiety is that there are very few bulls lurking in corners. You were mistaken; your mind created that fearsome bull out of shadows. That is the great secret about anxiety. Anxiety is a warning signal that ninety-nine times out of a hundred is warning you only about shadows.

These shadows cause gigantic reactions in us. The shadowy something that a spider represents can cause us to panic. The shadowy something that a bridge represents (the one-in-ten-billion chance of its fatal collapse) can prevent us from crossing the river. The shadowy threat that a performance represents can cause us to feel terrified before a one-minute speech. When you become the anxiety intuitive you have it in yourself to become, you'll learn how shadows are scaring you and millions of your fellow human beings.

The first thing I want you to examine is how your defenses work. We have evolved ego defenses whose main function is to *defend* us against threats to our self-esteem. A performance is a threat of this sort. When we fear flying, what we fear is the horrendous assault on our physical integrity that a plane crash implies. When we fear performing, the fears are very different: we fear that we will be exposed as incompetent; fail ourselves and others; become an object of ridicule and scorn; lose love, approval, and perhaps our job; and so on. These are exactly the kinds of threats that our defensive system was created to protect us against. Therefore we need to examine how our defenses work and how we can *transcend our defenses*.

OUR DEFENSIVE NATURE

Stella, an actress, enters a booking agent's office. She doesn't look nervous. Indeed, she appears confident, even cocky. If asked, she will say that she doesn't feel nervous in the least. But the agent soon comes to feel that Stella has an "attitude problem." Stella is a little too sarcastic and seems to think that she's doing the world a favor by being in show business. She disparages a prominent director, acting as if she and the agent secretly agreed that the director's work stinks. In parting, she tells the agent that he should get an office with a more convenient location.

What's Stella's problem? Is she dense? Immature? No: we should conceptualize Stella's problem as her particular mix of defensive reactions, meant to ward off the anxiety that is provoked when she tries to land acting roles. That's the psychologically acute answer. The defensive structure we build up to handle life stresses and to protect us from anxiety, shame, and guilt is an important facet of our personality.

EVALUATING DEFENSE MECHANISMS

Although defense mechanisms may serve useful protective functions, they usually involve some measure of self-deception and reality distortion and may seriously interfere with the effective resolution of the actual problem. For these reasons, ego-defense mechanisms are considered maladaptive when they become the predominant means of coping with stressors.

—JAMES COLEMAN, *Abnormal Psychology and Modern Life*

These ego defense mechanisms include all of the following, adapted from James Coleman's *Abnormal Psychology and Everyday Life*.

Denial of Reality

Here, an individual protects himself from some unpleasant reality by a refusal to perceive it or to face it. Often he engages in escapist activities that amount to an addiction, like an obsession with video games or shopping. Stella, for instance, may busy herself with thoughts and activities that prevent her from preparing properly for auditions. She doesn't allow the fact that she has no monologue prepared or that auditioning makes her anxious to enter conscious awareness and instead "denies" that auditions require preparation.

- *To what extent, if any, do you employ denial as a defense against threat and anxiety?*

  _____

  _____

- *Can you think of any concrete examples?*

  _____

  _____

  _____

  _____

PERFORMERS IN DENIAL

Denial is a primary ego defense, and people's use of it sometimes strikes us as remarkably strange (except when we use it in exactly the same way ourselves). How, for instance, can an actor deny that he will have to speak the words written for the character he is about to play in an audition scene? And yet actors do this all the time, so much so that acting teachers must remind them that they will have to speak the words written in the script. The actor and acting teacher Ed Hooks, for instance, explained in The Audition Book:

The best way to approach an audition is to take a long, cool look at what the scripted character is saying and doing in the scenes you will be reading and accept whatever is going on there as your behavior. Don't waste time denying that you would behave or speak the way that he does. Immediately embrace it. "But, I would never, not in a million years, talk and behave like the person in the script!" you complain. Oh, yes you would, and yes you will, just as soon as you get into the audition room. Those very words are going to come right out of your mouth, so you might as well motivate them. There is no gain in denial.

Fantasy

Stella fantasizes that she will have a great career, win Emmys and Oscars, and become a household name. These are fine fantasies, except when their primary purpose is to ward off knowledge about the anxiety you're feeling. If, instead of doing the work required to achieve our goals, work like learning our monologue piece or managing our anxiety, we spend our time gratifying our frustrated desires through imaginary achievements, we are using the defense known as fantasizing.

- *To what extent, if any, do you employ fantasy as a defense against threat and anxiety?*

_____

_____

- *Can you think of any concrete examples?*

_____

_____

_____

Compensation

Compensation is the defensive maneuver of covering up a perceived weakness (like our short stature) by emphasizing a perceived desirable trait (like our debating skills), or by making up for frustration in one area (that we aren't landing roles) by overgratification in another (like eating too many sweets). Stella compensates for the fact that she hasn't learned any audition pieces and that everything about her career makes her anxious by dressing sexily, talking a mile a minute, and acting chummy and conspiratorial with people she met only a moment ago.

- *To what extent, if any, do you employ compensation as a defense against threat and anxiety?*

_____

_____

- *Can you think of any concrete examples?*

_____

_____

_____

Identification

An individual using identification as an ego defense identifies himself with well-known people or illustrious institutions. He lets you know as soon as possible that he's had lunch with a certain famous actor, has the impossible-to-get home phone number of a certain famous director, and acted with a famous ensemble (without telling you that it was in a minor role). By boosting himself, he not only hopes to impress you but also defends himself against seeing his actual "low" status and the pain and anxiety that realization would bring. Stella, defending herself through identification, claims to be intimate with well-known actors, directors, and producers, on the basis of brief professional interactions or even just glimpsing them at publicity functions.

- *To what extent, if any, do you employ identification as a defense against threat and anxiety?*

_____

_____

- *Can you think of any concrete examples?*

_____

_____

_____

_____

Introjection

Introjection is the incorporation of external values and standards into your ego structure so that you don't feel at the mercy of them as external threats. If you were beaten with a stick as a child, you defend yourself against that horror by claiming that beating children with stick is good for them. If you grew up being criticized about everything, including even the color of your eyes, you defend yourself against that pain and humiliation by arguing that a little constructive criticism never hurt anyone, which is why you criticize others so freely. Stella has learned at the feet of her parents, who were used to conning people, to try con people in the business, and while this hasn't worked for her, she nevertheless can't graduate to another way of being because "conning people" is one of her introjected defenses.

- *To what extent, if any, have you introjected certain values as a defense against threat and anxiety?*

_____

_____

- *Can you think of any concrete examples?*

_____

_____

_____

Projection

Another common ego defense is blaming others for our difficulties or attributing our own unethical desires to others. Rather than acknowledge that you're afraid of the director, you label him as "unresponsive" and "out to get you" and attribute the distance between the two of you as all his fault. Stella, for instance, projects her feelings of animosity onto people in the business and imagines that they all secretly despise her. When she does manage to get some work, she alienates herself from the cast and crew by acting manipulatively and deceitfully, determined to "get them before they can get her."

- *To what extent, if any, do you employ projection as a defense against threat and anxiety?*

_____

_____

- *Can you think of any concrete examples?*

_____

_____

_____

Rationalization

Rationalizations are attempts to prove that our thoughts are rational and justifiable when, in fact, they may not be. A defensive lack of insight and awareness distinguish rationalizations from reasoned opinion. When we argue that we've failed because "those people had all the opportunities" and refuse to look at additional factors, as for instance that we never tried very hard, we are rationalizing. Stella rationalizes away her anxiety by arguing that people win auditions according to whom they know or how sexy they look, rather than according to how well they perform, so her only preparations are to look sexy and to find out beforehand who the auditors are.

- *To what extent, if any, do you employ rationalization as a defense against threat and anxiety?*

_____

_____

- *Can you think of any concrete examples?*

_____

_____

_____

Repression

Repression is the defensive technique of keeping aspects of personality at bay. If, for instance, your sexuality scares you, you repress your feelings by covering up from head to toe and dismissing all sexual thoughts as fast as you can. Similarly, you repress any memories of pleasurable sexual experiences. In Stella's case, she represses memories of her previous failed auditions, since to allow those memories into conscious awareness might provoke an unwanted, anxiety-provoking investigation of her motives and methods. As a result, she can't learn from her experiences, as she quickly banishes her experiences to memory and then represses those memories.

- *To what extent, if any, do you repress painful thoughts, feelings, and memories as a defense against threat and anxiety?*

_____

_____

• *Can you think of any concrete examples?*

_____

_____

_____

_____

Reaction Formation

When, in order to prevent dangerous desires from being expressed, you exaggerate opposite attitudes and behaviors and use them as barriers, that defense is known as reaction formation. You may mask your criminal desires by advocating the death penalty, keep your love of pornography at bay by joining watchdog groups, or remain "in the closet" by taking rabid anti-gay stands. In Stella's case, she defends herself against her deep desire to express her real love of theater—a desire that feels dangerous because, if expressed, it would open her up to ridicule and mockery—by mocking those actors who take acting seriously and openly express their love of their chosen profession.

• *To what extent, if any, do you employ reaction formation as a defense against threat and anxiety?*

_____

_____

• *Can you think of any concrete examples?*

_____

_____

_____

_____

Displacement

When you discharge your pent-up feelings of hostility on objects less dangerous than those that aroused the original emotion, that's called displacement. Classic examples are kicking your dog when you get home from work because you can't kick your boss or yelling at your kids because you can't safely yell at your father. Angry at not being asked to come back for a second reading after her audition, Stella allows herself to rant at slow drivers on her way home and lash out at her lover the instant he greets her.

• *To what extent, if any, do you employ displacement as a defense against threat and anxiety?*

_____

_____

• *Can you think of any concrete examples?*

_____

_____

_____

_____

Emotional Insulation and Isolation

Withdrawal into passivity protects the self from hurt. After Stella's performance in an off-Broadway play is criticized, she stops auditioning, arguing that she needs a little time to recover from the experience. As that recovery time begins to stretch out indefinitely, she finds more reasons not to audition, taking comfort in the defense of emotional insulation from hurt.

Rather than frankly admit that what she fears is the possibility of new wounding and the heightened anxiety that future performances might bring, she opts for the security of a closeted way of being.

- *To what extent, if any, do you employ emotional insulation as a defense against threat and anxiety?*

  _____
  _____

- *Can you think of any concrete examples?*

  _____
  _____
  _____
  _____

Regression

Regression is a retreat to an earlier developmental stage, resulting in immature responses and a lower level of aspiration. For example, passengers on a sinking ship, overwhelmed by their circumstances, curl up into the fetal position and give up trying to escape as they defend themselves against the realization that they are about to drown. Stella, too, appears like a helpless child as she shows up for her first cabaret appearance and is suddenly overwhelmed by the chaos of the club, the newness of the experience, and her fears about performing. Feeling like an adult moments before as she got out of the cab, her defenses kick in and, because the situation feels seriously scary, she lands on one of our most dramatic defenses, regression, and begins talking and acting like a little girl.

- *To what extent, if any, do you regress as a defense against threat and anxiety?*

  _____
  _____

- *Can you think of any concrete examples?*

  _____
  _____
  _____
  _____

Sympathism

Sympathism is the defensive attempt to gain sympathy from others so that you can bolster your self-esteem despite past failures or in anticipation of future failures.

A basketball player with a minor injury that doesn't require a brace but who fears that his performance will be radically affected by his injury hobbles onto the court wearing a brace, so as to simultaneously avoid playing and garner sympathy. In Stella's case, she complains to her fellow actors that the director can't direct, that the costumer hasn't fitted her properly, and that her role, though small, is incredibly demanding, all in an attempt to gain sympathy and ward off her feelings of anxiety.

- *To what extent, if any, do you employ sympathism as a defense against threat and anxiety?*

  _____
  _____

- *Can you think of any concrete examples?*

  _____
  _____
  _____
  _____

Undoing

Undoing is the attempt to atone for immoral desires or to make up for mistakes through some activity other than forthrightly addressing the desire or mistake and the anxiety it provokes. Rather than admitting to yourself that—because you were anxious when you mailed out your query letter to agents—you failed to include a return envelope, you write a long, detailed, apologetic letter of explanation to all

> ## TALKING CIRCLES AROUND ANXIETY
> *Intellectualizing and rationalizing are regularly employed by intelligent, fluent men and women who keep anxiety at bay by "talking circles" around the issues at hand. In Setting Free the Actor, Ann Brebner described the following interview with a young actor:*
>
> My first question to him was, "So, tell me about yourself." He responded by talking a mile a minute about the universe, life, goodness, truth, and the universe again. I soon lost track of what he was saying, unable to get any sense of who he was. I pointed out that I had asked him to tell me something about himself, and that he hadn't done that at all. Later he said he knew that he had blown many interviews with casting directors because he had tried to appear as he thought a good actor should appear—tortured and riddled with anxiety—only he didn't really know how to do that. Because he didn't feel adequately anguished, he would jump into his intellect as the next best thing.
>
> Here we have an elegant example of an actor providing rationalizations—that he is just not as naturally anxious as actors are supposed to be—to support his penchant for intellectualizing, which is his defense against the anxiety he claims not to be experiencing.

those agents (again forgetting to include a reply envelope!). In Stella's case, rather than acknowledging that she's stopped auditioning and trying to fathom the reasons for her avoidance, she spends the lion's share of her time trying to reconcile with an actress with whom she fought during the run of the last play she appeared in. Her attempts to undo the consequences of that conflict are a defense against examining the larger conflict she's experiencing, between wanting to perform and feeling too anxious to perform.

- *To what extent, if any, do you engage in undoing as a defense against threat and anxiety?*

_____

_____

- *Can you think of any concrete examples?*

_____

_____

_____

_____

Acting Out

Acting out is the attempt to reduce the anxiety aroused by threats and forbidden desires by taking indirect, oblique action meant to rid yourself of the threat or desire. Instead of acknowledging your fear of flying, you make a scene in the airport over the handling of your luggage and miss your flight.

Instead of acknowledging that you're afraid of public speaking, you write so poor a speech that your boss decides that you'd better not deliver it. Stella, who's fearful that she's going to forget her lines, acts out her desire not to come to the theater by arriving a little late for every rehearsal. When the director takes her to task, she stops arriving late but acts out in a new way, by getting irate at stagehands and causing production delays.

- *To what extent, if any, do you employ acting out as a defense against threat and anxiety?*

_____

_____

- *Can you think of any concrete examples?*

_____

_____

_____

_____

This already long list of ego defense mechanisms is hardly complete. Almost any human capability can be used in a defensive way. We can use humor defensively: as Mel Brooks put it, "Humor is just another defense against the universe." We can use anger defensively and ruin our chances: as the actor Alan Rich explained, "When you walk in with anger, everyone feels it. Lose the anger and you may win the part." It really isn't possible to produce a comprehensive list of the ways that we defend ourselves against unwanted information, potential blows to our self-esteem, perceived threats, and the experience of anxiety.

What we see when we look for performance anxiety is not just sweaty palms or shaking legs but all of our defensive antics meant to contain and ward off anxiety. We see inappropriate distancing, rationalizing, conforming, raging, and so on. This defensiveness binds anxiety and protects the individual but at many high costs, among them a lack of presence, an inability to access skills, difficulties in accurately reading the situation, and, as a bottom line, poor performance.

- *What defensive maneuvers do you employ to ward off threats and feelings of anxiety?*

_____

_____

- *Can you describe some negative consequences of responding defensively in performance situations?*

_____

_____

_____

- *Do you display a particular defensive posture before or during performance, for instance by adopting an aloof, angry, superior, scornful, wary, accommodating, cheerful, or meek persona?*

_____

_____

- *Does adopting this persona help you feel in control of the situation?*

_____

_____

- *Does it feel comfortable and familiar?*

_____

_____

- *Does it help you mask a more unacceptable attitude?*

_____

_____

- *What are the main disadvantages of adopting this characteristic attitude?*

_____

_____

_____

- *Is it offensive or otherwise inappropriate?*

_____

_____

- *Does it prevent you from doing your best work?*

_____

_____

- *Take a little time and chat with yourself about how your defenses operate. Get familiar with your particular tricks and think through what it would be like—and what it would take—to approach life less defensively.*

DANGER, DANGER EVERYWHERE

As you become wiser about anxiety, you'll begin to recognize that people are living their lives scared of shadows. Many psychological experiments have been conducted to prove this point. In one experiment subjects were shown a pair of lines, one of which was patently longer than the other. When a subject was shown the two lines in the absence of any pressure, he told the simple truth, that the line on the left was longer. When, however, subjects were put in a room with confederates of the experimenter who asserted that the lines were of equal length, they tended to crumble. Suddenly they felt compelled to say that the lines were of equal length. A "shadow" had entered their consciousness and paralyzed them with fear. Subjects became frightened that if they said something different from what other people were saying, they'd get gored.

THEY'RE OUT TO GET ME
Although defense mechanisms can provide relief from anxiety, they often make us feel unnecessarily psychologically constricted. Among the most common defense mechanisms are repression and denial (in which anxious feelings are blocked from conscious awareness) and projection (in which we attribute to other people feelings that are too threatening to admit to in ourselves). For example, "They're out to get me" was Charles's assessment of his jury committee before his end-of-semester examination. He was so absorbed in projecting his anger and hostility that he failed to acknowledge his own role in his predicament.
—PAUL SALMON and ROBERT MEYER, Notes from the Green Room

Their defenses "rallied" around them and caused them to lie. The nondefensive thing to have said was, "The one on the left is longer." Was there anything really to fear about making such a response? No. Not a thing. They could have said to themselves, "Wow, what's going on here? All these people telling lies about the length of those two lines is making me incredibly anxious. I wonder if I'll be able to stick to the truth!" That's how I would like you to think and talk. If they could have said something like that, the menacing bull would have vanished. When it was their turn to speak, they would have calmly asserted the obvious truth, unafraid of some amorphous social threat. No stumbles, no apologies, no embarrassed smiles—and no bull.

Consider another experiment. You're shown a painting. You like it. You say that you like it. Then the person next to you states his opinion. He says that he doesn't like it. What happens? A person who is easily threatened in such circumstances—a person who experiences shadows as threats—is going to change her mind. A person used to averting her eyes and living in fear of bull shadows is going to crumble. Internally she'll say, "Maybe I was wrong to like it," "Maybe I don't know how to judge a painting," or "Maybe that guy's right." When you ask her a second time if she likes the painting, she's going to tell you that now she likes it a lot less. In actual experiments, *all* subjects confronted by antagonistic views yielded at least a little in their stated preferences. That is, *every single subject started seeing shadows.* Their anxiety rising, they defended themselves by conforming.

When you lower your defenses, you will have to experience life as it is. All those shadows that you've been defending yourself against will suddenly appear—and at first glance they will indeed look like bulls. How will you handle this new reality and this new anxiety? First, you're going to say some new, helpful things to yourself. You're going to say, "Anxiety isn't the enemy. It's only a warning signal. Let me see if there's any real danger." If you remind yourself that the danger—and then the anxiety—are likely to vanish as soon as you look at those bull shadows directly, you'll start to grow courageous enough to do this life-changing work.

The mind makes anxiety. The mind makes anxiety because it makes big mistakes, translating little or no threats into big threats. The mind scares the body. People who may not look scared are in fact scaring themselves all the time. You can tell it by their behaviors. They're eating too much. They can't stop smoking. They can't sleep at night. They turn the house upside down to find a slip of paper they don't really need. They can't prepare a dinner for four without panicking. They can't smile. When pressed, they lash out. They see threats everywhere.

People who read my books write to me and say things like, "I never understood that I wasn't painting because of anxiety. Now it's so clear to me! If I just embrace my anxiety, I can paint." Recently I got the following email. The sender wrote, "I'm a creative potter. A painter friend and I have been reading your work and it's been amazing, almost magical, how the information is helping us! Taking your suggestions for working through the anxieties connected to each stage of the creative process, I've found myself able to walk through each and every anxious moment. It's great! A week ago I was feeling really tired and weak. Realizing that I was having starting anxiety, I read up on that chapter. The very next morning (and every morning since) I woke early with creating on my mind. Thank you!"

Learn all about anxiety and you'll have acquired the most important education of all. When the person in front of you on the supermarket line, who really must know that she's going to have to pay for her groceries, acts surprised when the clerk holds out his hand for money, realize that she's wearing her anxiety like a neon sign. What is she anxious about? That we don't know—all we know is that we are witnessing another anxious human being, another person trying to wall herself off from her experience of anxiety. How well is she doing? You can just tell that she isn't doing well; and when, a moment later, she pulls out a cigarette, we have further proof that this innocent moment provoked so much anxiety in her that now she needs to medicate herself.

You want to lower your defenses and notice what makes you anxious, not because you want the anxiety—you don't—but because lowering your defenses and unmasking threats are first steps in the process of transforming yourself into someone who isn't threatened by shadows. When you stop feeling threatened by shadows, you will feel much less anxious. Will yourself to look threats and anxiety in the eye. Begin right now. Go on an anxiety treasure hunt. Notice how anxiety inhabits—and inhibits—your sister, your father, your coworkers, and, when you dare look, you. Look for its obvious manifestations, in the way that people fumble through their presentations or refuse to fly. Look for it in its subtler manifestations, in people's anger, in their strange behaviors, in the way they brush you off or leech onto you.

Let me repeat the goals to keep in mind. Trying to ward off danger and keep anxiety at bay by defending yourself against every shadowy threat is a poor choice. This method prevents you from freeing yourself from threats that exist only because you aren't looking at them directly. The better choice is to look danger in the eye, even if that means that you will experience some anxiety. This is a better choice for many reasons, but the most important one is that you will begin to transform yourself into a less afraid person. Then you will experience less anxiety.

Chapter Five

CONTRIBUTING FEARS

What seems to frighten us about performing? Performance anxiety has its reasons, but they aren't as straightforward as "plane might crash, therefore I will die" or "loose tiger, better run!" What bothers us about performing are the following sorts of things: that we might fail; that we might look foolish; that we might suffer a blow to self-esteem; and so on. Let's look at some of these many fears and, by looking them in the eye, begin to master them.

The list of possible things that we may fear about performing is a very long one. That's good to know. It's good to know that a lot may be going on inside of us, psychologically speaking, contributing to our experience of performance anxiety. Otherwise we might just label ourselves as weak or even disabled. It is rather better to know that a specific fear, handful of fears, or constellation of fears is making us sweat than to suppose that we are ruined or broken.

On the other hand, seeing a list this long may make your heart sink. Don't let it. You won't have to master these fears one by one. They will all go away—or at least recede into the background—as you transform yourself into the stronger, more aware person that I hope you'll become. Even if you have to tackle certain ones head on, you'll find that you're able to do just that. So don't give the length of the following list a second thought.

OUR MANY FEARS

It would be nice if we could organize the following thirty fears into several neat categories, like not feeling ready to perform, not feeling like a strong person, or fearing the negative consequences of a poor performance. Unfortunately, while many of these fears seem to fit neatly into such categories, many do not. So I've chosen to list them alphabetically and then focus on four of them in a more detailed discussion.

Fear of annihilation

Fear of annihilation is the fear that if we fail at our performance we won't just "have a bad day" but rather will experience a terrible shattering of our being and complete annihilation.

Fear of being ignored

Akin to certain common nightmares, the fear of being ignored is the fear that when we perform people won't listen to us. We'll be singing, acting, or delivering our speech and our audience will be laughing and chatting among themselves. A related fear is that our message won't be taken seriously or that it will be dismissed out of hand as silly, unimportant, or flat-out wrong.

Fear of being in power

Sometimes we fear that by performing we will suddenly become the person in charge, thrust into a leadership role that we never wanted and to which we don't feel equal. This complex fear is made up of our unwillingness to take responsibility, our dislike of the spotlight, and our distaste for the feelings that acting powerfully provokes.

Fear of being seen as flawed

This fear, related to a fear of failure and to low self-esteem, can manifest itself as an obsessive worry about our physical appearance, the desperate attempt to hide a blemish, and an agitated concern about everything from our credentials to our accent. The flaw we fear revealing may be as small and real as an old scar on our cheek or as large and metaphoric as "our rotten insides."

Fear of criticism

This fear, which we'll discuss at length in Chapter 9, is one of the prime fears and connects to the many real instances of criticism we experienced as children in our home, at school, and on the playground. This may be more a fear of fair criticism (that is, that we performed poorly and that people noticed), more a fear of unfair criticism (that is, that we performed well and still got criticized), or a general, encompassing fear of both.

Fear of diminished self-esteem

This is the fear that our self-esteem or self-image, perhaps already fragile, will take a serious blow should we perform poorly, a blow we perhaps don't feel equal to surviving. A related fear is that our idealized self-image, which we maintain by avoiding situations that might test it, will get badly tarnished if we put it to the test in performance.

Fear of disappointing people

This is the fear that, even if we ourselves do not have that much invested in our performing brilliantly, others do—our parents, our teachers, our boss, our audience—and we'll badly disappoint them if we perform only adequately or, worse, poorly. This fear can make certain performances, when people whom we don't want to disappoint are in attendance, that much more nerve-wracking.

Fear of dying

It is strange that performing can provoke a fear this large, but it can. As one study subject put it, "When I look at all of my small fears they dissolve into one big fear, a fear of dying, and whether it's my literal death that I fear or something like my social or psychological death, the theme is death and the fear is of dying."

Fear of embarrassment and/or humiliation

No child has ever escaped childhood without experiencing moments of embarrassment and humiliation; and few adults forget how horrible those moments felt. The graver the humiliation we experienced, the more pointed that humiliation, the more vivid our memories of those terrible events, then the more likely it is that we will hold performance as a potential source of new humiliation and the more anxiety we'll experience in anticipation of performing.

Fear of evaluation (negative or positive)

Many people fear being critiqued and examined, even if the critique is ultimately a positive one and even if the examination ultimately leads to praise and applause. This fear is rooted in part in our basic privacy needs; in part on our fear that a negative evaluation, even if only marginally critical, will outweigh any positives that we hear; and in part on our innate nervous reaction to having a mirror thrust in our face.

Fear of failure

It may seem like an axiom of human nature that everyone fears failure. Yet when we look at the matter more closely, it appears that many confident, successful people—people who understand the natural and even inevitable place of failure in a rich, productive life—experience more fear about not trying than they do about failing at what they attempt. A fear of failure, then, seems to connect to a lack of confidence and a conscious or unconscious misunderstanding of the place of a certain amount of failure in a successful life.

Fear of fear itself

A surprising number of people fear performing because they fear—and hate—the experience of feeling themselves afraid before a performance. Perhaps unafraid in other areas of their life, they are forced to feel "weak," "cowardly," and "not all right" as performance anxiety wells up in them while they wait to perform. The anxiety itself becomes a reproach; and over time what they begin to fear is not the performance but the performance anxiety and the negative feelings it provokes.

Fear of imperfection

A fear of imperfection is a fear of the very idea of flaws. Not only do you fear being seen as flawed, but a "flaw" anywhere—in the adequacy of the publicity for your next concert, in the size of the audience in attendance at the concert, and so on—provokes anxiety. If you fear making even a single performance mistake, if your standards are the standards of controlled recordings and not live performance, if you really are inhibited by the need to be perfect, then this may be the fear that precipitates your bouts of performance anxiety.

> ## THE PERFECTIONIST
> *The perfectionist fixes one line of a poem over and over—until no lines are right. The perfectionist redraws the chin line on a portrait until the paper tears. The perfectionist writes so many versions of scene one that she never gets to the rest of the play. The perfectionist writes, paints, creates with one eye on her audience. Instead of enjoying the process, the perfectionist is constantly grading the results. For the perfectionist, there are no first drafts, rough sketches, warm-up exercises. Every draft is meant to be final, set in stone. Midway through a project, the perfectionist decides to read it all over, outline it, see where it's going. And where is it going? Nowhere, very fast.*
>
> —Julia Cameron, *The Artist's Way*

Fear of inauthenticity

Many people fear the demand that audiences, and especially mass audiences, make on performers that they look and act in certain stylized ways, in ways "appropriate," say, for a country-western singer or a pop lecturer. As one performer put it, "I have this fear of phoniness, of not staying true to my heart, of not being authentic. It's the fear that I have to put on my 'party' face and be nicer, more accommodating, and less smart than I really want to be."

Fear of lack of preparation

A fear of lack of preparation comes in two forms. One is a realistic fear based on our accurate understanding that we haven't prepared well enough and/or don't know our material adequately. The second is an unrealistic fear based on the shadowy worry that we aren't prepared, even though we are—or worse, that we can't ever be prepared no matter what efforts we make.

Fear of looking stupid or foolish

When we witness something go wrong in someone else's performance—when a prop falls apart, an amplifier conks out, a lecturer loses his place and gets that "deer caught in the headlights" look—many of us involuntarily think the following thought: "Boy, was that stupid!" If that's the kind of thought that pops into our head, we naturally leap to the conclusion that people will consider us stupid should we make a similar performance mistake or have a similar performance accident.

Fear of loss of control

Many performers fear that they will lose control of their emotions, their bodily functions, or their mind when they perform. The following report, from a well-known lecturer, is typical: "A fear of getting too emotional is very big for me. I get very involved in what I'm saying and get choked up, tearful, and turn red. This feels like a loss of control and also a loss of professionalism."

Fear of loss of love and approval

Many performers associate performing with winning love and approval and therefore naturally worry that a poor performance will lose them these precious commodities. The adult who, as a child, had to win love and approval from his parents, since it was never freely given, is likely to invest the performance arena with supercharged feelings from childhood, upping his experience of anxiety.

Fear of loss of the dream

For many people, performing connects to their deepest personal and professional dreams, so each time they perform, the chance exists that their dream may get tarnished a bit or, worse, burst altogether. The fear of losing their dream by performing poorly causes many people to avoid performing, as a dream never tested in the crucible of reality can remain a fine fantasy.

Fear of luck running out and other superstitions

Some people have early successes, easy successes, or a string of successes in performance situations and begin to fear that their luck is bound to run out. This natural superstitious fear can manifest itself in the fear that your voice is going, that people are tired of your message or your material, or, worse, in the inexplicable, obsessive, and corrosive fear that "something bad is due."

Fear of meaninglessness

Performers often invest great meaning in their performances and, as a consequence, fear that if a performance turns out poorly meaning will drain out of their life. A related fear is the fear that they are investing too much meaning in their performances, which similarly provokes existential anxiety. A third fear is that their life will seem dull and meaningless when the performance ends, making them anxious not so much about the performance but about the aftermath of performing.

> ## ANOTHER FACE OF PERFECTIONISM
> *Throughout the early phases of my career, the mirror was my nemesis, seductive to the point of addiction. Stepping through the looking glass meant confronting a double who exposed all of my flaws and pointed out all of my physical imperfections. The physical side of the discipline does involve a certain degree of tedium, to say nothing of the pain. But the hours of practice are minor compared to the emotional terror that can sometimes haunt a ballerina when she studies her reflection in the mirror. This anxiety is not due to simple vanity or fear of professional rejection. As in the myth of Narcissus, the beautiful youth who falls in love with his own reflection, the relationship between the dancer and her mirror image is an intimacy of extraordinary power and potentially perilous consequence.*
> —GELSEY KIRKLAND, *Dancing on My Grave*

Fear of mediocrity

Many people claim to be perfectionists, but in reality most people do not expect perfection from themselves. What they want is to do good work and, if possible, excellent work. The bar is really set at "good"; it is falling below "good" that terrifies many people. They hate the thought of doing mediocre work and viewing themselves as a mediocrity. This fear is exacerbated in those situations, which arise frequently enough, when the material they must present is mediocre and they might be tarred with the brush of their inferior material—as, for instance, an actor cast in a second-rate play.

Fear of memory loss

This common fear, a specific variation of a fear of "loss of control," is rooted in the natural worry that we may forget our lines, lose our place, or, worst of all, "lose everything" stored in our brain and our very ability to think. Since we've all suffered memory losses of this sort at one time or another, we each have a reservoir of bad feelings about our ability to store and recover information, especially when the pressure is on.

Fear of not being clear and/or being misunderstood

If the material we're presenting is complex, ambiguous, ahead of its time, controversial, or difficult in any way, it's natural for us to worry that we're not going to present the material well; that we're going to present it well but still be misunderstood; or that, because it's controversial, we'll create a tense atmosphere and provoke a negative response.

Fear of not repeating past successes

People who perform regularly get accustomed to having sometimes more successful and sometimes less successful performances. A budding fear can grow that the next performance will prove to be one of the unsuccessful ones, perhaps because the performer, on the lookout for "telltale warning signs" of failure, spots some. Past successes ought to serve as a kind of inoculation against performance anxiety, but a fear of not being able to repeat them can creep into consciousness and subvert those good memories.

Fear of rejection

It's one thing to get criticized and another thing to get rejected. It's possible to get criticized and not also rejected; but every rejection, even if it isn't accompanied by any criticism, amounts to a complete "No!" Therefore rejection feels worse; and a fear of rejection typically is rooted in a more serious precipitating cause, like parental rejection in childhood.

Fear of retribution

It is one thing to fear that you might perform poorly and that some negative consequence, such as not being invited back to perform, might result. It is another thing to fear retribution for a poor performance. To fear retribution is to have a super-sized worry about the severity of the punishment you might receive, a fear that likely originated in childhood experiences of extreme, outsized punishment.

Fear of success

A fear of success is most often a misnamed fear of failure. But sometimes it really is a fear of success: that is, a fear that with success will come unwanted duties and responsibilities, a changed lifestyle, a more public presence, and other perceived negatives. For some people, these negatives feel so burdensome that they feel obliged to sabotage their performances.

Fear of strangers

Many primitive fears, rooted in the ancient brain, can be activated when we perform. One is the fear that everyone who is not a blood relative or a member of the tribe is a threat and a danger. This fear can get activated when we perform in front of an audience different from the audiences we usually perform before, for instance before an audience of a different race or one whose beliefs we know to be different from ours.

> OBLIGED TO BE MEDIOCRE
> *A singer explained:*
> I have a hard time getting up and singing in front of people because I don't want people to think that I have an inflated opinion of myself. I almost feel obliged to be mediocre at things so as to avoid drawing attention to myself. What can I do with this fear? Well, it's easy to look at it right now and say that the fear is absolutely ridiculous. But I suppose the way I can deal with it is to concentrate on something other than my ego when I'm performing. I just need to breathe and concentrate on what I'm doing, not on what other people are thinking of me.

Fear of the unexpected and the unknown

We don't know and can't know what's about to happen when we perform, which means that we are at the mercy of our usual cognitive style of fortune-telling. As a rule, do you predict that good things are going to happen or that bad things are going to happen? If it's your custom to predict a negative outcome, irrespective of how past events have gone, then it's a short step to fearing every impending event and regularly experiencing performance anxiety.

FOUR PRIMARY FEARS

Real breakthroughs can occur just by realizing that a certain fear is circulating in your system. Here's a report from a study subject who took the time to think through which fears on this list might be implicated in her experience of performance anxiety. Nikki explained:

> *Looking at the list, what jumps out at me is that I have a fear of being misunderstood or a fear of not being understood at all. I'm a singer-songwriter and while I consider my style of music "pop," it's not run of the mill, average pop. I like to make music that is very much a challenge to the listener. The fear I have is that people will never "get it." What also jumped out at me was a fear of failure, a fear of imperfection, fear of loss of self-esteem . . . and then I began to see that the real fear was bigger than any of those fears.*
>
> *To fail would result in loss of the dream. If I never make the attempt, then the dream remains alive. If I make the attempt and fail, then the dream dies and the result is loss of self-esteem, hopelessness, and all the rest. Well, I can't operate this way, avoiding trying so as to secure my self-image and keep my dreams intact. I had no idea that's what I was afraid of! Knowing that is going to make*

a huge difference and I can already feel that I'm more eager to perform and more confident about performing than I've felt in a long time.

Next, let's take a look at four primary fears (from our list of thirty) that plague many performers.

Fear of the Unexpected and the Unknown

Anybody who's ever watched a horror movie knows what it feels like to anticipate the monster's arm crashing through the wall. We try to get ready for it, our body starts pumping adrenaline, but when the hairy arm appears, we still feel the urge to scream—and sometimes we do. If we aren't expecting that hairy arm, if the filmmaker has caught us off guard, we can almost experience cardiac arrest.

For many people, performance is a territory of monsters in the dark and primitive fears. For those who were frightened as children by traumatic events or who experienced childhood as a fearful time, it's understandable that they might bring a sense of dread to the performance arena. But a fear of the unexpected and the unknown need not have anything to do with traumatic events in childhood. It may arise simply because we're bothered by our insufficient knowledge of an upcoming event.

Consider the following example. A client of mine, an opera singer, had a benefit recital coming up at which her singing teacher would be honored. Many of the city's arts luminaries would attend. While she suffered from performance anxiety generally, she anticipated that in this case a really severe bout was likely. I gave her a menu of strategies to think about, of the sort we'll discuss in later chapters, and the following week we discussed the strategies in session.

One strategy had struck her as particularly useful, called "Bring a Friend," where the performer imagines that a supportive friend is in the audience. We went over in detail how she would use it and then I had her perform her recital, from entrance to exit, silently singing the pieces. During her silent recital, I'd stop her and ask questions.

"What was going on then?"

"That's a part I worry about. It's a hard part."

"What do you need to do with it?"

"I need to get ready for it. When it sneaks up on me, I get too nervous, and then I can't handle it."

"When do you need to get ready for it?"

She could pinpoint the moment when she needed to begin readying herself for the difficult passage, and that knowledge helped lessen her anxiety. We continued on to the end of the recital, identifying other moments of anxiety, and she expressed satisfaction with the knowledge she'd gained. But I could tell that something remained unresolved.

"Did we miss something?" I asked.

"I'm supposed to give my teacher flowers."

"Do you mean that you're supposed to bring flowers and present them?"

"No, someone else is bringing them. But I'm supposed to present them at the end of the recital."

"And say a few words?"

"Yes, but that's fine. I know what I want to say."

"But something about the flower part is making you nervous?"

Slowly it dawned on her that because she hadn't stopped to visualize receiving the flowers and handing them to her teacher and because those moments had remained an unknown to her, she had made herself anxious over "the flower thing." It turned out that she had to prepare mentally for the bouquet presentation just as she had to prepare for the singing. Once she could visualize what would happen, she visibly relaxed.

Fear of Loss of Control

Performers often fear that their body and/or their mind will slip from their control during performance. In one study, this fear ranked as the number one anxiety-producer for both male and female performers. Performers fear that they won't be able to control their bodily functions, their bodily movements, or their behaviors. For example one backstage observer reported that "an internationally renowned concert musician stayed off the concert stage for ten years because of the dread fear that he would accidentally expel flatus during a performance." He continued, "The fear of urinating on himself has prompted more than one performer to leave a bottle just offstage, into which he could relieve himself just prior to entrances."

Performers may also feel trapped before going on, as if caught in a snare. In such cases it isn't a fear of loss of control that disturbs them but rather the reality of a loss of a specific kind of control, that they have lost their ability to flee from danger. As Stephen Aaron explained, "The actor, waiting in the wings, can resort to neither fight nor flight. He is physically and emotionally trapped and there is an intimate relationship between such immobility and passivity, on the one hand, and panic anxiety on the other." Thus some cases of performance anxiety really should be thought of as cases of inhibited flight.

Paradoxically, a performer may feel anxiously eager to take flight and to remain passive at the same time. He or she is like the dog in laboratory studies that's been given frequent electric shocks to keep it from leaving and that, when the door to its cage is opened, makes no attempt to escape. A person suffering from performance anxiety may feel both panicky and defeated while he waits in the wings. He may look calm enough but in reality may only feel resigned to his fate. The fear of losing control has become, over time, a feeling of "learned helplessness" and of having actually lost control.

Fear of Strangers

An audience is a special set of strangers, and it's natural enough to experience some "stranger anxiety" before performing. Since the hall is not filled with your friends and family, who are these people? Should we presume them to be friendly or hostile, supportive or indifferent? Are they knowledgeable about your medium and message or basically ignorant? As the choreographer Paul Taylor put it, "I'm always puzzled by audiences. I really don't know who they are, why they're there or what they're thinking."

Our fears about hostile strangers can turn the audience into a primitive "other" and arouse in us the feeling that we are about to go into battle. Even being seen by them or directly looking at them can be experienced as a threat. One actor who had to leave the profession because of stage fright explained, "It occurred to me one night, while on stage and waiting for my cue, that if one looks at the two galleries in the dark, they remind one of an open mouth ready to swallow you up."

FOURTEEN TIMES I WITHDREW

A filmmaker explained:

I'm often afraid of not being prepared. When I thought about this problem today, I remembered fourteen different times when I withdrew from projects I'd started because I felt I lacked the knowledge, skill, training, talent, experience, or whatever. Oh my, if only I could undo the damage I did! I could have gotten all the knowledge and experience I needed just by following through and completing what I'd started. I could have learned what was necessary to do just by accepting the responsibility. I need to trust that the way to complete what I start will reveal itself to me if I just do the work—and I need to show up when it's time to perform.

Some scholars have argued that actors performing in the ancient Greek theater wore masks in order to protect themselves from the evil eye of the spectator. That stepping onto a stage can feel like going into battle is clear from the way that actors typically characterize the audience as people to be tamed or slain. Richard Burton, similarly, described the perfect audience as "sheep." Laurence Olivier would stand behind the curtain before a performance chanting "You bastards!" at the audience. Burgess Meredith described the audience as "the dragon to be slain." Expressions like "Kill them!" "Lay them out in the aisles!" and "Knock them dead!" are among the most common pre-performance exclamations heard backstage.

As Brian Bates explained in *The Way of the Actor*:

> Like an animal, the actor allows himself to be cornered, and then he performs and does battle with the audience. This is a sense of living with danger which creates a tremendous vitality and energy. But there is no doubt that there are elements of hostility involved—it is indeed a battle. Simon Callow has identified the aspect of competition, even aggression, that exists between the actor and the audience. "There's no getting away from the fact that theatre contains an element of hostility. Every actor knows that. Standing on the stage is an aggressive act. It says: Look at me. Listen to me. It says, I'm interesting, I'm talented, I'm remarkable." Callow points out that the audience naturally responds to this as a challenge. "Oh yeah?" says the audience. "You'd better prove it."

It is one thing to assume that some audience members, among them critics and competitors, may constitute something like your natural enemy. It is a different, darker matter to see all strangers as threatening and every audience as standing in opposition to you. Indeed, you may be projecting your own feelings of hostility onto the audience. This is a good way to make enemies where no enemies exist and to inflame your performance anxiety.

Fear of Loss of Love and Approval

The actor Burgess Meredith once observed, "If you're a hit, there's so much love around, you can't stand it. But if it's a flop, the audience is merciless and there's very little you can do about it." The actress Blythe Danner complained that after an unsuccessful performance she felt that people had stopped liking her. The fear that a poor performance will lead to a real loss of love, friendship, and approval is common among performers.

A musician offered the following observation in response to a column I'd written in *Callboard* magazine: "Over the past thirty years I've discovered that performance anxiety is largely due to being too eager to please others rather than myself." If you're burdened by a need to have the audience like you and if you believe that they won't like you unless you please them—by looking a certain way, by presenting inoffensive material, and so on—then you're setting yourself up for inauthentic performing. If, however, you're lucky enough to be loved in your everyday life, it may be less important that your audience also love you.

With enough love in your life, it may be sufficient that your audience respect or appreciate you. It may be sufficient that you move them, educate them, interpret music for them, show them a mastery of your material, or thrill and astound them—without also having to seduce them. If, however, you're missing that love and affection, then you may turn to your audience—as an anonymous whole or to specific members within it—to gain the love you lack.

DEALING WITH OUR MANY FEARS

You'll learn how to address these fears in subsequent chapters. For now, what I'd like you to do is to read over the list of thirty fears once again and write down whatever comes to mind. Here's how one client, a painter, responded to this exercise:

> When I first looked at this list of fears, I couldn't pick out the one behind my anxiety. I did a writing technique called "looping" to see if I could identify what it is that I'm afraid of. I wrote for five minutes and realized that I wasn't getting to the bottom of why I'm afraid of telling people the price of my original paintings. There were all kinds of possibilities but none of them felt quite real. (Maybe the fear wasn't real? But, no, the fear was real enough!)
>
> Then I tried another method, called BET, which stands for Body, Emotions, and Thought. I asked myself where I felt the fear in my body. I discovered that it was all located in my upper chest, throat, and head area. When I "looked" to see what the fear looked like, it appeared as a gray and black smoke, wispy and elusive. I couldn't get the feel of it, it just kept moving around.
>
> Then I asked it to take a face and it suddenly transformed itself into a nasty cartoon character. The face told me that he was there to distract me from knowing my own true worth but, if I wanted him to, he could help me finally accept that I was valuable. Rather than fleeing my body, I could inhabit it all the way down to the soles of my feet. I listened to him and understood what he was saying. After I did the exercise, I had the opportunity to call a prospective customer. I felt very connected during the transaction and, to my astonishment, made the sale. (So was the fear ever really real?)

Chapter Six

CONTRIBUTING FACTORS

Many things, among them the thirty fears described in the last chapter, can help precipitate a bout of performance anxiety. In this chapter I want to take a look at some additional contributing factors. The goal isn't to produce a comprehensive list but to continue to paint a picture of how the complexities of human nature are implicated in our experience of performance anxiety. The contributing factors that we'll look at are the following eight:

Feeling conflicted
Feeling ashamed
Feeling guilty
Feeling a burden of responsibility
Feeling unequal to independent action
Feeling increasingly pressured
Feeling anxious all the time
Feeling threatened all the time

FEELING CONFLICTED

Conflict raises a person's anxiety level. Just as a disagreement between two friends produces tension such that each gets a little nervous just thinking about encountering the other, so a disagreement between the leading lady and the leading man, between two "team teachers," or between a soloist and an accompanist can produce anticipatory tension.

Indeed, many performers are in conflict about even wanting to perform. They may not be performing of their own free will but rather because they are pleasing others or have been told one too many times that they are too talented not to perform. They may have been thrust into performing more than drawn to performing by choice; or they may have ended up in a performance career as the result of decisions made early in life, decisions, made either by themselves or by others, that are no longer valid.

Dr. Julie Nagel, a psychologist and pianist, has studied these particular conflicts extensively and described them in her article, "Medical Problems of Performing Artists." She found that among eighty students at the University of Michigan School of Music, one group experienced significantly less performance anxiety than did subjects in three other groups. This first group, dubbed the Identity Achieved group, she characterized in the following way:

> Identity Achieved individuals seek careers in music performance but also have tried or thought seriously about other options; they have weighed the pros and cons of their decision. Ultimately, they have arrived at their choice, perhaps despite parental objections, and, most importantly, are relatively conflict-free.

Conflict is a profound and enduring source of anxiety. Because your parents yelled at each other, and because this yelling made you anxious, you may now grow anxious if someone raises his voice in a seminar room or drops her musical instrument case. The more you experience life as conflictual—the more you see performing as a battle between yourself and the audience or between yourself and critics, or the more you're burdened by unresolved inner conflicts—the more likely you'll be to approach performing in a defensive and anxious way.

In Freudian psychoanalysis, a primary goal is working out inner conflicts through the insight gained in a dynamic relationship between psychoanalyst and patient. For Freud, neurosis in the individual resulted as much from painful unresolved conflicts as from any other psychological source. It is to the benefit of anyone suffering from performance anxiety to fathom what conflicts are simmering beneath the surface and how those conflicts may be affecting—and even creating—the anxiety.

- *Do you sense that you are harboring important internal conflicts with respect to performing?*

  _____

  _____

- *About what specific issues are you in conflict?*

  _____

  _____

  _____

  _____

- *If you are in conflict about wanting to perform, is this a mild, moderate, or severe inner conflict?*

  _____

  _____

- Consider how you currently handle inner (intrapsychic) or outer (interpersonal) conflicts. Do you deal with them:

By attempting to deny their existence?

_____

_____

By avoiding situations that provoke them?

_____

_____

Through other defensive measures?

_____

_____

By airing them and examining them?

_____

_____

- If you sense that a potent inner conflict is troubling you, what might you do to attempt to resolve it?

_____

_____

_____

_____

FEELING ASHAMED

In recent years we've grown more aware of the difference between guilt and shame. Simply put, a person feels guilty about having done or thought a bad thing but ashamed about *being* a bad thing. The ashamed person feels inferior, damaged, small, even worthless. He or she feels only marginally entitled to be seen or heard and scarcely competent to do anything—except, perhaps, make music, act, or dance. Music, acting, or dance may have been a place of refuge in the midst of a terrible childhood, a time when the young person focused her energies on performing and got proficient at it.

The time naturally came when public presentation became the next logical move. Stepping into the spotlight, however, activated her sense of shame. No matter how much this injured person may have practiced and no matter how large a talent she possessed, she nevertheless expected to be humiliated or punished for her performance, just as she had been humiliated and punished all along just for being. This fearful expectation naturally provoked performance anxiety.

In *Setting Free the Actor*, Ann Brebner pointed out, "For actors, shame as a constant companion can have deep consequences, endangering our dream of success. When an actor goes to an audition, the director is hoping to see the most intimate parts of an actor's soul. If what comes up is shame, the actor is not going to get a lot of work."

GUILT, SHAME, AND A FEAR OF EXPOSURE

Though Bruce's professional position called for him to speak publicly, he nevertheless could not represent his company well in public discussions. It was especially difficult to disagree or to be publicly critical of another; nothing terrified him more than a public debate. "What could happen in that situation?" I asked. "What is the ultimate calamity?" Bruce had no doubt about the answer. "Exposure." He feared his adversary would insouciantly read aloud a list of all the shameful sexual episodes in his life. He identified with the nightmare of James Joyce's Leopold Bloom who, when placed on trial for his secret desires, is humiliated when evidence of his many peccadilloes is paraded before the court.

—IRVIN YALOM, *Existential Psychotherapy*

Whether you work in the performing arts or only make occasional presentations, shame may be contributing to the fear you experience when you appear in public. If you have the sense that this is a reality for you, you may want to seek out a counselor or a therapist. The underlying issues are likely to be profound, ripe with many painful consequences (like self-debasing and self-sabotaging behaviors, from shoplifting to careless sex, from a drug addiction to uncontrolled rage), and hard to address without professional help.

- *To what extent were you made to feel ashamed of yourself as a child?*

_____

_____

_____

_____

- *To what extent do you feel ashamed of yourself today?*

_____

_____

_____

_____

- *Do you feel inferior to other people (even if, paradoxically, you also feel superior to them)?*

_____

_____

_____

- *If you are a performer, do you feel inferior to other performers?*

_____

_____

_____

- *To what extent do you expect to be punished for your performance efforts?*

_____

_____

_____

_____

- *What form do you imagine that punishment will take?*

_____

_____

_____

- *Do you recognize a relationship between shame and performance anxiety in your life?*

_____

_____

- *If so, what might reduce or eliminate your sense of shame about yourself? What might constitute small steps and what large steps in feeling less ashamed of yourself?*

_____

_____

_____

_____

_____

SHAME AND VULNERABILITY

An actor explained:

It is a challenge to my self-image to risk auditioning for a place in a theater program against twenty-year-olds. All of my fears and my experiences of humiliation show up more powerfully because I feel so vulnerable in this context. I'm confronted by my past experiences of failure, which in reality may not have been failures but only learning experiences badly handled. But competing with these young actors makes them feel like real failures and thoroughly activates my sense of shame.

FEELING GUILTY

Guilt and anxiety are intimate partners. A manager who is young, less experienced, and perhaps even less talented than his fellow workers may feel guilty about having been selected to address the annual sales meeting. A violinist may feel guilty about having a better instrument than his colleagues in the violin section. A college instructor may feel guilty about getting a coveted Ivy League job through a social connection. These guilty feelings provoke anxiety; our conscience is directly connected to our sweat glands.

What exactly is guilt? As with many of the concepts we deal with, including anxiety itself, guilt is not at all easy to define. The psychoanalyst Karen Horney likened it most to a "fear of disapproval" and a "fear of being found out." In this view, guilt is related to a fear of a loss of approval and to doubts about a person's competence. To the degree that we have been made to feel guilty in life or have gotten in the habit of "guilting" ourselves, the more likely we'll approach performances on the lookout for things to feel guilty about. As Linda Schierse Leonard explained in *Witness to the Fire: Creativity and the Veil of Addiction*:

> *Guilt is a lack, a debt, but not one that can be made up or paid off, although traditionally guilt has been understood in this way. But our existential guilt does not stem primarily from committed or omitted acts. We are not the source of our own being, nor do we have total control. We are not able to be perfect.*

In performance situations, where nothing less than perfection seems demanded, many "guilt possibilities" arise. Did you not really prepare enough? That's something to feel guilty about. Are you not really right for the role? That's something to feel guilty about. Are you unable to do justice to the music? That's something to feel guilty about. A person inclined to feel guilty can always find something to feel guilty about before, during, and after performing.

- *Are you regularly bothered by guilty feelings?*

  _____

  _____

- *What do you feel guilty about? What are the contents of your guilty feelings?*

  _____

  _____

  _____

  _____

  _____

- *To what extent do these pangs of conscience mask, distort, or protect you from other feelings?*

  _____

  _____

  _____

  _____

- *Do you sense a connection between your guilty feelings and your bouts of performance anxiety?*

  _____

  _____

FEELING A BURDEN OF RESPONSIBILITY

You may be a person who has learned to take personal responsibility for all aspects of a situation, including those that aren't even slightly in your control, like whether or not it rains on the day of the company picnic. You may also have learned to take responsibility for the actions of others, even though their behaviors aren't in your control and in most cases aren't even your business. This "burden of responsibility" is a common characteristic of people who grew up in families in which one or both parents were alcoholic or where the child had parent-like duties foisted on her at an early age. Those duties might have included minding younger siblings, providing emotional support for adults in the family, or working to augment the family income.

Suppose that you're grown up now and have become a musician. You may get nervous backstage if the person near you is having trouble with his instrument. You rush to help him without being asked and even though that means forgoing your own preparations—which naturally makes you more anxious. Or you may feel responsible for everybody's feelings in the band and try to make things "nice" between people who are feuding backstage. Not only don't you resolve the conflict, but suddenly it's time to go on and you aren't the least bit prepared—and panic sets in.

As a soloist or featured performer, you may feel a special and painful burden of responsibility for the performance, arguing to yourself that a muff will not only embarrass you but will cast everyone around you in a bad light. This burdensome "caretaker" identity, created in childhood, comes with a moral component attached: if you fail to take responsibility for everything and anything, then you are a bad person. This can also be thought of as a "tyranny of the shoulds": everywhere you look you see another thing that you should be paying attention to, taking responsibility for, and making right. Rather than possessing the freedom to decide in the moment whether you should or shouldn't shoulder a particular responsibility, you find that responsibility just attaches itself to you as if you were a magnet.

- *Do you hold as important parts of your identity the twin ideas that you are responsible for everything that happens and that you must take responsibility for whatever happens?*

_____

_____

- *What are the positive consequences of holding to those ideas?*

_____

_____

_____

_____

- *What are the negative consequences?*

_____

_____

_____

_____

- *Do you feel responsible for:*

The actions of others?

_____

_____

The feelings of others?

_____

_____

Events that you neither directly nor indirectly cause?

_____

_____

Events that you neither directly nor indirectly control?

_____

_____

- *Are you burdened by a tyranny of shoulds?*

_____

_____

- *If you feel burdened this way, can you identify the family dynamics or childhood events that might have contributed to this burden?*

_____

_____

_____

- *What might you do to overcome this problem?*

_____

_____

_____

FEELING UNEQUAL TO INDEPENDENT ACTION

A fear of taking independent action contributes to the experience of performance anxiety. When we perform, we must stand on our own two feet and accept responsibility for our performance. This felt sense of autonomy and independence may not come easily for the person who had poor role models, who learned to see the world as a terrifying place, or who was smothered and had little chance to practice independent behaviors. Nor may the ability to take autonomous action come easily to someone who grew used to hiding to avoid abuse or parental conflicts or who, having slid into drug or alcohol dependency, has become practiced at avoiding taking responsibility for his actions.

Individuation (that is, growing into our adult identity and taking on the responsibilities of adulthood) is a key task for the late adolescent and the young adult. Nowadays it seems that issues of individuation persist for a great many people, performers included, even into late adulthood. Some observers believe that we are in the middle of a "dependency epidemic" that manifests itself in a variety ways, from widespread drug and alcohol abuse to "codependent" relationships like those between a battered woman and the batterer with whom she continues to live.

Additionally, training in certain disciplines—dance, for instance—where a talented youngster may start a professional training program at the age of eleven or twelve and stay in that program all through adolescence, can easily foster dependency and prevent the artist from learning to think independently. As the dancer Vera Zorina explained, "Dancers are very obedient people. They don't go around making a fuss. They are not like actors who will say, 'I don't feel this line.' We simply stand around waiting for the choreographer to tell us what to do."

Conversely, a fiercely independent artist, fighting to retain a sense of her autonomy and independence, may aggressively act out. This artist experiences anxiety in situations where she has no choice but to conform. She may possess enough self-control not to engage in an outburst of "attitude" but may still feel a tremendous pressure at having to rein herself in. Such an artist may experience strange fears before performing: the fear that she will lose control and speak her own words and not the playwright's, insult the gallery owner to whom she is about to show her work, or in some other way thumb her nose at her audience.

> ## FEARING FREEDOM
> *Self-defeating fear is a natural consequence of being afraid of our own freedom to exist as a unique being or separate person. One anxiety sufferer wrote, "The thing I fear most is standing naked before my own freedom." The fear of freedom can lead to a passive, nonassertive approach to life. After all, if we are not even sure of our right to exist, how can we with any confidence ask others for good and fair treatment? And how can we be certain at any given moment that someone won't notice that we don't really have the right to be there. The enormous shyness that many of us have experienced as children or teenagers is a pure example of what the absence of freedom feels like.*
> —CHRISTOPHER MCCULLOUGH, *Managing Your Anxiety*

All performers must act independently at times and bow to the will of others at other times. For some, independent action is the edge and the source of anxiety. For others, bowing to another person's will and taking direction are the greater challenges. These are perennial life tasks that provoke anxiety in different measure according to the temperament and personality of the performer. If they are to be addressed and overcome, they require the performer's conscious attention.

• *Are you inclined to fear acting independently?*

_____

_____

• *Are you too obedient a person?*

_____

_____

- Are you too emotionally dependent on others?

_____

_____

- Are you so keen on maintaining your independence that you rebel inappropriately and refuse to conform?

_____

_____

- Have you established effective ways of dealing with people in authority, relating in ways that are neither too obsequious nor too rebellious?

_____

_____

_____

_____

- Can you tease out a connection between your performance anxiety and issues of dependency, authority and autonomy?

_____

_____

_____

_____

- If such a connection exists, what might you do to help yourself act both independently and appropriately?

_____

_____

_____

_____

FEELING INCREASINGLY PRESSURED

It would be nice to hypothesize that performance anxiety abates over time as a performer becomes more accustomed to performing and mastering his material. But neither performers' anecdotal reports nor studies confirm this hypothesis. For some performers the experience of performance anxiety actually intensifies over time. The actress Gertrude Lawrence, for one, complained, "These attacks of nerves seem to grow worse with the passing of the years. It's inexplicable and horrible and something you'd think you'd grow out of, not into."

Yet we can understand why this might happen. As a performer's career progresses, the real and felt importance of her performances may also increase dramatically. Suddenly she is performing before fifty thousand people, not fifty. People are paying a week's wages to hear her sing or traveling cross-country to see her act. Many people depend on her success and a great deal is expected of her band, dance company, repertory theatre, or ensemble. The publicity that precedes her touts her as the funniest woman alive, the greatest Blanche DuBois or Juliet of recent memory, a splendid interpreter of Beethoven's piano sonatas, or the best jazz singer around.

The pressure to live up to such billing can easily produce increased anxiety. She may also be asked to act as a spokesperson for her work and give interviews, appear on television and radio shows, help raise money for projects, and generally help promote and advertise her work. Performers are increasingly encouraged to undertake these tasks, each of which is a performance in its own right. While some performers relish these moments, others number them among their most anxiety-producing activities.

ADDED PRESSURE

An artist explained:

In a class I took, the instructor tried to convince us that working quicker was a plus, because the quicker you can produce pieces, the better your income will be. In order to teach us this lesson, he set up a contest: he did a demo, then we were to compete with each other to see who could finish our project the quickest. I was absolutely a mess. I had to stop working, set down my tools, and wait for the others to finish. I simply could not produce in that competitive environment. Weeks later, back at my studio, I took my time, practicing several times, and of course, did the project perfectly.

It turns out to be on the order of wishful thinking to imagine that your performance anxiety will vanish over time just because you perform more. The added pressures of a growing career, material that's more difficult to master, and heightened expectations can easily puncture that fantasy. That's unfortunate; but it's news that may allow an important message to sink in, that you will need to master *yourself* if you are to rid yourself of your performance anxiety. If you master yourself, primarily through the kind of detachment training you'll learn in Chapter 10, then you won't experience even a highly successful career as a reason to grow anxious.

- *Can you tell if your performance anxiety has decreased or increased over time?*

_____

_____

- *If it has increased, do you have any insights as to why that might be the case?*

_____

_____

_____

_____

- *In which performance situations do you experience extra pressure?*

_____

_____

_____

_____

- *Has this added pressure become predictable?*

_____

_____

- *Have you come up with effective ways of relieving or reducing this added pressure?*

_____

_____

_____

FEELING ANXIOUS ALL THE TIME

Because of childhood experiences and/or constitutional makeup, some people are regularly more anxious than other people. This persistent anxiety can manifest itself as obsessive thinking and compulsive behaving, in somatic ways, as constant headaches, stomachaches, panic attacks and phobias, and even as severe psychological disturbances that completely disrupt a person's life.

The effects of this anxiety may not reach a level that necessitates clinical treatment, but may still amount to the most serious psychological problem you face. You may suffer from a chaotic inner life, an inability to concentrate, or difficulty in making decisions. You may procrastinate and find yourself creatively blocked. You may experience a state of mild but ever-present anxiety that colors every facet of your life. It is natural and even inevitable that someone who is always at least somewhat anxious will become really anxious before a performance. How could that not happen?

The possibility of genetic and/or constitutional causes for the persistent presence of anxiety can't be ruled out. We simply don't know to what extent generalized anxiety is more a nature or nurture kind of thing. That it is prevalent in your family, for instance, isn't sufficient proof one way or the other, as a family picture of generalized anxiety might point to either genetic causes or environmental causes. What is clear, however, is that if you know yourself to be a highly anxious person, as someone who manifests more anxiety than the next person and manifests it more often than the next person, then the ball is in your court. Even more so than the next person, you will want to institute a long-term anxiety-management program of the sort outlined in Chapters 15 and 16.

- *Are you a generally anxious person?*

_____

_____

- *If you are, can you describe the relationship between that general anxiety and the performance anxiety you experience?*

_____

_____

_____

_____

• *Are members of your family anxious people?*

_____

_____

• *Do members of your family complain of panic attacks, phobias, and the like?*

_____

_____

• *Have any anxious family members been successful in effectively ridding them-selves of their anxieties or quieting their anxious nature? If so, what methods did they use?*

_____

_____

_____

_____

_____

_____

• *If you are a generally anxious person, what successful or unsuccessful measures have you taken to quiet your nerves?*

_____

_____

_____

_____

• *What new measures do you think you might want to take?*

_____

_____

_____

_____

People regularly "talk themselves" into additional anxiety. People who are anxious all the time do this to a fault. Cognitive therapists have identified many of these faulty self-talk patterns. Here are a few of them:

Fortune-telling

Catastrophizing

Mind reading

Discounting

Overgeneralizing

For instance, you might say to yourself, "I know I'll mess up this afternoon because I didn't get enough sleep last night" or "I never sing well after I eat a big lunch." These are examples of fortune-telling. By predicting failure and acting as if a bad performance is a foregone conclusion, you help raise your anxiety level.

You're catastrophizing when you say things to yourself like "This is the worst I've ever looked," or "This is the most boring piece of music I've ever played in my life." By magnifying the badness of the situation, you up the emotional ante and increase your anxiety level.

Mind reading takes place when you say to yourself, "I know the conductor isn't happy with my playing" or "I know the audience can tell I didn't rehearse enough," in the absence of any proof that people are thinking those critical things.

Discounting happens when you minimize your talents and your past successes. You may assert that you can't project your voice to the back of the hall or hold your own with the rest of the ensemble, even though you've projected well enough and held your own with this ensemble a hundred times already.

You overgeneralize when you leap from one or several negative events to an iron-clad rule about yourself. You say, "I never audition well" after fumbling two auditions. Or you say, "I always blow the joke at the beginning of my talk" when you've done so only twice in a row.

People who have adopted these ways of thinking keep making more anxiety for themselves. Not only are they generally anxious but they frame matters to themselves in ways that insure that they will become even more anxious.

- *Do you engage in negative self-talk of the above sort?*

_____

_____

- *What sorts of pessimistic and self-disparaging things do you tend to say to yourself?*

_____

_____

_____

_____

- *Do you foretell disaster?*

_____

_____

- *Do you catastrophize?*

_____

_____

- *Do you regularly conclude that others are harboring negative thoughts about you, even when you don't have any evidence?*

_____

_____

- *Do you discount yourself by the self-talk you use?*

_____

_____

- *Do you overgeneralize, leaping from a single instance of real or imagined failure to a general statement about your ineptness or unworthiness?*

_____

_____

- *Do you see a connection between your cognitive style and your experience of performance anxiety?*

_____

_____

- *If you do see such a connection, how might you begin to change your self-talk?*

_____

_____

_____

_____

FEELING THREATENED ALL THE TIME

If we've grown to feel threatened by life and to experience our daily routine as a series of responses to danger, we'll also have grown hypervigilant. We'll be on the lookout for threats that we presume are lurking around every corner. In order to remain this vigilant, we must keep our body in a state of readiness, which is stressful in its own right and depletes our immune system.

Equally unfortunate, by being this vigilant we'll create a self-fulfilling prophecy, as life will indeed seem threatening to us. As I walk along, calm and lost in pleasant thoughts, I may not notice the car weaving erratically three blocks away or the window washer dangling precariously thirty stories over my head. You, if you are hypervigilant, will; and so you'll experience your walk as dangerous and death-defying whereas I experience it as restorative.

Small bodily manifestations of anxiety are not that worrisome, and may not even be noticed, if we aren't on the lookout for threats. If we are on the lookout, then we'll spot that first butterfly fluttering in our stomach and have too large a reaction: "Oh, I am getting so anxious!" A hypervigilant person not only watches himself too closely; he is also likely to mislabel what he's experiencing. He may feel aroused, excited, enthusiastic, even exhilarated, and mistake the adrenaline rush that accompanies such states for the telltale signs of anxiety and danger.

When we mislabel butterflies of excitement as butterflies of anxiety, when we notice mild butterflies of anxiety and announce to ourselves that we are really anxious, and so on, we reinforce our sense of danger and provoke further bodily reactions. Now our palms begin to sweat and our breathing patterns change. This rapid, whole-body reaction to a heightened sense of danger is a profound one. As the psychologist Jeffrey Gray described it:

The body's emergency reaction functions to mobilize the body's resources for swift action that may be needed. There is an increase in the rate and strength of the heart beat, allowing oxygen to be pumped round more rapidly. There is a contraction of the spleen, releasing stored red blood cells to carry this oxygen. There is a release of stored sugar from the liver for the use of the muscles. There is a redistribution of the blood supply from the skin and viscera to the muscles and brain. And there is a deepening of respiration and dilation of the bronchi, to take in more oxygen. All this takes place in a matter of seconds or minutes.

The performer who is hyperaware of even her mildest symptoms risks taking her body to full alert every time she experiences even a twinge of anxiety. As a result of mobilizing to the hilt, she may begin to doubt her ability to function and fear that the situation is seriously worsening. In this way she turns mild anxiety (or even mere arousal) into a severe bout of performance anxiety. Indeed, some people argue that the primary benefit of beta-blocking medications used to control performance anxiety is not that they reduce somatic symptoms, per se, but rather that, by reducing the symptoms, these medications help reduce the workings of this insidious "feedback loop" in the hypervigilant performer.

- *Do you see threats everywhere?*

_____

_____

- *Do you understand that a hypervigilant response to life is likely to make more problems than it forestalls?*

_____

_____

- *When even mild symptoms of anxiety appear, are you very quick to spot them?*

_____

_____

- *Does your quick awareness of your own symptoms intensify your anxiety?*

_____

_____

- *Can you distinguish between the physical manifestations of arousal and the physical manifestations of anxiety? If they feel the same to you, how will you tell which are which?*

_____

_____

_____

_____

- *Is hypervigilance a problem for you?*

_____

_____

- *Can you identify any root causes of your hypervigilance?*

_____

_____

_____

_____

- *If hypervigilance is a problem for you, what might you do to lessen its impact on your life or to change how you view the possibility of threat?*

_____

_____

_____

_____

LOOKING AT CONTRIBUTING FACTORS

Think about the factors contributing to performance anxiety that were discussed in this chapter. You may discover, for instance, that you never really chose to become a performer but rather pursued a performance career because you were talented and because performing provided a means of escape from a turbulent childhood environment. Now, coming to grips with the psychological facts of the matter, you have the chance to fall in love with your art for the first time. You can recommit to your choice and, by recommitting to it, eliminate the anxiety associated with that long-simmering inner conflict.

If you do pinpoint specific factors contributing to your performance anxiety, that information can guide you to the kind of pre-performance anxiety-reduction techniques best suited to your circumstances. The techniques and strategies discussed in Chapters 13 and 14 cluster into twelve groups, and techniques from one group may prove more valuable to you than techniques from another. Strategies that are matched to the precise factors implicated in your personal experience of performance anxiety will yield the best results.

On the other hand, you may find it difficult to isolate the factors that contribute to your experience of performance anxiety. That's all right. You can manage your anxiety even if you can't pinpoint the sources of that anxiety. While there are no magic bullets available, there is a plan you can follow—whether or not you can identify what's going on. So don't worry if you find that you can't gain clarity about what is causing or contributing to your experience of performance anxiety.

Chapter Seven

THE HUMAN EXPERIENCE OF PERFORMANCE ANXIETY

If we want to understand performance anxiety, we need to understand what it means to be human. Birds do not obsess about how their warbling will be received, and golden retrievers do not obsess about whether or not they'll be able to locate the next downed duck. Human beings, on the other hand, are built to experience anxiety and built to make their own anxiety.

If a team of researchers descended from Mars with the job of learning what it means to be human, they would be hard-pressed to find a better field of inquiry than performance anxiety.

When study subjects join my performance-anxiety research project, I ask them two questions: "Is there anything autobiographical that you think bears on your experience of performance anxiety?" and "What have your experiences with performance anxiety been like?" In this chapter, we'll see how people just like you respond to this pair of questions. Then, at the end of the chapter, I'll ask you to answer these two questions yourself.

How do people connect the circumstances of their life with their experience of performance anxiety? Some see performance anxiety as a function of their shyness. They see themselves as just not being very comfortable around people and, as a consequence, consider performing in front of people their worst nightmare. Folks who hold this view typically consider their shyness to be constitutional, or primarily constitutional with an added-on environmental component. Take Carrie, a visual artist:

I've always been a shy, quiet person and I tend to keep my distance from most people. I stand back and watch everyone and everything before I feel comfortable joining in a group. I feel uncomfortable when a conversation is focused on me and I usually find a way to turn it around and refocus it on someone else. I also feel uncomfortable in crowds and I try to avoid them.

I think my shyness comes in part from my early socialization. My parents are both uncomfortable in social situations and I didn't have any role models to teach me how to be social. I remember being terrified when I had to go to school alone and be with other children. At that time I withdrew into art as an escape, and I have been involved in art ever since.

I am now fifty years old and I have learned to live with being shy. But still it is a hindrance when I need to talk about my art or, worse yet, do a presentation about my art to a group. There have been occasions when I have had to speak to groups, and it is always a nerve-wracking experience. I write down everything I want to say ahead of time but when I get up in front of the group I get so nervous that I can't even read my notes. I flounder and say stupid things and then I feel like an idiot afterwards.

Others who consider themselves shy have the sense that they were made shy by the dynamics in their family. Leanne, a singer, explained:

I've always been a very shy person. I think my shyness stems from my relationship with my father. I am the youngest of four and quite a bit younger than the other three. By the time I was born my father wasn't so keen on having a loud child around the house. I was always told to keep quiet, and bad behavior was just not tolerated. With no siblings around the house to play with, I often kept to myself. This is something I continue to do to this day.

I find myself dealing with performance anxiety quite a bit in my professional life. As much as I want to be onstage and sing for people, part of me is absolutely petrified to get onstage. Very often, I will talk myself out of going to auditions because of fear. When given the opportunity to perform, there is ALWAYS a part of me that wants to hide in the corner. Once I get to the stage I'm fine and happy to do what I love. But the moment before an audition or a performance terrifies me.

Family dynamics and childhood events of all sorts contribute to the experience of performance anxiety. Among these events are having parents divorce, having a parent die, or being regularly uprooted and moved from one community to another. Events like these contribute to a child's sense that the world isn't a safe place, that bad things are likely to happen, and that luck isn't on his side. As a consequence, he

A few years ago I participated in some screen tests for a new TV series. My job was to commit two scenes to memory and then play both with each of the six finalists for the lead role in the show. These were men who, by anybody's standards, would be considered successful. Therefore I was surprised to watch every single one of them struggle with tension. It was understandable that a new actor in town might be nervous in that situation, but these guys had been around. Still, it took hours to get through the tests because of botched takes, false starts, and too-sweaty faces.

—ED HOOKS, *The Audition Book*

is likely to experience more fear than the next person when it comes time to perform. Linda, an actor, expressed the connection between her childhood experiences and her experience of performance anxiety in the following way:

At age six, I knew I wanted to be an actor. But my parents divorced when I was seven, and as I grew older I began to develop anxiety around performing. Our mom struggled to make ends meet as a special ed teacher and then as a counselor. My dad always expected us to visit him regularly and had family court back him up on this, but he never had to pay appropriate child support. I now see him on a regular basis a few times a year, and we all pretend that everything's fabulous. I'm too chicken to tell him how painful those years were for me. When I got accepted into a Masters program in theater I showed my dad the brochure (silly me) and he tossed it in the trunk of the car without a word. I should have gone ahead and attended the program and I certainly regret that I didn't!

As a result of all of this, I have these underground thoughts about not being good enough, and I always feel that behind my back people are saying that I'm terrible. Then it comes time to perform and I'm paralyzed. When I try to perform, my hands shake almost uncontrollably, my mind goes blank, my mouth is bone dry, my heart pounds, and I'm plagued by thoughts of failure. Sometimes I can get past the anxiety if I'm in a class situation, but I never seem to be able to get past it in audition situations. I'm terrible in auditions! I recently had a film audition and I completely bungled it. It was embarrassing for ALL present. I was mortified. They'd said before the audition that they needed a second head shot; after the audition they said, "Never mind."

Many people come to the table burdened by a history of humiliations and the sense that they are stupid or otherwise inferior. Shelley, a painter, tells a characteristic story:

I experienced a lot of everyday but painful humiliation growing up. In high school I was the last one to be chosen for a baseball team and neither team would choose me. The teacher assigned me and the whole team that got me groaned and the other team cheered. I was always overweight and thought of myself as "the new fat stupid kid" whenever we moved to a new place. In junior high I had to have a "special desk" because I was too short and too heavy for the regular desks. And I was constantly humiliated by my alcoholic family and therefore never brought friends to the house. Today people perceive me as a very powerful woman, but I still think of myself as the fat new kid.

I completed a course in Teaching English as a Second Language so I could go overseas and teach, travel, and paint. My performance anxiety during the hours of student teaching became greater and greater as I went through the course and my last day of practice teaching was, from my perspective, an absolute disaster. I became progressively MORE anxious as time went on. The anxiety manifested itself as confusion, forgetting important things, and just wanting to avoid everything. And my biggest fear still today is looking stupid. Just this week I decided that there was no point in showing my work, that it just wasn't good enough, but I know that the real problem is that I feel too humiliated to go out and try again.

Some people lay their experience of performance anxiety at the feet of perfectionism and fear of failure. Sonia, a writer, explained:

I was raised by very strict parents. In our house children were supposed to be seen and not heard. We were expected to do things quickly as soon as we were told to do them, and to do them right. My mom's favorite saying was, "If you can't do it right the first time, don't do it at all." My father expected absolutely no dilly-dallying when he told us to do something. If he told us to get up and do the dishes and we were coloring, we could NOT finish the picture. We were expected to get up immediately and do the dishes. If we took even a minute, dad would beat us with a belt.

I tended to live in a fantasy world and I would make up stories about perfect worlds. And of course I would be punished for the stories I told. My mother still accuses me of making stories that are larger than life, and she still tells me, "If you can't do it right the first time . . ." The net result of all this is that every time I sit down to write I think that the writing must come out perfectly and that I must get it done in a hurry. So I rush something out and if it turns out to be garbage, which it often is because I'm feeling pressured and anxious, I feel like a total failure. Then, having failed, I don't want to write and I experience terrible performance anxiety if I even think about writing. I understand the why of all of this, but it is still horrible and paralyzing.

Some people see themselves as trapped in the following vicious cycle: their anxiety leads to a poor performance, which heightens their experience of anxiety, which leads to an even worse performance the next time. This vicious cycle often causes them to stop performing altogether. Joanne, a stand-up comic, explained:

I'm a relaxed and comfortable public speaker but doing stand-up has always produced a higher level of performance anxiety for me because of the judgment factor. The audience is going to decide whether each line you say is funny or not funny, and you get immediate feedback, so if it's not going well, you know immediately.

I had a couple of incidents last year that contributed to my current situation of seldom working. One time I was riffing (free-styling) and said something inappropriate— I'm white and I used the "N" word—in front of a black audience! I even shocked myself and immediately apologized but it created a tension I've never known before.

Every comic who got up after me (all black) remarked about my use of the word and joked about beating me up in the parking lot or walking me to my car to "prevent" me from getting beaten up. These were all friends of mine, so I had no actual fear, but this was a very uncomfortable situation and weighed heavily on my mind.

That incident and a few similar incidents triggered a major depression that lasted all year. I ended up canceling a lot of scheduled gigs, which created problems of its own because people began to think of me as unreliable. I need to learn to manage my anxiety—or else I can see how my career may go completely down the toilet.

Others see their current experience of performance anxiety as tied to a history of unexpected disasters and traumas, including, frequently, the trauma of suffering at the hands of cruel teachers. Leslie, a music teacher, explained:

I began my musical career as a singer. My first solo was at eight years of age. I had a big voice for my age and people were very impressed with the sound of my voice. I began voice lessons at age nine. I entered my first vocal contest and won an "A" medal and $100 prize at the age of nine. My voice teacher quickly understood that she had a student who could go far, so she began signing me up for singing engagements. I enjoyed performing and I was always rewarded by the positive responses I received. My fame grew and so did my repertoire. I was singing Italian arias by the time I was twelve.

Then my voice began getting hoarse. I had it checked out and the specialist told me that I had developed "nodes" on my vocal cords. When I mentioned it to other people, I got a reaction that told me this was a grave piece of information. I had to stop singing for six months, and when I opened my mouth again to vocalize I was shocked to hear the sound of my voice. It was gone. I had a contest that I was slated to sing at. My reputation had spread and I walked into a packed room. I sang my first song. I have never seen so many looks of disappointment, disbelief, and sorrow in my life! People in the room were shocked. Many left after my first song. Needless to say, I was devastated.

I still loved music and after that I began playing the organ. When I arrived at college I was assigned a teacher who was quite literally a monster. I cried after every lesson I had with him. He affected me in a major way. Nothing I played was ever good enough. He embarrassed me in front of others and put me "on the spot" several times. I almost didn't finish my degree but managed to play my Master's recital without his being present. That was the only way I could do it. As a result of that experience, I have never enjoyed performing on the organ. It is quite simply a huge chore. I feel that I can never reach the expectations of my audience.

The net effect of all of this is that I am always thinking that what I am doing is not good enough. When I perform, I'm always concerned about whether or not people are liking what they're hearing. I've gotten into a pleasing mode where I don't want to disappoint my listeners. I'm constantly worried that they're critiquing me even as I perform. So I get extremely nervous before I sing or play. My heart pounds, I get clammy hands, and I have difficulty breathing. Most people are totally unaware of this but it is not a pleasant experience for me at all.

Many people point their finger at existential issues, which are often the most important issues we face. The more meaning or importance a performance has for a person, the more his fears may be activated and the graver his experience of performance anxiety may be. Janet, an academic, described her experience of this painful dynamic:

> I was bright at school, particularly as a young child, and my parents pushed me to achieve, which I rebelled against as a teenager. Art was considered "not important" in my family. I was raised in a traditional, suburban home by judgmental, negative, critical parents. I was also overprotected and not allowed to experience anything they considered "scary." They seemed to be fueled by worry. I did feel loved—but conditionally, never unconditionally. "What I did" was valued, not "who I was." My braininess was valued, and my bookishness, and my ability to sit quietly and not make a fuss. My quirkiness, moodiness, and enthusiasms were tightly controlled. I spent most of my life wishing I were dead.
>
> What I've discovered over the years is that I have a very narrow gap between what I see as "unimportant" (which means I don't want to do it) and "vitally important" (which means I can feel crippled by perfectionism and performance anxiety). In that small but happy gap in the middle—when something is important enough that I can see a reason to do it but not so important that successful or timely achievement is vital—I think that's where my "best flow" lives. The crazy conundrum is that if something feels like fun, it automatically doesn't feel important enough, and if it feels important, that equates with "can't possibly be fun" and also with "very, very important." As I say, the gap is very narrow—because of the way my mind frames the issues.

As mentioned previously, we can experience performance anxiety whenever there is a performance element to a task: that is, whenever we do something that may be judged, even if only by ourselves. Therefore our territory includes the experiences of people who never get up on a stage. Take Lisa, for instance:

> I was an extremely shy, sensitive child, prone to pleasing people to gain love and acceptance. I had a rather dysfunctional family (lots of divorces, stepparents, etc.) so I didn't always feel secure. I still crave security and like to please the people in my life, including editors, to get it. When people are angry with me or don't like my work, I'm often devastated. I feel cast adrift and alone. I don't know if I was born with low self-esteem or if it developed because of insecurities in my childhood, but whichever it is, I know that I find the rejection that comes with writing tremendously difficult for me.
>
> I've held myself back to avoid rejection, for instance by not querying a particular high-profile magazine for fear they'll think I'm not talented enough or experienced enough to write for them. When I am rejected, my immediate reaction is that I'm a failure—I just don't measure up. When I do get a great assignment, I immediately start worrying that I won't live up to expectations. For instance, when I got my first book contract, I panicked and it took weeks to calm myself down. Every day I sat at the computer and heard a voice say, "How will you do this? You're not really very good." This fear is still paralyzing me. I keep hearing a voice telling me my idea stinks, that there's nothing there to explore, that the topic's already been done, and on and on.

BAD DREAMS AND PANIC

I am in my dressing room, getting ready for the performance. I realize that my costume is not there. I call for the wardrobe mistress; she doesn't answer. I go out into the hall to find her; she must have my clothes. She is nowhere to be seen. I begin to feel uneasy. I start walking down the hall and realize that I am completely alone backstage. Out front, I can hear the audience taking their seats. I wake up from the dream in a panic.

—An actor's recurrent nightmare, quoted in
STEPHEN AARON's *Stage Fright: Its Role in Acting*

Most people report that multiple factors are implicated in their experience of performance anxiety. In their opinion, many roads led to Rome: diagnosed and undiagnosed mental and physical ailments, constitutional style (shyness, introversion, sensitivity, artistic temperament, etc.), general and specific parenting issues, issues of loss and abandonment, specific traumas and traumatic performances, and more. Belinda, a painter, put it this way:

> *My mother's drive for order resulted in a need for unattainable perfection, which she mercilessly tried to induce in me. That need for perfection is what made me wake up upchucking the day of my Sunday School play, resulting in my understudy playing my part, which made my aunt and uncle mad at me, as they went to the play just to see me. (What kind of adult would blame a child for such a thing!) Plus my mother was angry with me because she'd worked hard to make my dyed blue sequined dress, which she had to drive all the way across town to deliver to my understudy. Thus began my performance career.*
>
> *In the many years since that event I've come to understand that I have ADD [attention deficit disorder], which makes transitions difficult. Even when walking into a room to meet just one person, I can lose myself in the two seconds it takes to step into the room. The years of depression, coupled with my ADD/creative brain, have trained my brain to check out, which makes thinking on my feet difficult. I also have a recently diagnosed mild bipolar disorder that led me into situations for which I wasn't prepared. When a manic phase hits, I can make decisions based on grandiosity. Then fear plunges me into depression and anxiety, which prevents me from taking the steps necessary to have the event turn out the way I want.*
>
> *Here, then, is the short list of factors contributing to my experience of performance anxiety. The list includes my controlling, perfectionist mother; an alcoholic, unloving, judgmental father; my unkind teachers; my sensitive spirit; my attention deficit disorder; my bipolar disorder; my basic depression; a worsening hearing problem; and the fear that I'm too old and too fat. Is that enough?*

Once a thought like "I dread what people will think" takes hold, people find themselves unable to focus on or enjoy their performance. They begin to obsess about "the audience out there" and how their performance will be received. Singer/songwriter Vanessa's experience is a good example of the syndrome:

When I was in school, I was thought of as a highly talented musician, and people's expectations at all my performances were very high. Classical training also focuses on perfection, so between these two things I sometimes thought that I would never be able to live up to what was expected of me, especially when I moved to a new area like songwriting. Now that I've put music aside for a rest, I'm finding some of these same issues cropping up in writing and submitting stories.

I can pinpoint the times when I experienced performance anxiety on the stage. As soon as I would start thinking, "I wonder what the audience is thinking?" I immediately got nervous and started to shake. It was horrible. The moment I started seeing myself as "on trial," with the audience as judges, everything fell to pieces. If I could manage to focus on the music, view the music as a gift I was giving to the audience, or remind myself that I had the ability to do the job, that helped. But the instant my mind went back to "What are they thinking?" I would lose it. It was totally amazing how a small shift in perception could completely change my experience of the performance.

I had to stop songwriting altogether because the anxiety became crippling. Before I even got pen to paper I was worried about what people would think of the song, what A&R reps would think, what critical reviews would say, what my friends and family would think. It was such a heavy burden that it stopped me in my tracks before a word or note got written. Now that I'm focusing on short stories, the anxiety rears its ugly head when it comes time to submit my work. My instructors tell me that I have several stories good enough for submission but I've stalled for months because the idea of what people might say about my stories scares the hell out of me.

Our final example is a success story. Human beings are built to suffer from performance anxiety, but they also can heal, grow, and master their anxiety. Consider Anna's journey from paralysis to success in stand-up comedy:

I grew up the only American-born daughter of strict European immigrant parents. I didn't speak English until I went to school. I spoke French, German, and Yiddish and we lived in a small town in rural Texas where multi-language speaking was not writ large as a talent. The kids at school threw rocks at me and called me a Nazi because I spoke German. I developed a mix of fear and anger, and my parents, fearing that I'd become unmanageable, sent me to a Catholic boarding school. The nuns wrapped my left arm to my body with clotheslines and cut off my left braid as first steps to "helping me" become right-handed. I began to stutter and stopped talking for most of seventh grade.

Early in my career, I worked for a huge multinational company. I developed a position that kept me in the background, which I loved. But one day I had to give a short speech myself. I couldn't. Right before I went on stage, I threw up and fainted. I was told that I had better learn to speak in public or I'd be fired. Another situation at work presented itself: a group presentation. I vowed to do better. The presentation was part of a competition, and I could tell that we were losing. I stood up, took the microphone, made a short presentation, and delivered a punch line that won us the prize. THEN I threw up and fainted.

I was transferred to another job in the company and a warning was put in my personnel file that I was not to give presentations. Knowing there was no advancement without that skill, I explored several routes to learn how to speak in public. Finally I went to an open microphone night at a comedy club in a nearby town. I began to do stand-up under an assumed name. At first it was horrible. Then it got easier. Two years later I could tell jokes to drunks in New Jersey bars. And once you can do that, you can speak anywhere. Now I teach people how to give effective presentations.

> ## I DON'T BELIEVE MYSELF!
> *The world-famous cellist Piatagorsky, admitting to being troubled by nerves before performing, was asked what he did to overcome the problem. He said he constantly reminded himself, "You are the great Piatagorsky!" "And does it help?" came the question. He replied, "No, I don't believe myself!"*
> —PAUL SALMON and ROBERT MEYER, *Notes from the Green Room*

Now it's your turn. Please take all the time you need and answer the following two questions:

- *"Is there anything autobiographical that you think bears on your experience of performance anxiety?"*

  _____
  _____
  _____
  _____

- *"What have your experiences with performance anxiety been like?"* (*You may have answered this question in an earlier chapter, but if you haven't, please answer it now.*)

  _____
  _____
  _____
  _____
  _____
  _____

Chapter Eight

PERFORMANCE SITUATIONS

Different performance situations elicit different sorts of threats. On a given day, Sharon, a professional singer, might take a class, call her agent, speak to schoolchildren about her life as a singer, be interviewed on the radio, give a recital, and attend a reception. Her performance on this day is not only the recital; she has been performing steadily from morning till night. Which one of these performance situations provokes the most anxiety in her?

Hopefully, none! But whatever the answer is, it's entirely a personal one. For Sharon it might be the call to the agent, whom she suspects doesn't remember her name. For another singer, it might be the "easy chat" with schoolchildren, because she has no idea what young children might want to know about the singing life. For a third, it might be the reception, because of her phobic dislike of small talk. Only for a fourth performer might the recital prove the greatest source of anxiety.

As we examine the range of performance situations likely to confront you, consider which are the really difficult ones for you, the ones that provoke the most anxiety. The question isn't which performance situations abstractly "should" or "shouldn't" make you feel anxious but rather which ones actually do—and why.

PRACTICE AND REHEARSAL

Private and public rehearsal are aspects of performing that can easily provoke anxiety. Many people experience practicing and rehearsing as negative, unpleasant events. Consider Carl, a young politician. Carl may feel incompetent as he learns to give speeches and muddles through the natural trial-and-error steps toward mastery. He may not like the way he sounds, and he may grow upset at his forgetfulness as carefully phrased passages concerning his political platform slip from memory. He may powerfully and negatively feel the pressure of an upcoming appearance as he sits with his advisers practicing his script. Despite all his hard work, he may not appear to be improving much; and while he practices he may find himself comparing himself to other politicians, peers and historical greats, and feel further diminished.

Carl may grow bored with the process and experience anxiety as a result, since boredom provokes existential anxiety and leaves a person with a whiff of meaninglessness. Or, in order to avoid additional anxiety, he may procrastinate and practice less than he should, which raises his anxiety level even more as he begins to fear that he'll fail when the campaign gets rolling.

To keep negative thoughts and disturbing feelings at bay, Carl may begin to practice mechanically, so as not to have to be present as he rehearses. With his eye focused narrowly on memorization and his mind trying to shut out negative thoughts, he may indeed manage to bind his anxiety. But in the back of his mind he knows exactly what he's doing and experiences not only anxiety but guilt as well. He *will* learn his prepared statements and he's managing to do exactly that, but he knows that he's unlikely to connect with voters if he gives a wooden, memorized performance. So now he has new reasons to feel anxious!

This is the rehearsal and performance experience at its worst. At its best, we can expect to get more out of practice and rehearsal sessions than the mere mastery of technique and the memorization of material (see box). According to Martin Seldman in *Performance Without Pressure*, a performer in practice sessions might attempt to obtain a clear, detailed picture of the desired performance; anticipate obstacles and areas where further preparation is needed; increase confidence by experiencing

---

PRACTICE

Our stereotypical formula "practice makes perfect" carries with it some subtle and serious problems. We think of practice as an activity done in a special context to prepare for performance or the "real thing." But if we split practice from the real thing, neither one of them will be very real. Through this split, many children have been irrevocably taught to hate the piano or violin or music itself by the pedantic drill of oppressively boring exercises. Many others have been taught to hate literature, mathematics, or the very idea of productive work. The most frustrating, agonizing part of creative work, and the one we grapple with every day in practice, is our encounter with the gap between what we feel and what we can express. "Something lacking," said the flute player's master. Often we look at ourselves and feel that everything is lacking! It is in this gap, this zone of the unknown, where we feel more deeply—but are most inarticulate. Technique can bridge this gap. It also can widen it. When we see technique or skill as a "something" to be attained, we again fall into the dichotomy between "practice" and "perfect" which leads us into any number of vicious circles. Competence that loses a sense of its roots in the playful spirit becomes ensconced in rigid forms of professionalism.

—STEPHEN NACHMANOVITCH, *Free Play*

success mentally; and reduce anxiety by making a mental "road map" and acquiring an "I've been there" feeling.

These extra benefits are available to the performer who chooses to accomplish more during practice than mastering material and who has managed to put anxiety in its place. At its best, rehearsing can be a joy. As the great keyboardist Wanda Landowska put it, "I never practice; I always play." We might hope to enjoy ourselves as we practice! We might even hope to have a soul-satisfying experience.

Public rehearsal—practice conducted in the presence of others—is anxiety-provoking in additional and different ways. These rehearsals take place in a field of interpersonal and group dynamics. The individual agendas of the participants come into play, as do power, control, and authority issues among individuals. Therefore conflicts arise, both interpersonally and within each individual.

For instance, making mistakes is permitted during rehearsals, and mistakes in the service of interpretation are even encouraged. On the other hand, mistakes by their very nature are disturbing, especially as the performance date nears. At each rehearsal, group members will have a different tolerance for mistakes and a different attitude about their permissibility.

Similarly, you are supposed to stand wholeheartedly behind the material you're presenting, for the sake of the group, the production, and your own ego investment in the project. On the other hand, you may clearly see its flaws, not really like or respect it, be bored by it, and so on. In addition, you find yourself in the company of your peers, pulling together to make a joint presentation, but you are also among competitors and critics who are watching you, noting your strengths and weaknesses, judging you, rating you, and marking you as better or worse than themselves.

Each of these dynamics can produce simmering conflicts, which raise everyone's anxiety level. In addition, there may be last-minute changes; new material added; the sense that the presentation is getting worse, not better; the sense that there isn't enough time to get ready; and much more. It turns out that everyone involved in a public rehearsal situation has the job of managing anxiety in addition to preparing for a performance.

• *How would you describe your experience of practice and rehearsal?*

_____

_____

_____

_____

• *What anxiety issues arise for you with regard to practicing?*

_____

_____

_____

_____

• Are the number of practice sessions you engage in sufficient?

_____

_____

• Do you practice and rehearse as regularly and as carefully as you would like?

_____

_____

• Do your practice goals include more than the mastery of technical matters and the memorization of material?

_____

_____

• What thoughts help you rehearse effectively? For example, do any of the following help:

I love the work I do.

_____

_____

I love hearing my instrument, expressing new ideas, etc.

_____

_____

I love interpreting Mozart, Shakespeare, etc.

_____

_____

Rehearsing is a kind of spiritual practice.

_____

_____

• What thoughts hinder you from rehearsing effectively? For example, do any of the following do so?

This is a lot of work.

_____

_____

This is too hard.

_____

_____

I can't get it right.

_____

_____

I'm not equal to this.

_____

_____

• *Do you have issues with procrastinating and practice avoidance?*

_____

_____

• *Do you understand procrastination to be an anxiety issue? If so, in what sense?*

_____

_____

_____

_____

• *What steps do you take to lessen anxiety so that you're less inclined to procrastinate?*

_____

_____

_____

_____

• *Is practice a time when you're permitted to make mistakes?*

_____

_____

• *What anxiety issues arise for you during public rehearsals?*

_____

_____

• *Which of these are particularly troublesome?*

_____

_____

• *Are you generally in good relationship with the people you practice with or do conflicts simmer beneath the surface?*

_____

_____

• *What ineffective or harmful measures do you employ to relieve anxiety during the rehearsal process?*

Do you use alcohol or drugs?

_____

_____

Do you eat too much?

_____

_____

Do you sleep too much because you're depressed?

_____

_____

Do you lash out at others?

_____

_____

Do you have somatic complaints or experience other health problems?

_____

_____

Do you experience any specific thought difficulties?

_____

_____

- *Can you pinpoint any specific strategies you employ to manage your performance anxiety during practice and rehearsal that seem particularly effective?*

_____

_____

_____

_____

LESSONS AND CLASSES

Performers often continue to take lessons and classes even after their professional careers are launched. An actor coming to Los Angeles from New York is likely to make it a priority to locate a good acting class. An opera singer may return to a voice teacher at any point in her career, perhaps to prepare for a difficult role, perhaps because something about her singing seems "off" to her. A dancer may take classes every day as part of the process of staying in shape.

By the same token, performers often become teachers and give private lessons; work in colleges, conservatories, or acting schools; teach workshops and classes; and provide master classes at festivals. Like any teacher, the performer-turned-teacher can experience performance anxiety.

Sometimes student-teacher relationships are among the most stressful relationships we enter. Performers bring with them any of the contributing factors discussed in the last chapter and may then be met by a teacher who harshly criticizes, who looks on indifferently or reads a letter during a practice session, who offers dogmatic or contradictory advice, or who is both unpleasant and rejecting.

Margret Elson, a pianist and artists' counselor, described several of these harmful student-teacher interactions. One she calls the "move over, darling" tactic, where the teacher makes use of your time and money to satisfy his or her own need to perform.

ACTORS AND DIRECTORS ON REHEARSALS

Carole Rothman, director:

The first day of rehearsals is always a nightmare, yet you've got to be coherent and excited about the play. It's very nerve-wracking.

Gregory Mosher, director:

The whole idea of rehearsing a play in four weeks is a ridiculous convention; it has nothing to do with the needs of the play. Some plays need three weeks' rehearsal, some need three months.

Tom Hulce, actor:

What's really difficult is when something is changed or removed that was a vital step in the race you were running. It's as if they take out part of the track and you have to make this great hurdle in the middle of the race.

Hume Cronyn, actor:

Sometimes, even with work, you not only don't improve the piece, but can actually dig the hole deeper. You can't take something the playwright has conceived, tear it apart in rehearsals, and start all over again. You end up with a patchwork quilt, and it ain't very pretty.

Donald Moffat, actor:

Overnight, I was presented with a new poem. It took me some time to learn the poem and fill it out. It's always a shock to be thrown something on such short notice—especially the night before the critics come.

—LEE ALAN MORROR and FRANK PIKE, *Creating Theater*

Elson writes:

> *No sooner does a student play a few notes before a teacher whose heart lies in performing, not teaching, than the teacher vigorously shakes his head and says sweetly while dusting the student off the chair: "Move over, darling." He then proceeds to show what music really sounds like in the hands of a master.*

On the other hand, some teachers *never* demonstrate, refusing to expose themselves to scrutiny and judgment and thus remaining high on their perch of perfection. The teacher may interrupt repeatedly and give full vent to criticisms, making use of a vocabulary heavily laden with "never" and "always." He may demand that performers do things that they patently cannot do, like sing beautifully in an unsupported falsetto, or he may demand that they follow rigid instructions. Envious of their students' talent, teachers may even seek to subvert them. As the pianist Rosina Lhevinne put it, "There are no jealous students, only jealous teachers."

Critical and controlling teachers may have been psychologically injured themselves and may have as a central item on their agenda the desire to put and keep students in their place. Conversely, teachers may hold to certain beliefs that are appropriate but that also put real pressure on students. They may, for instance, believe that performers should practice only the very best music, even if it is also the most difficult. The pianist and teacher Leon Fleischer articulated this point of view in the following way:

As far as my ideas on degree of difficulty are concerned, the music must be difficult both physically and musically, like late Beethoven sonatas, Rachmaninoff's Third Concerto, and Brahms's B-flat Concerto. I think you should study them at a young age, because if you learn something and then drop it, during the dropped period whatever you tried to learn begins to grow, ripen; it matures, so that in a year or two when you pick it up again, you see it in a different way and it becomes part of you in an almost genetic sense.

Of course, people who are not in the arts also encounter teachers and enter into student-teacher relationships. Psychotherapists in training, for example, engage in supervision and for an hour each week present cases and client material, often in the form of tapes of actual sessions, to a seasoned therapist who asks questions and wonders aloud about the appropriateness of the trainee's actions. The situation for the trainee is very like the situation for the performer. What exactly is the supervisor's agenda? Does he or she need to show off, keep the trainee subordinated, or push a theoretical position? Trained as a psychotherapist and not as a supervisor, does he or she use methods of supervision that are effective, appropriate, or fair?

Each such situation—for the singer or counseling trainee, for the actor or employee answering to a mentor at work—demands that the student keep good boundaries and maintain a healthy objectivity about the teacher. Part of the maintenance of boundaries involves asking oneself questions when made anxious by a teacher's comments, questions like "Is the teacher being fair here?" "Is what I'm being told to do good for me?" and "Is this the best way to help me learn?"

Classes, in contrast to private lessons, can be both less intense and more intense. When you're not on, you can be invisible, but when you're on, many people are watching you. Additionally, classes in the performing arts often demand that students access feelings, "open up," and in other ways allow themselves to be vulnerable—demands which provoke anxiety.

In both individual lessons and classes, the focus most often is on technique, so questions of technique may loom very large in both the teacher's and the performer's mind (see box). As a violinist, you may not be worried about your bowing, but isn't there something about your fingering to brood about? What about your tone? What about the way you handled the fast passages? What about the way you handled the slow passages? Like an iron filing in a shifting magnetic field, anxiety can jump about as you move from one technical issue to another, turning lessons and classes into torture sessions.

With respect to lessons:

- *Are lessons sometimes, often, or always anxiety-provoking experiences for you?*

_____

_____

- *Can you pinpoint what exactly about the experience produces anxiety?*

_____

_____

_____

_____

• *Is one of the following a more important factor than the others?*

Fear of fair criticism

_____

_____

Fear of unjust or unwarranted criticism

_____

_____

Fear that you'll be found lacking

_____

_____

Fear of the teacher's "hidden agenda"

_____

_____

Mistrust of the teacher's style or expertise

_____

_____

Dislike of the teacher's attitude

_____

_____

• *Do you usually come prepared for lessons?*

_____

_____

• *If not, can you identify the factors, possibly including performance anxiety, that contribute to your lack of preparation?*

_____

_____

• *Are you less assertive during lessons than you would like to be?*

_____

_____

• *Are you too eager to please teachers?*

_____

_____

• *Are you too quick to take every suggestion?*

_____

_____

- *Would any of the following make the student-teacher experience a less anxious one for you?*

Better teacher selection

_____

_____

A different attitude with respect to "authority figures"

_____

_____

More serious preparation

_____

_____

More ease about "being seen"

_____

_____

Better ways of accepting criticism and dismissing criticism

_____

_____

With respect to classes:

- *Are classes sometimes, often, or always anxiety-producing situations for you?*

_____

_____

- *Are you worried more about how your classmates view you or more about how your teacher views you?*

_____

_____

- *Do you see class as a place to learn, experiment, and enjoy, or as a place where you will be scrutinized and judged?*

_____

_____

- *How does your anxiety manifest itself with respect to classes?*

_____

_____

_____

_____

- *Do you fail to adequately prepare for classes?*

_____

_____

- *Do you cut classes or get sick on class nights?*

_____

_____

- *Do you rarely volunteer and hope not to be seen?*

_____

_____

- *Do you experience physical and mental symptoms of performance anxiety during class?*

_____

_____

- *What one thing might you do to help make class a less tense experience?*

_____

_____

_____

_____

INTERVIEWS

An interview is a special presentation of yourself. The interview situation might be a formal job interview; it might be an informal job interview at a party or conference, where you find yourself chatting with someone in a position to hire you; or it might be an on-the-air interview where you try to sell your ideas, your current film or your upcoming concert or event. In each case, the task of presenting yourself in a good light, in a situation that matters with regard to your career, naturally provokes performance anxiety.

WHY AREN'T ACTORS' VOICES BETTER?

Julia Wilson-Dickson explained:

People sometimes ask me why by the third year of drama school all our actors' voices aren't of a very high standard, or why in the professional theater not all voices are what they should be. If I were to list all the things one is actually up against, one would wonder how most actors do as well as they do. It takes many years to overcome obstacles and get to a state of equilibrium. So when people say, why isn't the standard higher, I say I have been working on my voice for twenty years and I am just beginning to be able to tolerate it. It's very difficult to get the voice to do what you want it to do. As it is, drama schools are working miracles—and so are all the students who commit themselves to working on their voices.

—EVA MEKLER, *Masters of the Stage*

Informal interviews are often a part of the networking and auditioning processes. When someone in a position to help your career casually talks to you and asks seemingly idle questions about your recent work or future commitments, you are being interviewed; your mental preparation for such interviews and your presence of mind during them are important ingredients in your recipe for success.

Performers are at least partially aware of this and often experience performance anxiety before and during social situations like receptions, benefits, opening nights, galas, fund-raisers, and so on, where informal interviewing is likely to occur. Indeed, many of us have felt anxious before a party or gathering that puts us together with others in our profession and that falls into the category of networking event.

- *Imagine that an impromptu interview is occurring. Are you prepared to give a compelling answer to the innocent-sounding though unnerving question, "Tell me a little bit about yourself"?*

  _____

  _____

- *Do you have a good sense of what to present and what to withhold at such times?*

  _____

  _____

- *Do you have a good sense of how diplomatic and/or assertive to be?*

  _____

  _____

Studying up a bit on the interview process (see box) and making an effort to find opportunities to do interviews will help you better understand how to handle yourself in any interview situation, whether formal or informal, expected or a complete surprise. Still, whenever you're interviewed you're in the territory of improvisation. For example, I've found myself in the following situations:

- *Just as she goes into a commercial, a radio interviewer says that she'd like to cover a certain question after the break. That is the question I think about during the break. After the break, she asks an entirely different question.*

- *On the other end of a radio interview conducted by phone, five people—two co-hosts and three in-studio guests—ask me questions. The questions come from "different directions" with lightning rapidity.*

- *An editor and I are discussing manuscript changes. At the end of the conversation he asks, "What do you think your next book will be about?"*

- *I meet with a publisher in his office for an hour. This is a social visit, but at a certain point I present a book idea, and he in turn asks me questions about the book's structure, contents, and audience potential.*

These and similar situations arise for each of us. You may not find yourself interviewed on radio or television, but many situations present themselves that are the equivalent of interviews. We can be carefully prepared for some of these interviews, generally prepared for all of them, and for the rest we must trust our ability to improvise and our in-the-moment anxiety-management skills.

- *Can you identify which aspects of the interview process are the most anxiety-provoking for you?*

_____

_____

_____

_____

- *How does that anxiety manifest itself?*

_____

_____

_____

_____

- *Do you regularly search out interview possibilities, either of a formal or an informal sort?*

_____

_____

- *If not, are you avoiding them because of anxiety?*

_____

_____

- *If you presently avoid them and it's in your best interests not to, will you begin to seek them out?*

_____

_____

- *Might you prepare and rehearse answers for the sorts of questions that are likely to arise in interview situations?*

_____

_____

- *Might you rehearse or role-play interview situations with a friend?*

_____

_____

- *Are you prepared to be informally interviewed right now?*

_____

_____

During the next week, find someone to interview you. Prepare the questions but not the answers, so that you can experience answering them cold. Tape record the interview, listen to it, and think about it. If it goes as might be expected—rockily—think about what you need to do to prepare yourself to speak confidently about yourself and your work.

AUDITIONS

Auditions are especially grueling performances. They are especially grueling because:

- *The work that a performer is hoping to get is not just "some old job" but an opportunity tangled up with her deepest hopes and dreams.*

- *The competition is fierce, and scores if not hundreds of qualified performers may be competing for a given role or position.*

- *Often a performer is to come in with memorized pieces and perform them "perfectly" and "without anxiety."*

- *At the same time she must present herself as someone human and easy to work with, so she has the contradictory-feeling tasks of looking both "perfect" and "human."*

- *Many audition situations are not strictly about the talent of the performer. It may be that an actress with a certain look is wanted, or one with a certain twang or lilt to her voice. Band members holding auditions for a lead singer may be looking for a singer who has a certain presence, who can be a leader, who has good connections, who can project an image, who can contribute money for studio time and, only incidentally, who can sing.*

Given these many added difficulties and uncertainties, it's no wonder that performers number auditions among their most stressful experiences—a fact that acting teachers know well (see box).

- *Do auditions regularly make you anxious? If so, how does that anxiety manifest itself?*

  _____
  _____
  _____
  _____

- *Do you regularly avoid auditions because of anxiety?*

  _____
  _____

- *Do you see auditions as job interviews? Would you say that you've learned how to effectively manage anxiety before and during job interviews?*

  _____
  _____
  _____
  _____

- *Do you know what is required of you at job interviews? For instance, do you have clear ideas about what your auditors want and need?*

  _____
  _____

- *Do you have clear ideas about how best to present yourself at a job interview or audition?*

  _____
  _____

- *Do you have clear ideas about what constitutes inappropriate behavior or self-defeating behavior at a job interview or audition?*

  _____
  _____
  _____
  _____

- Have your most successful job interviews or auditions been ones where you felt most confident and relaxed?

_____

_____

- If so, what steps do you take to bring those feelings to all of them?

_____

_____

_____

_____

THE EXPERTS ON AUDITIONS

If you were to tell an actor that he or she would be auditioning for a Broadway musical in the next few days, you would probably swear, from the reaction, that this was a fate worse than an IRS audit. Successful actors with credits ranging from Antigone to Zorba become petrified at the thought of having to give a vocal audition. I have seen stars dissolve in tears at the prospect of having their work judged and found wanting. The terror of having to put oneself on the line and face rejection can cause mental distress varying from mild stage fright to total emotional and physical collapse. Some performers give up in despair and vow never to be put in that thankless position again—while a few who have done their homework can't wait for the chance to show off their talents and skills.

—FRED SILVER, *Auditioning for the Musical Theater*

Most actors come into the interview situation wearing a thick mask, spending their energies protecting themselves. It's rough interviewing someone who is determined to keep himself hidden. Try to give. Try to open up. Try to see who the interviewer is. I've had many occasions to interview actors all day—thirty, forty of them—and then at lunch or at the end of the day run into the same actors. I say hello and they look blankly at me, as if I were a mugger: I remember them, and they never saw me. I've interviewed thirty people, and they've had one interview, and they don't know what the guy who interviewed them looks like.

—MICHAEL SHURTLEFF, *Audition*

The interview is a business meeting, but it is also very personal. It's our best opportunity to let the casting director know who we are. Instead, we sometimes spend it looking up fearfully at the ceiling, clearing our throats, coughing, muttering, or otherwise acting as if we've been asked to talk about something we know nothing about. In some ways, the interview represents everything that is frightening about being a creative person. It demands a great deal of self-revelation, it requires that we be present in the moment and respond to changing circumstances, and it reminds us that we have to sell ourselves over and over again in ways that people with "regular" jobs never have to do.

—ANN BREBNER, *Setting Free the Actor*

- *Have your most successful job interviews or auditions occurred when you were most prepared?*

_____

_____

- *If so, is it the case that preparation is your best anxiety-reducer?*

_____

_____

- *If you could change one thing that is in your power to change to make job interviews or auditions less anxiety-producing, what would that one thing be?*

_____

_____

_____

_____

PRESENTATIONS AND PERFORMANCES

Most presentations and performances have certain structural elements in common. The presentation or performance happens on a certain predetermined date at a certain predetermined time in front of a group of people who are obliged to be there or have chosen to be there—in the case of a theatrical or musical performance, they have likely paid to be there. In the period before the lights in the hall dim, the person slated to appear waits anxiously in the wings. The technical preparations commence, the audience begins to settle down, and, finally, he or she (along with his/her fellow performers) begins the ritual countdown.

Each of us will have a different sense of whether or not a performance is imminent. Some of us will feel that it's imminent weeks before it arrives. Others will consider it imminent hours, minutes, or even seconds beforehand. For people who experience significant performance anxiety, that feeling of imminence triggers their anxiety—so if they can train their mind not to start shouting "It's almost here!" weeks before the performance happens, the better off they will be. This ability to control the mind and have it think what you would like it to think, rather than what it, out of fear and anxiety, is driven to think, is the key to anxiety management.

- *How does your performance anxiety manifest itself in the days before a performance?*

_____

_____

_____

_____

- *Does the approaching performance seem to become more real to you or less real?*

_____

_____

- *Do you rehearse and prepare more often or less often as the performance draws near?*

_____

_____

- *Does your mastery of your material seem to deteriorate or to improve the closer you get to the performance?*

_____

_____

- *What is your experience of performance anxiety on the day of the presentation?*

_____

_____

_____

_____

- *What symptoms do you experience?*

_____

_____

_____

_____

- *Do you isolate yourself, medicate yourself, pace restlessly? How do you spend the time?*

_____

_____

_____

_____

- *What worries, if any, occupy your thoughts on that day? Can you identify your negative self-talk?*

_____

_____

_____

_____

- *What is your experience of performance anxiety in the period just before going on (during the last fifteen minutes or so)?*

_____

_____

_____

_____

- *What symptoms of anxiety do you begin to manifest?*

_____

_____

_____

_____

- *Does the anxiety intensify markedly during these last fifteen minutes?*

_____

_____

- *Do you employ some strategy to reduce the anxiety or do you "white-knuckle" it?*

_____

_____

- *What do you tend to focus on during this period?*

_____

_____

_____

_____

- *What external factors seem to affect your experience of performance anxiety during this period?*

The size of the audience?

_____

_____

The compositional makeup of the audience?

_____

_____

How often you've performed the material before?

_____

_____

The quality of the material?

_____

_____

Whether critics are in attendance?

_____

_____

- *What is your experience as you begin the presentation? Does your anxiety peak and then begin to abate?*

  _____

  _____

  _____

  _____

- *Does your anxiety tend to completely disappear once you begin?*

  _____

  _____

- *If you are still anxious once you're into the performance, how does the anxiety manifest itself? What symptoms are present?*

  _____

  _____

  _____

  _____

- *If the anxiety is still present, about what in particular are you worrying?*

  _____

  _____

  _____

  _____

- *Does your anxiety level rise and fall during the presentation, depending on, say, whether a difficult passage or scene is coming?*

  _____

  _____

- *Are you relatively aware of the audience? Or unaware?*

  _____

  _____

- *Does becoming aware of them make you more or less anxious?*

  _____

  _____

- *Does your anxiety increase markedly according to external circumstances, say if someone forgets a cue or fumbles a passage?*

  _____

  _____

- *Do you feel yourself in control or out of control during performances?*

  _____

  _____

- *While you're performing, what strategies, if any, do you employ to reduce anxiety?*

_____
_____
_____
_____

- *How do you feel once the performance is over? Greatly relieved, even giddy with relief? Still anxious?*

_____
_____

- *Do you analyze the performance or tend to forget about it immediately?*

_____
_____

- *Recalling an important performance, how would you like to have handled it differently?*

_____
_____
_____
_____
_____
_____

- *What can you do to better manage your performance anxiety before, during, and after performances?*

_____
_____
_____
_____
_____
_____

FOUR RULES FOR "SPEAKING EASY"

The Speakeasy approach revolves around four basic concepts: Energy, Awareness, Strength (or Self-Esteem) and You. Together, the first letters spell EASY—the way speaking should and can be. Energy: To make an audience listen, a speaker must have energy. The energy necessary for effective speaking can best be defined as intensity or involvement. Awareness: If you stop thinking about yourself and pay attention to what is going on out there, your gut will respond to your audience. Strength: Strength, or self-esteem, means having a strong, secure sense of self which you will not allow your audience to threaten. You: Like it or not, it all comes back to you and how much time and effort you are willing to devote to improving your spoken image.

—SANDY LINVER, *Speak Easy*

PUBLIC SPEAKING

Most people fear speaking in public. This fear may prevent you from teaching workshops, fronting your band, advancing at work, successfully promoting your products, and, more generally, realizing your dreams and achieving your goals.

Professional performers greatly benefit from creating public-speaking opportunities, accepting them when they arise, and mastering the anxiety that accompanies them. A performer may profitably invent lectures to give and workshops to teach as a change of pace from regular performances and as new performance experiences in their own right. Confidence is bred in the person who manages to speak successfully in public, a confidence that spills over into artistic performance and everyday life.

- *Do you currently have occasion to lecture, teach, or give speeches?*

  _____

  _____

- *What is your experience of anxiety in these situations?*

  _____

  _____

  _____

  _____

- *Have public-speaking possibilities presented themselves that you've avoided because of anxiety?*

  _____

  _____

- *Have you thought about offering classes or workshops but avoided them because of anxiety?*

  _____

  _____

- *Before speeches, lectures, or workshops that you give, how does your performance anxiety manifest itself?*

  _____

  _____

  _____

  _____

- *What ineffective or harmful strategies do you use to reduce this anxiety?*

  _____

  _____

  _____

- *What effective strategies have you learned to use at such times?*

_____

_____

_____

_____

- *If you perform for a living, what one thing might you do to begin to add public speaking to your repertoire of performances?*

_____

_____

_____

_____

BUSINESS SITUATIONS

Professional and business relationships often include charged and complicated performance moments and high anxiety. For instance, an actor walking into an agent's office or returning an agent's call may experience severe performance anxiety. As the talent agent Lester Lewis put it, "Most actors when they come into my office are so damned nervous they can hardly respond. I've had actors read for me and their hands are shaking. I tell them, 'Look, we're not the enemy . . . yet! Just relax.'"

Can you calmly confront your boss, business colleague, or fellow band member when confrontation is required? Can you casually speak to your agent without anxiety or listen to criticism from your coach, choreographer, or faculty chairman without anxiety? Generally not. At such times there may be so much at stake or so much going on between the lines that, while ordinarily cool under fire, you begin sweating through your shirt as you attempt to fire the drummer or return a record company executive's call.

Many business negotiations are enacted through subtle, nuanced rituals in which a lot is said in a few words (see box). Most people are made anxious by these rituals; they don't engage in them often enough to really understand them; and feel too invested in the outcome to maintain appropriate distance. For instance, a

---

AN AGENT AND AN EDITOR DO LUNCH

Sometime around ten-thirty or eleven, your host or hostess calls you with the traditional phrase, "Are we on for today?" The time and place are then agreed upon. But not always easily. To wit: "How does Italian sound to you?" "Had it last night. Mexican?" "I'm on a diet. There's a great fish place around the corner from my office." "But that's all the way on the other side of town from me." And so it goes. Sometimes there is more to these negotiations than two busy people trying to find common ground. Nothing serious, just a subtle game of chicken: I am more powerful than you because I made you come to my side of town at an inconvenient hour and eat a cuisine that gives you heartburn.

—RICHARD CURTIS, How to Be Your Own Literary Agent

practiced literary agent and a practiced editor in a book contract negotiation are likely to present disputed points clearly and quickly, as they know the shorthand of the business, and don't have the kind of personal stake in the outcome that an author does. But a writer involved in such negotiations is unlikely to understand what's going on and feel a great stake in the outcome.

We're challenged to normalize these professional relationships as best we can, so that we neither fall in love with nor fear people simply because of the positions they hold in the world. The power that once resided in the person of kings now resides in people able to provide us with roles, promotions, contracts, lucrative deals, and all the rest, and we must learn to manage our anxiety and maintain our counsel in their presence.

- *Do you regularly experience performance anxiety before and during business situations?*

_____

_____

- *Since a fair number of business situations can be avoided, does your anxiety manifest itself as procrastination and avoidance?*

_____

_____

- *Which business situations cause you the most anxiety?*

Phone conversations?

_____

_____

Face-to-face meetings?

_____

_____

Money talk?

_____

_____

Small talk?

_____

_____

Hiring and firing situations?

_____

_____

Choosing projects and making commitments?

_____

_____

Taking a stand or exerting leverage?

_____

_____

• *Do you regularly practice and rehearse business performances?*

_____

_____

• *What ineffective or harmful strategies do you employ to reduce the anxiety before or during business performances?*

_____

_____

_____

_____

• *What effective strategies have you learned to employ at such times?*

_____

_____

_____

_____

• *What one thing might you try to do to help reduce your anxiety about business situations?*

_____

_____

_____

_____

OPENING NIGHTS

"Opening night" as metaphor stands for all those occasions when a presentation is made for the first time "for real" in front of its intended audience. The occasion might be a first kiss with that new someone or the first time you perform a particular violin concerto in public. Opening nights tend to generate an inordinate amount of performance anxiety. As a result, the performance often doesn't go quite as expected or intended. For example, the stage manager Thomas Kelly observed in *The Back Stage Guide to Stage Management*, "Often performers throw a lot of curves at the stage manager during the first performance in front of an audience. Actors have a tendency to either speed up or go slower, and speak louder or softer than they had at rehearsals."

Performers need to be alert to the fact that on opening night extra adrenaline is pumping through their system, a biological fact bound to affect both the performer's experience of anxiety and the performance itself.

- *Do you experience "opening nights" as particularly nerve-racking?*

  _____

  _____

- *What ineffective or unhealthy strategies, if any, do you employ to help with the anxiety of opening nights?*

  _____

  _____

- *What effective and healthy strategies do you employ to help with the anxiety of opening nights?*

  _____

  _____

  _____

  _____

CHANGING AND EXCHANGING ROLES

Another situation that heightens performance anxiety is the changing or exchanging of roles. The actor who takes on directing, the musical performer who begins to conduct, the middle manager who gets promoted to vice president are all likely to experience anxiety that comes with added responsibilities, new tasks, and a step into unknown territory.

A performer who has always wanted to step forward in some way but who has never taken a shot at it may not realize that it's the anxiety associated with changing roles and adding responsibilities that's preventing her from trying. To front her own band, she will have to choose among the musicians she auditions, to name just one of her new tasks. Will she choose the most versatile performer, the one who best understands her concept for the band, the one not on drugs, the friendliest one, or the one who comes with a little capital to invest in the band? These are questions that she didn't have to tackle when she was just one player among many. The thought of having to tackle issues of this sort may provoke considerable anxiety and cause her not to go forward with her dream.

- *Can you identify times when you changed roles or "switched hats"?*

  _____

  _____

- *Did such changes—from performer to creator, from follower to leader—increase your experience of performance anxiety?*

  _____

  _____

- *Do you avoid making changes of that sort in order to avoid the experience of anxiety?*

  _____

  _____

- *If you undertake to make such changes and find them anxiety-provoking, what measures do you think you ought to take to reduce that anxiety?*

_____

_____

_____

_____

THE CREATIVE ACT AS PERFORMANCE

A successful playwright came to see me. She had two play commissions overdue, one for a Chicago theater and one for a San Francisco theatre; a very personal but probably noncommercial "second stage" piece in its early stages; and several screenwriting ideas that intrigued her and on certain days even obsessed her. But she wasn't working on any of these many projects. She was blocked creatively.

It seemed reasonable to attribute her creative block to the fact that her plate was too full and that she was finding it hard to settle on any one project. But the situation turned out to be more complicated than that. With respect to each piece of work, she felt torn between her idea about how to create the piece and contradictory ideas about what the audiences for each piece—artistic directors, theater subscribers, her fellow playwrights—were expecting of her.

Once you begin to wonder what reception your work will garner, once you make a distinction in your mind between what you want to do and what you believe the marketplace will permit you to do, your art-making is bound to take on the flavor of performance. At such times the creative blockage you experience may well be a special case of performance anxiety. If you find that you're treating your creative efforts as performances, the same remedies that work to reduce performance anxiety in any situation will help you face the blank page or the blank canvas.

- *As a creative artist, do you tend to think a lot about who the audience is for your work and what they're expecting?*

_____

_____

- *Do such thoughts lend an air of performance to your art-making efforts?*

_____

_____

- *Do you experience much creative blockage?*

_____

_____

- *Thinking about that blockage now, is it perhaps more a variety of performance anxiety?*

_____

_____

- *If this is true, how might you handle your creative blocks differently?*

_____

_____

_____

_____

Everything from dating to preparing Thanksgiving dinner, from playing in a company softball game to asking for a raise can feel like a performance. What can we do to reduce our experience of performance anxiety in these many disparate situations? It's time for us to focus on solutions.

PART TWO

Performance-Anxiety Solutions

Chapter Nine

HANDLING CRITICISM

In order to reduce performance anxiety, you need to enter into a new relationship with criticism. You need to fear it less. The equation is simple: a fear of criticism equals a fear of performing. If you allow past criticism to haunt you, a fear of future criticism to worry you, or your own "inner critic" to hold sway, you will fear performing. It is important to be able to handle the criticism you receive—to know how to make sense of criticism, to discern what part of it is useful and what part of it should be discarded, and to get the part you want discarded quickly out of your mind and out of your system.

But even more important than learning how to handle criticism is learning not to fear it. If you can rid yourself of *that* fear, you might eliminate your experience of performance anxiety entirely.

- *What would it be like not to fear criticism?*

_____

_____

_____

_____

_____

The goal is to eliminate the fear, not the criticism. It is not possible to eliminate criticism in life. Even if we were to perform splendidly each time, which isn't realistic, we might still be criticized unfairly. History is replete with stories of great works that were mercilessly panned. So it is pointless to imagine that there is some way to avoid criticism. We can't even avoid criticism by not performing, as then we can be criticized (by others and certainly by ourselves) for not performing. It is time to let go of the hope that you can avoid your share of criticism. It's also time to embrace the idea that not fearing the criticism is your number one goal.

- *Write "I do not fear criticism" one hundred times. If that feels too silly . . . do it anyway.*

_____

_____

_____

_____

_____

_____

_____

_____

THE TERRITORY OF CRITICISM

Criticism comes at us from the past, in bad memories and from our own introjected "inner critic." It comes at us every day, at work and at home. It colors our sense of the future. Some of it is minor and only ruffles our feathers a little bit. But a surprising amount of it is toxic, as bad for our system as any poison. Toxic criticism, the sort of criticism that gets under our skin and lodges in our mind, can fester like an open wound. It is so devastating a problem that millions of people alter their life plans because of the criticism they suffered as a child, adolescent, or adult. Because it is toxic, it does three things: it harms our self-image, reduces our motivation, and causes us to fear criticism in the future. This translates to not feeling equal to performing, not wanting to perform, and experiencing performance anxiety before we perform.

Every day, I see how criticism affects people who perform. A writer presents her new idea for a novel to her critique group, the idea is panned, and the writer goes into a month-long funk. A singer is praised for her performance but receives one offhand criticism, from her father—and can't schedule new gigs. A painter who would love to approach gallery owners with his newest paintings finds it impossible to proceed—he just knows that he's going to get criticized for changing his subject matter. An actor stops auditioning because her "inner critic" has gotten so loud that she doubts her abilities, her chances, her look—everything.

The identical critical comment can sting only a little or it can do us real harm. The power of criticism to hurt isn't an objective matter. It's not about who delivers it, how nasty it is, or in what circumstances we find ourselves. It's about how we take it in, what it means to us, how it gets a grip on our mind, and how it eats away at our being. Toxic criticism is the criticism that affects us powerfully, whether or not it is truly biting, whether or not it was meant to hurt, and whether or not it was even meant as criticism. If it gets inside and does damage, it is toxic. Similarly, our fear of criticism only sometimes rests on objective concerns. From an objective standpoint, it may be sensible for us to fear for our future career when we audition for a premiere symphony orchestra, but is it equally sensible to fear that someone may walk out on us at a small church recital? No—such are the fears that really must be exorcised.

The first thing to notice about criticism is that it falls into three broad categories: actual criticism, anticipated criticism, and self-criticism. Examples of actual criticism are getting a poor job performance review, having your painting attacked in painting class, being held up to ridicule by a sibling, or hearing from a friend that your latest dinner party was your least successful so far. Examples of anticipated criticism are worrying what people will say should you present your ideas at work, fearing an attack by critics if your novel gets published, or imagining the critical things your parents will say if you tell them that you're thinking of switching careers. Examples of self-criticism are demeaning your efforts, calling yourself names, and presuming that you'll never reach your goals.

WRITING "DEAR CRITIC" LETTERS

One way to deal with criticism is by writing a letter of a certain sort, a "dear critic" letter. Here are all the instructions you need in order to get started: "Please write a letter to someone real or imagined who has criticized you in the past or who might criticize you in the future." That's it. Give it a try.

Here's a "dear critic" letter written by Isabelle, a musician:

Dear Jack,

I wish you could be happy for me. I stood up in front of a large group of people last night to sing and all you could say at the end was, "You didn't pick the right songs." I really needed your support last night. Would it have put you out too much just to wish me well? Everyone else did, but you couldn't.

You are the person I most want to please and it just seems impossible to do so. Can't you stop and think about the things you say before you say them? I have to believe you would never want to hurt me, but you did. I just want you to think about one thing: how would you feel if someone said that to you?

Isabelle

All three kinds of criticism can produce devastating effects. A particular piece of actual criticism can cause you to stop a creative career or decide that you aren't good enough to rise to the top of your profession. Your fear of future criticism can cause you to let go of your dreams or not go public with the efforts you make. Your experience of self-criticism can color your days in a negative way, causing you to be more pessimistic and depressed than you otherwise might be—and also more critical. These are three equally toxic poisons, and to eliminate only one from your system isn't enough. You need to break free of all three.

These three brands of criticism come in two flavors, "fair" and "unfair." It is very important that you understand that both "fair criticism" and "unfair criticism" produce toxic effects. If you give a presentation at work for which you didn't prepare and which you deliver poorly, a fair criticism is that your presentation wasn't up to snuff. On the other hand, if you do an excellent job and your boss admonishes you for not starting with a joke, that's unfair criticism. It turns out that *either* criticism can prove toxic—and for *different* reasons.

Fair criticism can prove toxic because it possesses real power to make us angry with ourselves and disappointed in ourselves. We hoped to perform well—and we didn't. We wanted to prove an excellent leader—and we didn't. We dreamed that our children would excel—and they didn't. The sting of fair criticism also causes us to fear criticism in the future. Why try again if we're likely to fail and receive more criticism? When fair criticism grows to toxic proportions, it has the cognitive effect of amplifying a truth (that something we did went poorly), and transforming it into a falsehood (that we are doomed and a failure).

Unfair criticism can prove toxic because it makes us angry with other people and with the world. We start to harbor powerful resentments, we begin to doubt the basic integrity and fairness of our fellow human beings, and we entertain the painful possibility that no matter how well we perform "they" will still criticize us and "get us." This everyday paranoia causes us to retreat, to lose interest in the things we love, and to sink into a semi-permanent depression. We acquire an attitude of "learned pessimism" as a result of being unfairly treated and an attitude of "learned helplessness" as a result of having no satisfactory ways to redress the injustice.

What if we get criticized and can't tell in our own mind whether the criticism was fair or unfair? That's the worst! Then we both demean ourselves and rage at others. On top of that, we get to call ourselves additional bad names for not being able to tell whether the criticism was appropriate or not. The chaos and confusion that result from not being able to determine in our own mind whether a given criticism was fair or unfair weakens us and adds to our sense that we aren't equal to life's demands. Better that the criticism we receive be clearly fair or unfair!

When we fear future criticism it is both fair criticism and unfair criticism that we fear. Fair criticism will mean that we've made mistakes and messes. Unfair criticism will mean that we've been treated unjustly again. Neither is pretty to contemplate. It is not pretty to picture ourselves failing, and it is not pretty to picture ourselves attacked for no good reason. The identical situation arises with respect to our "inner critic": some of the criticism we level at ourselves will be apt and will hurt because it is apt, and some of it will be unfair and will hurt because we sense how unfairly we're treating ourselves.

A "DEAR CRITIC" LETTER TO AN "INNER CRITIC"

Dear little crappy voice inside my head:

WHY do you constantly put me down and tell me that my art "isn't good enough"?! Who are YOU to judge my art? Have YOU ever sat down with nothing but a pencil and a piece of paper and created a portrait? I DON'T THINK SO! Why must you constantly torment me? You think you're terribly clever, but I have news for you. I'm going to beat you. I don't know when and I don't know how but I know that I will. YOU WILL BE HISTORY! I may always hear you, but that doesn't mean I will always have to listen. I'm becoming stronger—and I'm seeking ways to lessen your voice. AND I WILL WIN!

Go to hell!

Lenore

Because criticism regularly produces devastating effects, and because these effects cause us to fear future criticism, it's vital that we know how to handle criticism so that we don't have to fear it ever again. But by "handle criticism" I mean "handle it effectively." Everyone already knows how to handle criticism ineffectively, as that's the way we usually handle it. Let's look at some of our common ineffective strategies for coping with the criticism we receive.

INEFFECTIVELY HANDLING CRITICISM

Our first line of psychological defense with respect to criticism is to try to "not hear" it and somehow ignore it. We try our best to not hear caustic comments, not notice a snicker or a roll of the eyes, not take in the negative comments penned at the end of our essay. Defending ourselves this way has its pluses, especially if the criticism is unfair, but by resorting to "blindness" we lose out on vital information and put ourselves in danger of repeating our mistakes. We also make ourselves tense and miserable as we try not to hear what people are saying to us. Worse yet, when some piece of criticism manages to get through our defenses, it cuts much more deeply and *really* takes hold.

A "DEAR CRITIC" LETTER TO A PARENT
Dear Mother,

Thanks for attending my writing group's poetry reading. When you said that my poems were the best, I was thrilled. But when I asked you what you liked about them, your reply was that they were the "shortest," as if you just couldn't wait for the whole thing to be over. This isn't the first time you have made comments which, though not outright negative, seemed to belittle my creative work, as if you find it insignificant.

I think my poetry and my painting are not unlike your flower gardening, relaxing to the spirit, and yet purposeful because they create more beauty for the world. I would hope that for these reasons alone, you would value my creative efforts. However, barring that, I would hope that you would want me to be happy, and my artistic work does make me happy.

Therefore, I would appreciate it if you could make more supportive comments about my work. (As you have often said, "If you can't say something nice, then don't say anything at all.") Finding the courage to do my art is difficult for me, and yet it is so rewarding when I do. So please encourage rather than discourage me to continue. Only by continual practice can I create work that might one day even meet your standards of excellence.

Gratefully yours, your daughter,

Laura

A second line of defense is to notice the criticism and then get angry with the person doing the criticizing. This method of dealing with criticism strains relationships, makes enemies out of friends and loved ones, and eats away at our insides. We start to live with a simmering anger or even in a perpetual rage. Millions of meek-seeming people are secretly revenging themselves on their critics, boiling them in oil and tearing them limb from limb. Anger is our most usual response to criticism, and because we don't dare vent that anger—as it would harm us and others if we turned violent—we live with that anger roiling inside of us, toasting our stomach lining.

Another way we operate is to try to "stuff" the criticism, to take it inside and hide it away as if it were dirty laundry stuffed out of sight in a closet. It isn't really out of sight, though—it's as if the closet had no door and a searchlight were permanently trained on the dirty laundry. We obsess about the criticism, prepare responses that we don't deliver, and get caught up "dealing" with the criticism by never letting it out of our sight. Just as a person with a toothache can't think of anything else, a criticized person trapped in his own mind can think about nothing but the criticism he received. This inner pollution feels terrible and is bound to make us sick from one stress-related illness or another.

A fourth characteristic response to criticism is to take the criticism to heart, feel wounded and diminished, and stop acting in that arena so as not to get criticized again. If the criticism occurred in painting class, we stop painting. If we got criticized about our weight, we stop dating and even stop going out. If our intelligence was attacked, we lower our sights academically. Not only do we not exorcise the criticism, we let it dictate how we'll live our life and what we'll consider available to us as options and dreams. The criticism wins—and depression sets in.

Similarly, we may become our own worst critic. No longer is it John in painting class or Mary at work who is doing the criticizing—we do it ourselves. We shake our head at our own efforts, declare ourselves unequal to our dreams, and half-heartedly move through life. At this point we've acquired a self-critical style and a way of looking at the world rooted in pessimism, anger, and despair. It is easy to see how criticism that becomes toxic not only affects us moment-in and moment-out but also ruins our future and transforms the very way we think about ourselves.

Doubting that the future will be any different from the present, we make a secret pact with ourselves to avoid further criticism. We don't date, even though we want love and affection. We don't voice our beliefs or act on our beliefs, even though we have beliefs. We don't stand up for ourselves, even though we know that self-advocacy is the path to success. Even if we understand that we're hiding, we nevertheless feel powerless to try, since our paramount concern is to not get criticized again. At this point toxic criticism has turned from wound to scar: our future is scarred.

Another way we deal with the possibility of future criticism is by sabotaging our efforts. We bravely accept a new position at work, one with more responsibility and more possibility of criticism, and instantly have a car accident. At first glance there might seem to be no connection between the two events. At an unconscious level, however, we may have been looking for a way to avoid the criticism that we know will come with our new job. Our panic and our secret wish to undo our decision made us just impulsive enough that we tried a driving maneuver that we would otherwise never attempt. Did we actually want the accident? No!—but maybe. When we fear future criticism, see it looming on the horizon, and don't know how to avoid it, one of the tricks our mind plays is to precipitate an event-ending crisis.

Another characteristic way we deal with the specter of future criticism is by getting ourselves sick with worry. If we have a presentation at work that we must give and if we really don't want to sabotage ourselves, we may spend the two weeks before the presentation sick to our stomach, trying to "get it together" but fearing and visualizing the worst. We worry about everything from what we're going to wear to whether the equipment will work on the day we present. Because we are so concerned about the potential for criticism in the situation and because we have such a dread of that criticism, we spend those two weeks in agony.

A "DEAR CRITIC" LETTER TO A FUTURE CRITIC

Dear Imaginary Someone:

I don't thank you for your criticism of me and my work. I was extremely upset and hurt by your implicit rejection, your snickers behind my back, your looking down your nose at me, calling me an inferior musician with your eyes. I do not thank you for calling my show a disaster, calling me an amateur, and not inviting me to participate in the next group show you're putting together.

I do not thank you for encouraging my desire to give up this business altogether, for making me feel even more justified in holing myself up in my room and not practicing what I most need to learn. The vision of your face makes acid rise in the back of my throat. I do not like feeling judged by you. I do not like that you threw yourself onto my heap of bad memories, that you increase my dread of walking around during the day. I hate the idea that we will come face to face one day and I will be the one running from your line of sight.

I do not thank you.

Esther

Sometimes we choose a path in life where so little is at stake that no one bothers to criticize us. We hide out in a routine civil service job, an uneventful corner of an academic field, or a low-level job devoid of responsibility and scrutiny. Or we become the building inspector who gets to criticize rather than the contractor who must deal with the criticism, the professional critic rather than the artist, or the hypercritical teacher. It may seem odd at first glance to imagine that a person might pick his profession simply because it allows him to avoid criticism or permits him to dole out criticism, but people often select their profession for just such reasons.

Last but not least, people regularly deal with the specter of future criticism by "acting out" and "getting in the first blow." They become oppositional, let their anger drive their actions, and grow a thick skin to deal with the negative reactions that their acting out provokes. They dress in jeans when they should appear in a suit, stride in with a dirty look, and dare anyone to criticize them for their inappropriate dress. They fail to prepare and then act as if their performance deserves a standing ovation. They become the "difficult" person everyone knows to avoid and not to trust. They inoculate themselves against criticism through narcissistic grandiosity that masks their fear and pain.

None of these methods serve you. What methods do?

EFFECTIVELY HANDLING CRITICISM

There are three keys to effectively handling criticism: a dynamic key, a mindfulness key, and a holistic key.

The first key to dealing effectively with criticism is growing into the sort of person who can put criticism in its place. This growth does not happen all at once. It is a process that includes consciously breaking free of the past, noticing and eliminating patterns of thought and behavior that serve you poorly, and healing from the effects of shame, guilt, and other psychological impediments. I'm calling this the *dynamic* key, named for the field of psychology known as psychodynamics, which deals with childhood experiences, personality formation, and enduring psychological issues.

The second key is becoming aware of how the mind works; learning how fears, worries, doubts, and negative self-talk are generated by the mind and maintained in the mind; and engaging in practices that return your mind to your conscious control. I'm calling this the *mindfulness* key, hinting at a practice combining the insights of cognitive therapy with Eastern ways of thought. This practice involves identifying and disputing negative self-talk, learning when and how to detach, and adopting mindfulness practices that promote centering.

The third key is arriving at an understanding of how allowing criticism to deflect you from your life path amounts to spiritual or existential self-sabotage. This is the *holistic* key, named to underline the idea that you are a whole person with strengths, desires, dreams, and goals, and not just the wounded part of you that is susceptible to the sting of criticism. The better you understand your life purposes and commit to living life in accordance with those purposes, the less likely you'll be damaged or derailed by criticism.

You learn to deal effectively with criticism by taking charge of your personality and taking charge of your mind so that you can live the life you intend to lead. As you grow in this direction, you learn to deal with criticism in new, more effective ways. Here are some practical strategies that you would want to learn as you transform yourself into a person who handles criticism well.

You effectively handle criticism by:

- *Learning your idiosyncratic reactions to criticism.*

- *Learning to accurately detect what troubles you the most about a piece of criticism.*

- *Learning to distinguish between fair criticism and unfair criticism.*

- *Learning to remain calm and focused in the face of criticism.*

- *Learning to separate the criticism from the critic.*

- *Learning not to argue with your critics.*

- *Learning not to magnify or dwell on criticism.*

- *Learning to relish criticism as a natural consequence of setting goals and taking risks.*

- *Learning to reframe criticism as stepping stones to a better understanding of the truth.*

- *Learning not to talk too much about the criticism you receive.*

- *Learning to respond to criticism assertively, briefly, and clearly, when you choose to respond.*

- *Learning to set limits on the criticism you receive.*

- *Learning to gracefully accept and grow from fair criticism.*

- *Learning selective inattention and the power of ignoring unfair criticism.*

- *Learning to write "dear critic" letters that ventilate your feelings and point you in the direction of growth and change.*

- *Learning new internal language for thinking about criticism and responding to criticism.*

- *Learning to "put criticism in its place" so as to serve your emotional, spiritual, and existential needs.*

- *Learning to evaluate your progress in handling criticism.*

Consider the following story. A client, a world-famous musician, came to see me in my capacity as creativity coach. He wanted to take his music in a new direction but didn't feel equal to dealing with the criticism he knew he would receive—from the people around him, from his audience, and from media critics—if he moved his music in this new direction. He'd already grown tremendously in our work together, so much so that he dared contemplate this break with his popular music, but this was a new—and terrifying—edge for him.

We agreed that he really had no choice in the matter. In order to grow musically, he had to face his fear of criticism and he needed to develop new tools to deal with the criticism he was smart enough to know would come his way. He couldn't just dash off a "dear critic" letter to an imaginary critic or add an affirmation to his self-talk vocabulary in order to prepare himself for this new adventure. He understood that he would have to transform himself into someone who stood in a new relationship with the idea of criticism: someone braver, more detached, and savvier than he currently felt himself to be.

With my help, he did this work. About a month later we chatted on the phone. He explained that he was ready to unveil his new musical ideas to his business manager and to some other close confidantes. I asked him if he could explain to me how he'd changed. He replied instantly, "My new mantra is 'I invite criticism.' And I mean it. I've come full circle from fearing it like the devil to opening the door wide. If I don't take risks, I'll die. If I do take risks, people are bound to have plenty of negative things to say. I've nailed that equation in my head."

You could hear the new strength in his voice and the new wisdom in his words.

EXTINGUISHING YOUR FEAR OF CRITICISM

The less you fear criticism, the less you will experience performance anxiety. If you do nothing else, please think about the relationship between a fear of criticism and performance anxiety. Imagine for a second that there was no way that you or anyone else could criticize your performances, not because your performances were invariably excellent (since excellent performances can still be unfairly criticized) but rather because criticism had vanished from the face of the earth. How much easier would it be for you to perform? Infinitely easier!

You can't get rid of the criticism—that isn't in your control. But getting rid of your fear of criticism is functionally the same thing. If you do not fear criticism, you do not have to spend even one single second worrying about whether you or anyone else will criticize your performance. What you say to yourself is, "If I get criticized, I'll deal with it. I refuse to fear it and, you know, I don't really fear it!" When, one day, you hear those words coming out of your own mouth, you may find yourself completely rid of your performance anxiety.

- *Please describe your plan for fearing criticism less.*

_____

_____

_____

_____

_____

Chapter Ten

DETACHMENT TRAINING

When you can't get a thought out of your head—for instance, that an upcoming performance is frightfully important—you are obsessing. The thought is intrusive, a pressure, a pain. You have the sense that your mind isn't really in your own control. You know that nothing is being served by cycling that thought over and over again and that real anxiety symptoms are being provoked by cycling that thought. Yet you can't seem to do anything about it.

The Buddha, for one, recognized this grave dilemma and commanded, "Get a grip on your mind!" He taught that we either manage to control our thoughts or we don't manage to control them and that those of us who can't are doomed to live in pain and misery. He didn't name performance anxiety as one of the miseries that would afflict us if we lost control of our thoughts, but he might have.

Healthy mind control means that you think about what you think about only when you want to think about it and only in the ways that you want to think about it. You don't *avoid* thinking about an impending performance, as avoidance is a form of defensiveness and leads to procrastination and anxiety. Rather, you think openly and frankly about that performance but exactly as you wish to think about it and only when you want to think about it.

Say that you have an audition coming up tomorrow for a role that you really want. "Really wanting it" is not a problem; the detachment I'm describing is not a detachment from desires, dreams, and goals. You can want to do well and you can dream about succeeding. Rather, the issue is the extent to which you allow negative or nerve-racking thoughts to intrude. You've thought about how you want to present yourself. You've rehearsed your audition pieces. You know what you're going to wear and you intend to leave early enough to get there in plenty of time. Nothing is a problem—unless you let the wrong thoughts in.

Do you want to picture yourself tripping over the doorstep and entering the audition room on your face? Do you want to entertain the thought "I should have lost seven more pounds." Do you want to "remind" yourself that you've had a streak of bad luck and will probably lay an egg? No. Those are the sorts of thoughts not to entertain. The essence of detachment is not thinking thoughts that do not serve you. It isn't so much that you are detached but rather that you have the power to detach "wrong thinking" and send it packing. Isn't that a tremendous power to cultivate? Can you think of a single power whose possession would do you more good?

EIGHT THINGS ABOUT YOU

I use the following structured "disidentification" exercise. I choose a quiet peaceful setting and ask the participants to list, on separate cards, eight important answers to the question, "Who am I?" I then ask them to review their eight answers and to arrange their cards in order of importance and centricity: the answers closest to their core at bottom, the more peripheral responses at the top.

Then I ask them to study their top card and meditate on what it would be like to give up that attribute. After approximately two to three minutes I ask them to go on to the next card and so on until they have divested themselves of all eight attributes. Following that, it is advisable to help the participants integrate by going through the procedure in reverse.

—IRVIN YALOM, *Existential Psychotherapy*

Detachment is not just a "mind" sort of thing. We may be frightened of a performance and yet have no identifiable thoughts that signal our fear. Our mind may be a blank as the anxiety courses through our body. Our fear is hidden from us even as it is made manifest through symptoms. Therefore successful detaching means more than gaining control of our thoughts. It means gaining control of our silent, frightened orientation in the world and detaching from the doubts, fears, worries, and shadows. This is a taller order—but the right goal. Let's begin our examination of how to successfully do this by looking at the concept of *disidentification*.

DISIDENTIFICATION

Disidentification is a useful concept elaborated by the Italian psychiatrist Roberto Assagioli as part of a therapeutic model he called psychosynthesis. Assagioli argued that people often become over-invested in and identified with transitory events and states of mind and that the cure for their mistaken identification involves consciously disidentifying.

For someone giving a performance, this means disidentifying from the performance by consciously saying *and believing*: "I am not my performance. I am separate from my performance, I am different from my performance, and, most importantly, I am more than my performance." You are not the equivalent of your singing voice—you are infinitely more than your singing voice. You are not the equivalent of any poem you write—you are infinitely more than any poem you write. You are not the equivalent of any of your strengths or weaknesses, any of your personality parts (Assagioli called them subpersonalities), or any of your failures or successes. You are greater than the sum of your parts, however your parts are named and identified.

According to Assagioli, the process of disidentifying unfolds in the following way. He wrote in *Psychosynthesis*:

> The first step is to affirm with conviction and to become aware of the fact: "I have a body, but I am not my body." For instance, we say, "I am tired," which is nothing less than a psychological heresy; the "I" cannot be tired; the body is tired. The second step is the realization: "I have an emotional life, but I am not my emotions or my feelings." To say "I am content" or "I am irritated" is to commit an error of psychological grammar. The third step consists in realizing: "I have an intellect, but I am not that intellect." Ordinarily we identify ourselves with our thoughts, but when we analyze them, when we observe ourselves when we think, we notice that the intellect works like an instrument. These facts give us evidence that the body, the feelings, and the mind are instruments of experience, perception and action which are deliberately used by the "I," while the nature of the "I" is something entirely different.

This way of looking at life allows us to create the following "disidentification affirmations":

"I perform but I am not my performance."
"I may have negative thoughts but I am not my negative thoughts."
"I may find myself in a given situation but I am not my situation."
"I am more than the part of myself that is anxious."
"I may have fears but I am essentially unafraid."
"I am more than any mistake I might make."
"My body may be acting up but I am all right."
"My emotions may be acting up but I am all right."
"Whatever happens, I will be fine."

This process of disidentification does not contradict the idea that you want to do well and that you want what you do to matter. You can want what you do to matter and you can want to do well while still remembering that you are not the thing you are doing. You can *care* without *over-identifying*. This is a life-altering lesson to learn.

RIGHT MIND

The goal of detachment training is not to become a Pollyanna. You do not replace wrong thoughts with happy thoughts. You replace them with affirmative thoughts full of true understanding and an appreciation of reality. You do not replace "I can never learn that role" with "If I whistle a happy tune, I can learn that role in three minutes flat!" You do not replace "No one will like my performance" with "Everyone under the sun will love my performance!" You replace the first with "I can learn my role if I buckle down and work" and the second with "I'm sure I'll have a good experience." Right mind is not smiley-face mind. You face the world optimistically while treating reality with respect.

Another way to say this is "I do things, but I am not the things I do." For instance, you can tell yourself the following: "I sing but I am not my concert, and I will not live and die according to how much applause I get." "I paint but I am not my painting, and I will not live and die according to whether it pleases me or pleases others." "I am more than anything I do and I am different from anything I do."

- *Do the ideas of over-identification and disidentification make sense to you?*

_____

_____

- *Have you tended to over-identify with your performances and has that over-identification played a part in your experience of performance anxiety?*

_____

_____

- *Create a few "disidentification affirmations" like the ones listed above. If you come up with one that you really like, commit it to memory, write it out and put it up in a prominent place, and begin actually using it.*

_____

_____

_____

_____

_____

_____

- *Dream up some ways of disidentifying from your performances. What comes to mind?*

_____

_____

_____

_____

_____

_____

Some people instantly resonate with the idea of disidentification and agree that it might be a very smart technique to master. For example, Anne, a painter, explained:

Learning about disidentification proved very useful. I've been working on a solo painting exhibition that will happen in June. I had the usual problems getting the good work to come out, although when it did I really liked it. Then I started to doubt it, which of course interferes with the process. I started having thoughts like "Maybe this body of work isn't cohesive" and "Maybe people won't accept it." I can see how I over-invested in the event itself. Does it really matter what people think? Well, yes, it does; but it also doesn't. In reality a show is over in a flash, and then I'm working on the next one.

I think that the lesson for me to learn is that "I am not my exhibition. There is me in all of my work but my work is not me." The affirmation I want to create is this: "I will keep this exhibition in perspective. I am more than this work and more is yet to come." One life lesson I already knew is that whatever disturbing event is coming up will soon be in the past and another one will start looming on the horizon. I already knew this but framing it in terms of disidentification proved really helpful.

Other people understand and appreciate disidentification as a concept but run up against a profound problem: if they are not any one of their composite parts, who or what are they? Here is how Andrea, a musician, wrestled with this issue:

I'd heard of disidentification before but hadn't studied it in any detail. It makes great sense to me. My problem with it (and one of the reasons that I'm still in long-term psychotherapy) is that I don't know what the "I" is when I'm detached from whatever I'm doing/thinking/feeling. I absolutely understand and believe that I am not my performance, my presentation, the chapter I'm writing, the Ph.D. I acquired, or the concert that I give. But I don't know what I am. So I could truthfully utter all of the affirmations you mentioned but I gain little comfort from them, because my issue is with the "I" that's underneath.

So my challenge with the practice of disidentification is to experience, or uncover, or become comfortable with—I don't how to phrase it—the "me" that is not my thoughts, feelings or deeds. If I truly am "more than anything I do and different from anything I do" (and I honestly believe this to be the case), I need to find out and get comfortable with whatever the heck "that me" is!

Right now, focusing on my performance—identifying with it, I guess—grounds me and gives me a reason to exist in the moment. What I find more useful for the stage I'm at is to say something like "This really matters to me. In this moment I'm totally involved in my performance. I will act as if it's all that matters, while knowing at the same time that there's so much more to life." You can see how much trouble I'm having letting go of investing in the importance of my performances!—no doubt because I just don't have a solid sense of who I am, separate from what I do.

Some people, like Andrea, have trouble comprehending who or what "I" remains if and when they disidentify from their actions, behaviors, feelings, thoughts, and performances. Others, like Suzanne, whose response follows, are troubled by the thought that by detaching they actually suck the meaning out of what they do. How can they care whether or not they perform well if they are "so much more" than their performance, if mistakes don't matter, if their audience doesn't matter, if the performance itself doesn't matter? Suzanne wrote:

This lesson on detachment is the hardest lesson so far. I notice that all the examples say, "I am not my X, I am more than my X." Doesn't it stand to reason that I am also less than my X? And where does that leave me? If I am both more and less than my X, why try at all? What puts power into my performance is that I DO care, that I WANT to be good, that I WANT to make a good impression. If I say to myself, "I am not my presentation," then I feel I am not responsible for doing my absolute best for the presentation.

I tried to say "This matters to me but I am not my presentation" the last time I had to present. It was a very difficult presentation, one I started by discussing an important mistake I had made in front of a lot of people. Suddenly, thinking "I am not my presentation" sucked the meaning out of what I was saying. If I'm so much better than anything I do, who cares if I make a mistake? I substituted "I care about the audience; I want to help them be their best." And that worked pretty well, but I still had the feeling that disidentifying was ruining something for me. This may all be about my anxiety and not anything about detaching, but whatever it's about, I'm sure I didn't land on the right way of thinking about this.

These three examples alert us to some of the challenges that confront us as we try to detach. If I want to do well, mustn't I necessarily be invested in the quality of my performance? If performing is my life's work, how can my sense of identity and self-worth not get tangled up with outcomes? What sort of person would I be if didn't care about my efforts? Before I disentangle these issues, I'd like *you* to try your hand at disentangling them.

- *Write at some length in response to the following question: How can I honor my performances as events that matter, while at the same keeping them in healthy perspective?*

_____

_____

_____

_____

_____

_____

_____

_____

CARING AND NOT CARING

You are obliged to believe that your performances are important to you, as otherwise you will not be motivated to do them or to do a good job on them. At the same time it's wise to believe that they aren't important to you, in the sense that making a mess, receiving a negative evaluation, or having a less-than-perfect experience mustn't be allowed to harm you emotionally or badly unsettle you. One shorthand way of stating this is "My performance matters to me and it doesn't matter to me." Another is "I care about my performance and I also don't care."

I would like this to be a strong, useful book. In that sense, what I write matters to me. But it surely wouldn't be a good idea for me to worry if a typo appeared, if some sentences proved ungrammatical, or if some number of you disagreed with my ideas. More important—and this is hard to take in and believe—it would not serve me to worry even about making a complete hash of this book. I do not want to do that, and I will work hard not to do that, but should that happen I would need to disidentify from the result and get right back on the writing horse. If, instead, I said to myself, "Oh, I'm so embarrassed!" or "I must not know what I'm talking about," I would be setting myself up for blocked creativity and an inability to perform. I'm eager to work well on this book—that is my intention, my goal, and my responsibility—and *then* I must let go of needing it to turn out well: *then* I must stop caring.

ROYALLY MAGNIFICENT ALONENESS

I read somewhere: "You are tried alone; alone you pass into the desert; alone you are sifted by the world." But let a man once look within in all sincerity and he will then realize that he is not lonely, forlorn, and deserted: there is within him a certain feeling of a royally magnificent aloneness, standing all by himself and yet not separated from the rest of existence.

—D. T. SUZUKI, *Zen Buddhism and Psychoanalysis*

The phrase that I'm using to articulate this idea is "My performance matters to me and it also doesn't matter to me" or, alternatively, "I care but I don't care" about how well I perform. The task I want to present you with is finding your own phrase for this idea. If you can land on a truly resonant phrase, one that gives you real permission to work well without worrying about outcomes, you will have arrived at a "miracle phrase" of inestimable value to you.

- *Create your own resonant phrase that does the work of reminding you that your performance matters to you but that you have permission to make a hash of it and that you are not afraid of outcomes.*

_____

_____

_____

_____

There are many subtleties at play here, as you can well imagine. For example, your phrase might work for an everyday performance but not work for a performance that "really" matters. For that reason, you might want to create two phrases, one for "everyday performances" and one for "special performances." Conversely, you may reason that maintaining a "permission to be human" is the right way to go with respect to all of your performances and maybe with respect to the "most important ones, especially.

- *Think through whether you feel that you need two phrases or only one phrase and, if you feel that you need two, please arrive at a pair of phrases that work for you.*

_____

_____

_____

_____

_____

_____

Tackling questions of "mattering and not mattering" and "caring and not caring" naturally provokes some big meaning questions, as does the whole idea of detachment. Here is the report of one artist who wrestled with these issues:

I start from the place of assuming that the beads I make MUST be good ones, that I can't afford to make mistakes. As I process this assumption I realize that of course that matters, but that learning also matters. The only way to make any progress is to learn, and the only way to learn is to try things and make mistakes. Yes, it matters that some of what I make must be good enough to sell, but it's also my goal as an artist to grow and mature, and that can't happen unless I try new things. So this is a perfect opportunity to improve my skills and also learn new techniques.

I also stop and question my fear of working in front of others. My assumption has been that when I give demonstrations I'm supposed to be the expert and look like I know what I'm doing. And of course that's true in an important sense. However, mistakes happen, and they happen to everyone. I just saw one of those TV chefs make a mistake and he didn't even bother to edit it out. Maybe it's only human to make mistakes and not as big a deal as I make it out to be. So my new "permission" phrase is "People are glad to have somebody show them how to make these beads and they don't need the demonstration to be perfect. They'll even learn from my mistakes how to fix things on the fly!"

But as I work on this issue, an underlying problem rears its ugly head, a meaning problem. Since 9/11, a meaning switch flipped for me, and I haven't been able to find my way out of the dark. The world has become so focused on safety and survival that art feels like an unnecessary luxury, especially when our leaders and institutions make it clear that they don't put a high priority on the arts. I've gone from art meaning too much to me, to the point of paralyzing myself, to it meaning absolutely nothing, and I can't seem to reach a sane middle ground. Therefore, I'm having a hard time getting through the inner dialogue that is needed to establish a resonant phrase to deal with the paradox of creative performance. Without a foundation, I've got nothing to stand on.

Detachment training can bring up the specter of meaninglessness, as the "not caring" and "not mattering" components of the equation can create a slippery slope toward a meaning crisis. The solution is to hold the "caring" and "mattering" components of the equation simultaneous with and just as strongly as you hold the "not caring" and "not mattering" components. If you can do this, you will find yourself in an entirely new relationship to your performances, motivated to perform because "you care" and also fearless because you "don't care." Here's how one singer/songwriter framed the issue:

I've been struggling with this issue for months now. I thought that my goal was to widen the gap between "important" and "not important." Unless something is really important to me, I'm not motivated to even attempt it. Conversely, unless something is "unimportant" to me, I can feel crippled by perfectionism and not start. So I thought that my task was to somehow widen that gap and make a space between "important" and "unimportant." Now I see that the real goal isn't to widen the gap but to hold both concepts as true at the same time.

This realization is a genuine breakthrough for me and removes the need for the "gap" I was trying to invent. But it also requires me to do something that I'm not yet adept at doing: holding two contradictory viewpoints in the same moment. I have become very good at holding contradictory points of view in succession, even in very quick succession, but have not yet mastered the knack of holding them at one and the same time. I'm ready to develop that ability. I know that it would be a great gift to really possess the simultaneous holding of "important" and "not important" and to hold them in just the right way, so that I feel motivated but not overanxious.

THE FOUR PILLARS OF DETACHMENT

Detaching is a larger idea than disidentifying from your performances. It's really about adopting a certain stance with respect to life and instituting a certain philosophy. Four separate elements make up a "philosophy of detachment." In order to achieve right detachment you need to cultivate a compassionate appreciation for the human predicament, strength of conviction, clarity of intention, and clarity of mind.

A woman stands at the podium facing her audience. She smiles at her audience because she has a compassionate appreciation for their humanness. She understands that the fellow in the front row may be undergoing radiation treatment for an inoperable cancer, that the woman in the red dress may be having terrible spats with her teenage son, that the dour gentleman at the end of row four may have painful kidney stones. She doesn't see these people as her judges; she sees them as her fellow creatures, exactly her equal in this essential regard, just mortals like herself who have entered and will pass through this mortal coil.

EGO ATTACHMENT

A concert violinist came to see me, complaining bitterly that she hated turning the pages of her score during performance. Why? Because she was obliged to turn the pages not only for herself but also for her seatmate. He was higher ranking and she was lower ranking, so he didn't have to lift a finger. She wanted to kill him.

"I hate turning the pages!" is ego attachment. It is the mind making unnecessary pain, anxiety, and suffering. She could have detached and said, "I am playing in an orchestra, I am doing what I love, and I am being paid." Would that have been any less true?

She also has the clear conviction that she is walking her path. This performance is something that she is doing because it supports her way of being. If she is a musician, she believes in her path as a musician and sees it as a good thing that she is a musician (and maybe a magician and healer, too). If she is an actor, she believes in her path as an actor and sees it as a good thing that she is an actor (and maybe a shaman and priestess too). If she is a writer at a book-signing event, she believes in her path as a writer and sees it as a good thing that she is a writer (and maybe a leader and cultural meaning-maker, too). Because she quietly but deeply believes in what she is doing, she quietly but deeply believes that it is right that she engage in this performance.

Maybe this isn't a terribly important performance. Maybe this particular performance is more of a chore than a joy. Maybe this performance is only tangentially related to her path and so she finds it something of a stretch to call it meaningful. Still, she is satisfied that she is living a consciously created life and that this performance is part of that adventure. Therefore she can detach from the details of the performance—that the audience is rather small, that the room is chilly, that her new material may not prove interesting—and bask in the good feeling that she is living her intended life.

She stands there with the clear intention to live according to her cherished principles. Her intention isn't to avoid mistakes, perform perfectly, make a good impression, or anything of that sort. Those aren't principles upon which to base a life. Her intention, if she is a musician, is to communicate beauty and the spiritual or existential nature of the universe. Her intention, if she is an actor, is to make magic. Her intention, if she is a writer, is to communicate ideas, tell moving stories, stand as a truth-teller for her culture, and prove a positive force. Because she holds these principles dear to her heart and because she has the clear intention to manifest them, her mind doesn't wander into the territory of fear.

Her mind is clear. She experiences this clearness as a certain emptiness from clutter or, to use the language of this chapter, detachment. There are no extraneous thoughts percolating, no doubts, no idle worries about whether someone will walk out from boredom or leap up and boo. She knows that, when it is time, she will launch into her performance; and so she waits, calmly, a beneficent presence. She experiences no stage fright as she waits, and her audience experiences her as powerfully present and a calming influence. They begin to relax because they sense her mastery, her mastery of herself and, they predict, her mastery of her material. She is comfortable and that makes them feel comfortable. She is quiet and that stills their nerves. She is good-humored and that lightens their mood.

She is detached. One proof is that she has it in her to calmly walk off the stage and do something else if need be. She is in the moment but not trapped in the moment. She is not a prisoner of the performance situation, she feels no special obligation to perform, she has a larger sense of her path and of the universe than that. Of course, she will only walk out for good reasons, but she is not a slave to her circumstances. The audience senses that, too, and feels less trapped as well. There is a certain freedom and good humor on both sides, something that the audience appreciates so much that they give her a standing ovation when she is done.

In order to achieve right detachment, you need to cultivate a compassionate appreciation for the human predicament, strength of conviction, clarity of intention, and clarity of mind.

Please describe your plan for cultivating these qualities. If you can't come up with a complete plan, at a minimum describe some of the things you intend to try in order to move in the desired direction.

- *What will you do to deepen your compassion for the human predicament?*

_____

_____

_____

_____

- *What will you do to strengthen your convictions, both generally and with respect to the performances that you give?*

_____

_____

_____

_____

- *What will you do to cultivate clarity of intention?*

_____

_____

_____

_____

- *What will you do to cultivate clarity of mind?*

_____

_____

_____

_____

Chapter Eleven

TEN-SECOND CENTERING

I've already mentioned the benefits of cognitive change—thinking differently about performing—and incorporating relaxation techniques into your life to help calm yourself before and during performances. I want to marry these ideas and present you with a simple technique that will help you on both fronts. Once you learn and practice this technique, you'll possess a truly powerful tool for calming and centering yourself.

TEN-SECOND CENTERING

You can dramatically improve your ability to deal with performance anxiety by taking ten-second pauses of the sort that I'm about to describe. You'll be amazed to learn that such a life-altering strategy can come in a package as small as ten seconds, but it can. Hundreds of my clients have discovered this and so have hundreds of subjects who've volunteered to try out this technique. They've used this technique to center, calm, and ground themselves while caught in traffic, sitting in the dentist's office, preparing to record a new album, or readying themselves to talk to their teenager. They know that this technique works—especially in the context of dealing with performance anxiety.

This ten-second technique has two components, a breathing part and a thinking part. The basis of ten-second centering is using a single deep breath as a container for a specific thought. First you practice deep breathing until you can produce a breath that lasts about five seconds on the inhalation and five seconds on the exhalation. Learning to do this will take you only a few minutes. Then you insert a thought into the breath, thinking half the thought on the inhalation and half the thought on the exhalation. This, too, will take you little time to learn. In an afternoon you can familiarize yourself with the program outlined in this chapter.

This sounds very simple, and it is. This ten-second centering technique is simple to grasp, simple to use, simple to practice, and simple to master. It's nevertheless profound in its benefits. You will be able to do things that previously felt too painful or too difficult to attempt. You will be able to calm and center yourself before an important meeting or conversation. You will change your basic attitudes about life, moving from pessimism to optimism, from procrastination to effort, and from worry to calm. These are the benefits that await you.

I'm adopting a word from the world of magic to describe these breath-and-thought bundles. The word is incantation. An incantation is a ritual recitation of a verbal charm meant to produce a magical effect. This is exactly our method and aim. The magical effects are instant centering and instant calming. The ritual we use is breathing a certain way and thinking a certain thought for ten seconds at a time. The verbal charms are the specific thoughts that I'll teach you, twelve incantations in all.

Each of these twelve incantations is a centering charm. I hope that you're a little skeptical about the promises I'm making regarding the profound effectiveness of ten-second centering. Then, when you see that it works, it will strike you as that much more magical.

MARRYING EAST AND WEST

We know from Eastern practices like yoga and meditation the importance of the twin concepts of *breath awareness* and *mindfulness*. Breath awareness is simply paying attention to the way we breathe with the object of reminding ourselves to breathe more deeply and more fully than we usually do. As we rush through life, we breathe shallowly, our mind chatter propelling us forward. Burdened by what Buddhists call "monkey mind"—that worried, needy, grasping, anxious, unaware mind of the everyday person—we fall into the habit of automatic shallow breathing.

A vicious cycle evolves in which we maintain this shallow breathing as a defense against knowing our own thoughts. In a corner of consciousness we know that if we were to slow down and breathe deeply we would become truly aware of our thoughts and learn too much about what we're actually thinking. Out of a genuine fear that acquiring such an understanding would upset us, we make sure not to engage in deep breathing.

If we were willing to engage in conscious deep breathing, we would become more mindful. We would begin to see our own tricks; how what we hold as facts are mere opinions; how our usual ways of operating often sabotage us; how pain, resentment, and disappointment course through our system. You can see why mindfulness is easy to champion as an abstract idea but much harder to tolerate in reality. Mindfulness implies that we grow aware of how our mind works, which is a scary proposition.

I'm employing a very simple version of breath awareness as a core element of ten-second centering. You have nothing arcane to learn, no long sitting meditations to endure, no distinctions to make between emptying your mind and concentrating your mind. You will simply learn and practice "one long, deep breath," a breath longer and fuller than you are used to experiencing. This simple addition to your breathing repertoire is all you need to take away from Eastern practice in order to begin your transformation to mindfulness.

From Western thought I'm taking the basic ideas of cognitive therapy. The main idea of cognitive therapy is that what we say to ourselves—our self-talk—is the prime and actual way we maintain our problems, defenses, flaws, and blocks. If we manage to change our self-talk, we have done something profound for ourselves, something more substantial than just making some innocent linguistic alterations.

The incantations that follow function in the way that "thought substitutes" function in cognitive therapy. A cognitive therapist (and I am one) teaches you to identify "maladaptive self-talk," confront and dispute "wrong thinking," and substitute new language that supports your intention to move in a certain direction. You learn to notice your characteristic forms of "distorted thinking" and create "thought substitutes" which in form and content are often indistinguishable from affirmations. These are the key ideas from cognitive therapy that underpin ten-second centering.

Ten-second centering does not demand a full practice of mindful meditation or a complete course in cognitive therapy. In an important sense, I have done the work for you, by presenting you with these twelve incantations. When, for instance, I teach you the incantation "I expect nothing" and explain to you why it is important to let go of expectations (but not of goals or dreams), I will be presenting an idea that you might have arrived at through years of ardent practice. The work has been done for you and you can reap the benefits.

This is not an illegitimate shortcut. Suffering is overrated. I would prefer that you change your life in a day and not in a decade. I hope that you agree. I hope that you concur that you have already earned your merit badges in suffering and that it is legitimate to quickly learn a way of centering that works, rather than arriving at one by studying everything that the East and the West have to offer.

BEING UNCENTERED

As we grow centered, our anxiety decreases markedly. "Centered" and "uncentered" are useful words that conjure a way of dividing our experiences into the kinds we want to nurture and the kinds we hope to avoid. We would prefer to feel less scattered, chaotic, distracted, anxious, nervous, irritable, and unsettled. We would like to be able to marshal our inner resources, focus our attention, make strong decisions, and act when action is required. We would love to feel more grounded and calm. People understand these distinctions without needing to have them explained. However, until you take the time to describe in writing your own experience of uncenteredness, you won't possess a clear personal picture. Do that right now.

- *Take a few minutes and describe what it feels like when you're uncentered.*

_____

_____

_____

_____

_____

Here are some reports from my clients and study subjects. Jessica, a painter from England, explained, "When I feel uncentered, I feel chaotic, fragmented, and unable to move forward. There is an ominous feeling of impending failure and a keen sense of paralysis." Linda, a writer in South Florida, described this unwelcome state in the following way: "When I'm uncentered I feel off-balance, as if I can't right myself. I feel like I'm searching for something but I'm completely lost. Sometimes my uncenteredness manifests itself as disorientation, confusion, or, worst of all, disconnection from my emotions."

Annie, a poet from the Ozarks, described her experience metaphorically: "I'm floating along a calm river, watching birds, marveling at the stark beauty of the limestone bluffs, when at a bend in the river I get caught in a roiling eddy. In the force of the whirling vortex, my self-esteem is torn away. I'm spinning so fast I can't focus. I tell myself 'if you paddle, you can get out of this' and I reply 'I can't paddle well enough, so there's no point.'"

- *Why is it so important that we rid ourselves of uncenteredness? First, you have accidents that you might otherwise have avoided, mental accidents and physical ones as well (see box). Second, when you're uncentered, you do things that you regret, things that come from the shadowiest part of your personality (see box). We make some of our biggest decisions—to marry, to pursue a new career, to move to a different city, to stop performing—while uncentered. Stop now and write about the mistakes you've made and the accidents that have befallen you while you were uncentered. Stopping to remember these painful experiences will help remind you why it is so important to learn how to center.*

_____

_____

_____

_____

_____

_____

_____

_____

TRADITIONAL SOLUTIONS

Most people don't know what to do to center themselves and simply hope and pray that their anxiety, agitation, and confusion will pass of its own accord. Some try to alter their state of uncenteredness chemically, risking addiction and achieving something very different from the experience of centeredness. A large majority of people do not even recognize that they're uncentered, either accepting their rushed, harried, fractured state as the norm or misnaming their uncenteredness as personal style. They think of themselves as "just anxious," "overly sensitive," "obsessive-compulsive," "a worrier," and so on, not realizing that their uncenteredness is a state and not a trait.

A minority of people are aware that they need to become centered and try to practice healthy methods of grounding themselves. They try meditation, yoga, tai chi, and other practices that share a commitment to slowing down, reducing mental chatter, and becoming present. People who try these methods almost always find them valuable. They also typically report that these helpful strategies are hard to sustain over time and hard to employ in real-life situations.

UNCENTERED ACCIDENTS

Annette, a musician in Seattle, explained:

In March 1997, leaving work in a "hyper," agitated, uncentered state, I approached an intersection. I stopped, looked both ways, and saw what appeared to be a fairly slow-moving vehicle quite a way down the street coming in my direction. Debating about whether to wait or not and too agitated to really think straight, I said "To hell with it!," hit the gas and pulled out. Little did I know that the driver of the other car had just hot-wired it from a local car lot and was making a high speed getaway.

I looked up just in time to see a huge, red steel wall slam into me. My car was hit in front, spun around, hit in the side, then traveled down the hill into a telephone pole. Lucky to be alive, I suffered a closed-head injury that kept me off work for six months and recuperating at least another year. I have no doubt that had I been at least aware of the degree of my agitation, I would have waited to pull out no matter HOW slow I thought the other car was going. My logical mind was swept away by my jangling thoughts and by the intensity of my agitation and I was just uncentered enough to make a really poor decision.

Barbara, a singer from Chicago, complained: "I practice tai chi, yoga, and qigong regularly, plus my own form of meditation. I have routines that are part of my day that are designed to keep me centered, and I currently spend some time each evening meditating and reflecting on the day's events. This keeps my general level of stress low. And still I don't have a mental practice that I can call on when I'm really off center and need to shift my state of mind on the spot."

Traditional solutions tend to require time—a half hour listening to a relaxation tape, fifteen minutes going through postures, twenty minutes quieting mind chatter—and are not designed to be used in public. They do not help you become centered, except in a residual or cumulative way, when your boss throws a new project on your desk, your daughter tells you that she's just been in a fender-bender accident, or you feel scattered and anxious during an important meeting.

Leslie, a visual artist in Ontario, observed: "I've created several guided meditations that I currently use to calm myself, to regain my confidence, and to bring me back to the present moment. I simply put on some relaxing music and visualize my way through one of these meditations. This works wonderfully but it takes at least a half hour of time, which I don't always have. I would love to find something that can bring me to a similar place but doesn't take so long."

Traditional solutions fall short for an even more important reason. They have no thought component. They help you relax, calm your nerves, and so on, but they are not designed to meet your centering challenges by providing you with a repertoire of useful thoughts. We need certain thoughts if we are to center ourselves, specifically the dozen thoughts I'll name shortly. For instance, we need to make use of the power of the phrase "I am completely stopping" when we find ourselves rushing around madly. We need to hear ourselves say "I expect nothing" before an important presentation, so as to make our points clearly, compassionately, and powerfully. Phrases of this sort are crucial components of a real centering program.

STRUGGLING WITH TRADITIONAL CENTERING PRACTICES
Andy, an actor, explained:

Over the years I've tried many things with varying degrees of success. I've read a lot of Eastern philosophy, which makes sense and appeals to me very much on an intellectual level, but I can't seem to sustain the practice very well. "Mindfulness" or "Insight Meditation" appeals to me very much and I sense that I need it, but even after four years I don't seem to be able to sustain the focus necessary. I've tried guided visualizations, yoga, mantras, chanting, journaling, and just plain surrendering. But nothing really works when push comes to shove.

Many people grow frustrated in their attempts to use traditional solutions like yoga or meditation and conclude that they are doomed never to feel centered. Lucinda, a painter from Milwaukee, explained: "I've tried many things but nothing seems to keep me focused. Sometimes I feel that being centered is something that just happens to a fortunate few while the rest of us are doomed to wander around in a daze."

ONE LONG, DEEP BREATH

The "ten-second" part of ten-second centering refers to a single breath of ten seconds' duration that you use as a container to hold a specific thought. The first thing I'd like you to do is familiarize yourself with what ten seconds feels like. Look at the second hand of your watch and experience ten seconds.

What I think you'll notice is that ten seconds is a significant amount of time and even a surprisingly long amount of time. It probably feels longer and more substantial than you expected it would.

The customary breath you take is on the order of two or three seconds in duration. This is normal, natural, automatic, and does a fine job of keeping you alive. Exactly because it is natural and automatic, a breath of this length does nothing to interrupt your mind chatter, alter your sense of a given situation, or support change. When you consciously decide to breathe more slowly and deeply, you alert your body to the fact that you want it to behave differently. You are not just changing your breathing pattern, you are making a full-body announcement that something is up.

The long, deep breath you take serves as a container for specific thoughts, but before it does that it serves as the best way to stop what you are doing and thinking. If you have been doing something compulsive and harmful to yourself, this alteration in breathing gives you the chance to bring awareness to your behavior. If you have been obsessively worrying about something, the conscious production of one long, deep breath interrupts your mind flow and provides you with a golden opportunity to counter your anxious thoughts. A long, deep breath is the equivalent of a full stop and is the key to centering.

There are certain considerations in producing this long, deep breath. The first is whether to breathe through your nose or through your mouth. I suggest that you inhale through your nose and exhale through your nose, keeping your lips lightly shut. As with the other suggestions I'll be offering, I think your best policy is to try it my way several times before making any changes. Once you've given my method a reasonable try, by all means personalize and customize your breath so that it suits your style and physiology.

The next matter is whether to keep your eyes open or shut. I suggest that you close them so as to shut out the visual stimuli around you. This will increase the benefits you obtain from deep breathing and, when you introduce a thought into the deep breath, will allow you to focus on the thought without distraction. You can either sit or stand, but I recommend that in the beginning you practice your deep breathing while seated in a chair, your feet planted squarely on the ground.

Your inhalation should last about five seconds and your exhalation another five seconds. If you have experience with traditional practices, you will know that many of them ask you to concentrate on the inhalation and let the exhalation take care of itself. I suggest that you give the inhalation and the exhalation equal weight and equal consideration. Each is going to serve as a container for "half a thought" and each needs attention. You'll want to inhale slowly and deeply, pause slightly before you exhale (this pause, too, is important), and exhale in the same slow, deep, controlled way that you inhaled. Practice until you have this long, deep breath, inhalation and exhalation both, under your conscious control.

You may want to build up to your long, deep breath with several preliminary breaths that you use to progressively deepen your breathing pattern. I predict that ultimately you'll find this unnecessary and that you'll be able to switch from your ordinary breathing-and-thinking pattern to your centering incantation from one breath to the next. For now, though, if it helps you to arrive at a long, deep breath by progressively breathing more deeply, by all means allow yourself some warm-up breaths.

The first few times you practice producing a long, deep breath you may notice that you're rushing yourself or that anxiety or stray thoughts are preventing you from patiently inhaling and patiently exhaling. Try to consciously quiet your body and your mind. Suggest to yourself that you grow calmer, more peaceful, and more focused. If you have ongoing trouble producing a long, deep breath, you might try counting slowly to five on the inhalation and to five on the exhalation. Two slow, unrushed counts of five should produce the deep inhale and the deep exhale that make up one long, deep breath.

- *Please practice now. Please don't read on until you've "mastered" one long, deep breath. It's the basis of ten-second centering and the only physical component of the program. If you find it hard or awkward in the beginning, just keep practicing. You'll master it if you give it an honorable try. Please practice now.*

Welcome back from your practice. I hope it went well. If you do nothing more than incorporate a few long, deep breaths into your day, you will become more centered.

For example Sandi, a study subject, explained, "When I first learned to actually breathe (at age thirty-seven!), I remember that it made such a huge change in my life. I'd had no clue how much I was holding back and how pinched and sour my breathing actually was. Now, six years later, I'm a much more relaxed person."

LEARNING TEN-SECOND CENTERING

Leslie, a nonfiction writer, described her initial experiences trying out the ten-second centering process:

First I returned to the long, deep breath exercise. After three or four breaths I felt that I was doing a good job. It was so calming that I almost feel asleep in my chair! Then I tried to "comfortably fill a long, deep breath with a thought" and that was easy too! I found the concept unique and began to wonder if I could get more creative by using this breath-and-thinking technique to envision my work. It was very powerful to say "I am an artist" and "I am perfectly fine." I can see how breathing with affirmations or incantations can set you on a clear path. This breathing-and-thinking takes you to a very deep place.

Lenore, a musician, explained: "This exercise was easy for me, as several years ago I learned breathing techniques to master control over anxiety and panic issues. I am currently a practitioner of yoga as well as a teacher, and I know that breath is the key to everything. Breath is the first thing I teach my students. I had to take several long cleansing/releasing breaths before I could actually focus on 'one long, deep breath,' but then I felt energy and warmth coming into my body."

Francine, an environmental lawyer, reported: "At the beginning I felt a bit of dizziness so I started counting as suggested, which took my focus away from being dizzy. I was managing well by the sixth go but wanting to know what came next. I got rather impatient with this practice exercise and my mind was saying, 'Okay, I've got this, what's the next bit? Do I have to do the same thing over and over again?' I realized that this is how I approach a lot of things in my life!"

BREATHING AND THINKING

The meat of ten-second centering is using the long, deep breath you just mastered as a container to hold a specific thought. Let's consider two different sorts of thoughts: "stained glass window" and "I am perfectly fine." The first task you face when you insert a thought into a long, deep breath is deciding how to break it up so that it divides naturally and rhythmically between the inhalation and the exhalation. You'll discover, for instance, that "stained glass window" divides most naturally as "stained glass" and "window" and that "I am perfectly fine" divides most naturally as "I am perfectly" and "fine." Give this a try and see if you agree.

The most natural way to break up a given phrase is not by mechanically dividing it in half according to its number of syllables but by testing it out and allowing it to divide as it wants. Consider the phrase "a crisp walk in the country." As an exercise, try dividing it up so that it comfortably fills one long breath. I think you'll discover that it naturally divides into "a crisp walk" on the inhalation and "in the country" on the exhalation. Any other division feels awkward and unnatural. Try some variations, like "a brisk" on the inhalation and "walk in the country" on the exhalation and "a brisk walk in" on the inhalation and "the country" on the exhalation. I bet these won't feel right to you.

A second challenge is not seeing images. When we think a thought, sometimes we see an accompanying image and sometimes we don't. "Stained glass window" is the kind of phrase that naturally conjures an image. "I am perfectly fine" is the kind of phrase that doesn't tend to spark an image. The centering incantations are of the second type, and you should have no problem "not seeing" images as you breathe-and-think. If you're a very visual person and accompany all of your thoughts with images, you'll want to make an effort to "think without seeing."

- *Let's practice breathing-and-thinking right now. First, practice your long, deep breath. Then insert each of the following phrases into one long breath, letting the word or phrase divide naturally between the inhalation and the exhalation:*

"Stained glass window"
"I am perfectly fine"
"A brisk walk in the country"
"I am an artist"
"Amazing"
"A special meal with my best friend and her two cousins"
"Big dog"
"I am calm and contented"
"Two toads and an alligator"

I'm sure that you noticed several things. Single words (like "amazing") and short phrases (like "big dog") had to be stretched to fill up a long breath. With "big dog," for instance, you were actually thinking "biiiiiiiig" on the inhale and "dooooooog" on the exhale. A long phrase (like "a special meal with my best friend and her two cousins") could hardly be squeezed in at all. Some phrases may have surprised you by their power, others by their ability to make you smile.

Amanda, a reporter, explained: "I found that if the phrase was rhythmic and evenly divided, it was easy to do. If it wasn't, I had problems. Either I sped the breath up too much or my mind went off on a tangent. Also, when I visualized images, I had to work harder to keep myself focused. For instance, I bounced from

---

CENTERING AND JOY

Alexis, a singer, explained:

Using ten-second centering has reminded me that I have more choices and more control over an experience than I sometimes realize. I make assumptions that because something is challenging, there can be no joy. But I noticed that I actually got more joy from challenges than from anything else and that's a good thing to remember. Intentionally centering myself makes it possible for me to open myself to the joy that performing can bring.

one image of a stained glass window to another and ended up at the Cathedral of Notre Dame. Before I knew it I was off thinking about French food and wine. This was a lovely mini-vacation but not exactly centering!"

THE TWELVE INCANTATIONS

Now we're ready to look at the twelve incantations. I'll use parentheses to indicate how the phrases naturally divide. Please note that Incantation Three functions differently from the other eleven. It is a "name your work" incantation. You think something different each time you employ it, depending on the work you intend to accomplish. For instance, if your work is an imminent performance, your phrase might be "(I am ready) (to sing)" or "(this audition) (will be excellent)." I'm using "(I am) (doing my work)" as a place marker to stand for the idea that you name specific work each time you use this incantation.

Here are the twelve incantations:

1. (I am completely) (stopping)

2. (I expect) (nothing)

3. (I am) (doing my work)

4. (I trust) (my resources)

5. (I feel) (supported)

6. (I embrace) (this moment)

7. (I am free) (of the past)

8. (I make) (my meaning)

9. (I am open) (to joy)

10. (I am equal) (to this challenge)

11. (I am) (taking action)

12. (I return) (with strength)

- *I suggest that you try out these incantations right now. Take the time to go through the list slowly, incorporating each phrase into its own long, deep breath. Begin with some preparatory centering breaths, breathe-and-think the first thought "(I am completely) (stopping)," and pause for reflection before moving on to the second incantation. Take your time and begin to experience the power of these twelve phrases.*

Each phrase stands by itself and can be used to reduce performance anxiety in a variety of ways. You may discover that one or two of these phrases feel particularly powerful or useful to you, and these may become your prime centering mantras. Clients and subjects have found that the first six phrases, used in sequence (what I call the centering sequence), do a great job of centering you and take only about a minute of your time. Here are a few uses for each phrase, provided to give you a basic sense of when—and why—to use one incantation versus another.

1. (I am completely) (stopping)

- *Because of anticipatory anxiety, you may keep yourself in a rush and rarely get around to practicing your speech or your song. Use this incantation to calm yourself, stop yourself, and remind yourself that it is time to rehearse. Or you may find yourself "trapped" backstage before a performance and notice your anxiety mounting. Use this incantation as a way to "completely stop" all of your racing thoughts and calm yourself just before you perform.*

2. (I expect) (nothing)

- *By going into a performance not needing any particular outcome—not needing an error-free, perfect performance, a crescendo of applause when you finish, and so on—you reduce your experience of anxiety. Use this incantation to remind yourself that expectations are burdensome and a significant source of anxiety.*

3. (I am) (doing my work)

- *Forthrightly naming the performance work you're about to undertake and framing that work in a positive light are important calming strategies. You might create personalized incantations like "(I will perform) (with strength)," "(I am ready) (to sing)," "(This audition) (will be excellent)," "(I am excited) (to be acting)," or one of your own choosing.*

4. (I trust) (my resources)

- *You may be adequately prepared to perform but not feel prepared. This incantation reminds you that you are ready and in possession of everything you need in order to perform. You can also use this incantation to assure yourself that fate, the gods of whimsy, your instrument, and the alignment of the planets are on your side.*

5. (I feel) (supported)

- *Rather than focus on the negatives of a performance situation, for instance that the room is smaller or colder than you would have liked, reorient toward the positive, especially toward the humanness of your audience. You can also use this incantation as a shorthand reminder of your spiritual beliefs.*

6. (I embrace) (this moment)

- *You can fight the moment and fervently wish that you were anywhere but about to perform. Or you can surrender, relax, and embrace the moment. Fighting the moment produces tension; embracing the moment produces lightness and calm. Use this incantation to fully accept that you are where you are.*

7. (I am free) (of the past)

- *Preparing for an upcoming performance, you may suddenly find yourself bombarded by an unwelcome thought about a past performance that went poorly, something in your childhood or upbringing that still haunts you, or some other memory or visceral sensation connected to the past. Use this incantation to instantly rid yourself of that thought or feeling.*

8. (I make) (my meaning)

- *Often when we experience anxiety about an upcoming performance we start to second-guess our reasons for performing, cast doubt on our motives, and precipitate a meaning crisis. This incantation helps remind us that performance is a natural and even vital part of our meaning-making efforts. Reassured that performing makes existential sense, we discover our anxiety waning.*

9. (I am open) (to joy)

- *For the lucky few, performing is a painless, joyful experience. This incantation helps remind you that there is joy to be found in the present moment and that you can experience making music, acting on stage, or presenting at work as not only a positive experience but even a joyous, heartfelt one.*

10. (I am equal) (to this challenge)

- *Many performers like to conceptualize their performance as a kind of heroic challenge that allows them to test their skills and their mettle. If you number yourself in this category, this incantation may work well for you. Even if you don't conceptualize performance this way, asserting that you are equal to your upcoming performance can prove a powerful calming thought.*

11. (I am) (taking action)

- *Action reduces our experience of anxiety, which is one reason why performers tend to experience significantly less anxiety performing than waiting to go on. Virtually any action you take, whether it's walking around the block or stretching a few times, will reduce your experience of anxiety. This incantation reminds you that taking action is a powerful anxiety-management tool.*

12. (I return) (with strength)

> • *Maybe your acting role calls for many exits and entrances or your part in the symphony requires that you jump in scores of times. This incantation helps you calm and center yourself as you await your next entrance or return. It also serves as an excellent "transitioning" incantation as you move from one situation to another throughout your day.*

Whether you use the phrases I provide, each of which has a rationale and a certain resonance, or phrases of your own creation, I hope that you will make ten-second centering an integral part of your program to rid yourself of performance anxiety. The marrying of a deep breath with a useful thought is simplicity itself—and shouldn't be scorned because of its simplicity. If you can get into the habit of breathing deeply and thinking "I am equal to this challenge," "I trust my resources," or your own favorite incantation as you ready yourself for a performance, you may discover that your performance anxiety has vanished.

[For more information on ten-second centering, please consult my book *The Ten-Second Pause* (Sourcebooks, 2006).]

Chapter Twelve

SLEEP-THINKING SOLUTIONS

In my book *Sleep Thinking* I championed the phrase "sleep thinking" to stand for our brain's natural ability to think while we sleep. People immediately understood the phrase and responded to it because it corresponded to their felt experience. In that book I introduced an eighteen-step program made up of simple, sensible steps that people can employ to help themselves sleep think. People responded to this Sleep Thinking Program because it helped them institute a new routine and solve problems of all sorts. You can use sleep thinking to solve any kind of problem, whether personal, relational, professional, or intellectual—and you can use it to rid yourself of your performance anxiety.

Since I wrote *Sleep Thinking*, important new research has confirmed my contention that we do some of our most important mental work while we sleep. Until 2004 there was no significant scientific evidence to support that contention. Then, early in 2004,

---

SOLVING PROBLEMS IN DEEP SLEEP

When people are awakened during slow-wave sleep, they report some sort of mental activity just before awakening in roughly half of the cases. Such reports are usually not of true dreams but of sleep thought, which is more akin to day-time thinking. Often the subject of sleep thought is some problem that had been of concern during the day. For example, a student who had been cramming for a math exam might report working on a calculus problem while sleeping.

—Peter Gray, *Psychology* (Third Edition)

the following report, previewing an article that would appear in the prestigious journal *Nature*, garnered worldwide attention:

German scientists say that they have demonstrated for the first time that our sleeping brains continue working on problems that baffle us during the day. The German study is considered to be the first hard evidence supporting the common sense notion that creativity and problem solving appear to be directly linked to sleep. Previous studies have shown that seventy million Americans are sleep-deprived, contributing to increased accidents, worsening health and lower test scores. But the new German experiment takes the subject a step further to show how sleep can help turn yesterday's problem into today's solution.

The exact process in the sleeping brain for sharpening these abilities remains unclear but the changes leading to creativity or problem-solving insight occur during "slow wave" or deep sleep that typically occurs in the first four hours of the sleep cycle. Other researchers said they long suspected that sleep helps to consolidate memories and sharpen thoughts. But until now it had been difficult to design an experiment that would test how it improves insight. The German researchers "have applied a clever test that allows them to determine exactly when insight occurs," wrote Pierre Maquet and Perrine Ruby of the University of Liege in a commentary on the research. They concluded, "The results give us good reason to fully respect our periods of sleep."

ON SLEEP THINKING, PART 1
Sleep seems to hammer out for me the logical conclusions of my vague days.
—D. H. LAWRENCE

Here are some true stories from people who solved problems while they slept. These vignettes will give you a sense of the power of sleep thinking. Yolanda, a fifty-five-year-old teacher, explained:

The problem was how, when, and where to tell our children that their father was dying. While sleeping I had a dream about running and having fun at Half Moon Bay beach. As a young family, this was a cheap and fun way for us to spend time together. In my dream, my husband did not appear physically consumed by cancer. We both talked to our children about his impending death. They asked questions about why he had to be the one to die and what would happen to us. We talked for several hours. No one cried. Then we all started to have fun again.

The next day I told my husband that we needed to go to Half Moon Bay, maybe for the last time. The following weekend I scheduled an outing with our children, giving them the news while we were on the beach. We talked; their father was too ill to do any walking. When we left the beach, he wanted to have lunch, so we had our last lunch together as a family. We were able to support each other and openly discuss his death and dying. Before this dream I just couldn't figure out how to share this information with them.

> *I often think that the night is more alive and richly colored than the day.*
>
> —VINCENT VAN GOGH

John, a thirty-five-year-old hi-tech worker, recalled:

> *I had to make a decision whether to take a position at a new company or to stay where I was working. I was very torn over making the decision and I tried to weigh both sides of the issue but was still unable to feel confident about making a decision. Then I had a dream about an upcoming party for the company where I currently worked. In the dream my boss came up to me and said, "I don't think things are going to work out here." I woke up from the dream with a peaceful feeling. To me, it was as though I knew inside what the right decision was but I had just been unable to see it with my eyes open. I did give my notice the following week and left the company on good terms. My new job is providing me with all of the opportunities and benefits that my former company was unable to give me.*

> *Researchers suggest that novel solutions are possible in sleep because we give our thoughts and images free rein without distractions from the environment.*
>
> —JAMES B. HAAS

Sarah, an office manager, remembered:

> *I often go to bed thinking that I want to solve my problems while I'm asleep. I've even prayed before I go to sleep to have a problem solved. One particular night stands out, where I had to arrange the following day to fit everyone's needs. I had no idea how I was going to get that done. After stressing about it all day, I prayed about it and just let it go. When I awoke my day was arranged for me. Everyone's needs were met. I find that whenever I have a lot of things on my mind, I sleep think. All night it's as if I'm discussing my problems with someone. I'm talking to someone and being fed the answers. This invisible person whispers the answer and then I say it or think it out loud. Usually it happens when I'm concerned about something and then I receive the guidance I need as I sleep.*

> *In the night there is counsel.*
>
> —Latin proverb

Angela, a twenty-eight-year-old single mother, remembered the following incident:

> *I had to decide how I was going to deal with moving out on my own with my son, Jason. While I was asleep I thought of all of the things I could do and needed to do. I thought of how I was going to get an apartment of my own. I knew exactly how I*

would handle the break-up with my ex-boyfriend. During my sleep I solved every issue that I was going to come across while moving out on my own. I think we think about things in our sleep because our unconscious mind has no other outside distractions. During the day, outside distractions keep us from a proper, clear-minded process.

"Let me sleep on it" is not always a way of postponing a decision. It may also be a recourse to the folk wisdom that knows that there is more than one way to think about a problem.

—A. ALVAREZ

Let me teach you how to use your ability to sleep think to reduce your experience of performance anxiety. In the following pages, I'll introduce you to the steps of the Sleep Thinking Program. If you'd like a more detailed discussion, please consult *Sleep Thinking*.

THE STEPS OF THE PROGRAM

Step 1. Commit to self-awareness.

The first thing you need is a willingness to think about what's going on in your life. Freud and the psychoanalysts who succeeded him were right when they said that we are defended against knowing ourselves. Jung and the depth psychologists were also right to propose the idea of blind spots, those areas of our life that we have trouble spotting. The first step of the Sleep Thinking Program is disputing your natural tendency to keep your guard up. Are you ready to do that? Ready yourself by saying "I am willing to know myself." Take a little time and chat with yourself about committing to self-awareness.

Step 2. Affirm your desire to answer your own questions.

Our worries are with us much of the time. But we tend not to be interested in addressing them because we realize that the answers we come up with may be difficult to implement. Maybe we'll have to say a hard thing to our boss, our mate, or our child. Maybe we'll have to make some big changes in our own personality. Bite the bullet and affirm that you *do* want answers. Inject a dose of optimism into your system and let your brain know that it has your permission to start thinking.

Step 3. Brainstorm current issues and questions.

Sit down with a pad and a pen and ask yourself, "What questions do I want to answer?" or "What problems do I want to try to resolve?" The few minutes that it takes to sit with yourself and generate such a "master list" of current issues and questions is a tremendous use of your time and serves to break through your defenses. Right away important connections begin to be made, ones that your brain will continue working on while you sleep.

Step 4. Identify particular issues and questions to focus on.

It's possible to sleep think without a particular issue or question in mind. However, it's more productive to identify issues that concern you, select one issue to work on, ask yourself some questions about that issue, and select one of those questions to be your sleep-thinking prompt. Maybe, as you look over your list of current issues, you come to the conclusion that your performance anxiety is indeed the problem that most concerns you. Next you would generate a list of questions like the following:

- *Why do I experience so much anxiety, even though I know my material so well?*

- *Could I stop feeling anxious just by snapping my fingers?*

- *What would help me to get rid of my performance anxiety?*

- *What do I need to learn in order to break free of anxiety?*

- *Could I trick myself into performing without anxiety?*

- *Am I missing something important about why I get so anxious before performances?*

From this list (which can be as long or as short as you like) choose the question that feels like the most resonant one to use as your sleep-thinking prompt.

Step 5. Manage anxiety.

One of the great impediments to thinking is anxiety. (Yes, anxiety again!) When you're too anxious you can forget your own telephone number or have trouble with the simplest calculations. Since thinking about your problems provokes anxiety, learning effective anxiety-management strategies is an important part of the Sleep Thinking Program, just as it's an important part of your performance anxiety–management program. There are many effective stress reduction techniques available to you, such as progressive relaxation exercises, meditation practices, guided visualizations, affirmations that you create, and so on. Pick one or two that work for you and incorporate them into your new bedtime routine.

Step 6. Refashion bedtime so that you're prepared to sleep think.

Your bedtime habits affect how well you sleep think. If you go to bed too late, watch programs that agitate or upset you, end each night with a fight with your mate, or in other ways produce stress or unhappiness right before you go to sleep, you are hurting your chances of inducing helpful sleep thinking. Create a new evening routine that supports your sleep-thinking efforts and eliminate those things that produce stress at bedtime.

Step 7. Fall asleep with a wonder, not a worry.

The most important step of the Sleep Thinking Program is falling asleep with a wonder rather than a worry. The performance anxiety questions that I listed above all started out with the phrase "I wonder . . ." Your sleep-thinking prompt should be crafted the same way. You want your attitude to be one of lightness, wonder, and even joy. If you can make this movement from worry to wonder as you fall asleep, you will give your brain a real invitation to think. When you go to sleep worrying, you invite anxiety dreams. When you go to sleep wondering, you invite answers.

Step 8. Surrender to nighttime brain work.

Think back to a time when you stopped struggling with a problem and surrendered to the fact that you couldn't force an answer. Maybe you were wrestling with a problem in class and couldn't come up with the solution. Finally you said something like "I give up" and had the answer come to you the very next instant. You hadn't given up but instead had surrendered to the idea that more struggling wasn't the answer. Maybe you had a tough decision to make, found yourself unable to choose, and said, "I've got to clear my head." Once your head cleared, the right choice became apparent. By letting go and acknowledging that you couldn't force a decision, it became easy to decide. The same is true for sleep thinking. If you surrender to the night and let go of your tense struggle with problems, your brain will feel free to solve problems.

Step 9. Arise during the night to record your thoughts, if your thoughts awaken you.

Only rarely will thoughts wake you up from a deep sleep. This may not happen more than once every six months or once a year. But when a thought does wake you up you'll want to write it down, because it may be a very important one. Why wouldn't you do just that? For several reasons. First, many people are worried that if they come fully awake they'll have trouble getting back to sleep. Second, it feels a little silly to write down things in the middle of the night. Third, and most important, people are unaccustomed to taking their own thoughts seriously. Commit to the idea that when a thought awakens you, you'll write it down and think about it in the morning.

Step 10. Spend time the first thing each morning processing the night.

One of the most important steps of the Sleep Thinking Program is allowing time the first thing each morning for thoughts that may have been generated during the night to make themselves known to you. If you wake up and immediately start worrying about the day, you'll have silenced your sleep thoughts. Instead, make a commitment to spend a little time, as little as five or ten minutes, with a pad and pen learning from the night. Don't interrogate yourself about the night, just gently repeat your sleep-thinking question and begin writing.

Step 11. Make sense of the information you receive.

Sometimes your sleep thoughts will be very clear to you. You will know exactly what they mean and what you're supposed to do with them. You go right to the laboratory and launch an effective experiment or go right to work and say the perfect thing to resolve a conflict between two employees. Often, though, the information isn't transparent. Instead you receive tantalizing clues that must be unraveled if you are to solve the mystery. Part of your job as an effective sleep thinker is learning how to accomplish the detective work required of you. "I wonder what this might mean?" is the phrase that opens the door to your own deep understanding of the information you just received.

Step 12. Make use of the information you receive.

What you learn from your sleep thinking needs to be applied to your life problems, intellectual problems, or creative problems if the information is to prove useful. You may learn that, in order to change course at work, you have to bring new confidence to the job. You still have a lot of thinking to do, however, in order to figure out how you will go about acting more confidently. You may learn that the novel you're writing requires a different antagonist. There is still a lot of work left before you effectively craft that new antagonist. Sleep thinking gives you the answers you are looking for but it also presents you with new work to do. Be prepared for this new work and even welcome it.

Step 13. Plan for any necessary work or change.

Planning is an important part of the Sleep Thinking Program. The plan that you decide to put into place can be very simple, as simple as identifying two or three steps you mean to take to make a change. Your plan might prove as simple-sounding as "Today I am going to clean out my file cabinet, tomorrow I am going to label file folders for my long-term anxiety management program, and Wednesday I'm going to spend two hours putting that program together." A plan even this short is infinitely better than no plan and can make all the difference between reaching or not reaching your goals.

Step 14. Accomplish the work and make the changes.

It is one thing to plan for change. It is another thing to actually make those changes. One goal of the Sleep Thinking Program is that you gain insight into your problems, but another important goal is that you solve those problems by making necessary changes. No weight is lost by planning alone. You also have to exercise and eat less. No relationship is improved by planning alone. You also have to talk to your mate, express your feelings, and work out compromises. No play is staged by planning alone. Props must be found and scenery painted. And no performance anxiety is managed unless you do what's necessary to manage it, whether that's consciously creating affirmations, practicing your deep breathing, or rehearsing your guided visualization. Sleep thinkers become doers who take effective action to meet their goals and solve their problems.

Step 15. Keep track of your progress.

Keep a sleep-thinking journal in which you make many kinds of entries. In it you'll do your morning writing, record meaningful dreams, discern what issues are up in your life, record sleep thoughts, plan for change, and so on. You can also periodically summarize your progress. As you summarize you will learn whether you want to change your sleep thinking question, work on a different issue, alter your bedtime routine, or make a new commitment to your morning writing. This conversation with yourself provides important feedback, alerts you to changes that you may want to make, and becomes a record of your progress.

Step 16. Sleep think new issues and questions.

Each of us is faced with simultaneous problems, recurrent problems, and new problems. A novelist has to wrestle with her current novel and then with her next one. A parent has to deal with her three-year-old's behavior, then, ten years later, her thirteen-year-old's. Some issues may not get resolved easily, which forces us to sleep think them in different ways. Some issues get resolved completely, but then another problem requiring our sleep thinking rears its head. The Sleep Thinking Program is available to solve current problems but it's also a lifelong self-help program that you can use to think about anything.

Step 17. Bring sleep-thinking fundamentals to your daytime thinking.

The skills you learn as you work the Sleep Thinking Program can be applied directly to your thinking processes while you are awake. You can wonder rather than worry. You can make lists and identify your most pressing concerns. You can use your stress-management tools to put yourself in a better frame of mind to think. You can surrender to your natural ability to solve problems rather than trying to squeeze out solutions. The Sleep Thinking Program helps increase your sleep-thinking skills and all of your other critical thinking skills as well.

Step 18. Live an examined life.

Sleep thinking is simply your brain working effectively while you sleep. For it to work effectively, it needs to be pointed in the right direction. If you stay curious, commit to self-awareness, desire answers to your own questions, work on anxiety management, and live an examined life, you will be primed for excellent sleep thinking every night of your life. You will learn for yourself how to be creative, productive, intimate, mentally healthy, and happy. These are the fruits of living an examined life.

THE ANCIENTS ON SLEEP

In Eastern philosophies and religions sleep has sometimes been depicted as the real and true human state, in which the universe and the individual are at one. The Chinese philosopher Chuang-tzu (300 B.C.) wrote, "Everything is one: during sleep the soul, undistracted, is absorbed into this unity; when awake, distracted, it sees many things and hence far less." In a passage in the ancient Indian philosophical texts of the Upanishads, deep sleep and the real self are connected: "Now when one is thus sound asleep, composed, serene, and knows no dream, that is the Self (Atman), that is the immortal, the fearless, that is Brahma."

—Alexander Borbely, Secrets of Sleep

SLEEP THINKING AND PERFORMANCE ANXIETY

You can reduce or even eliminate your experience of performance anxiety by using the Sleep Thinking Program in a systematic way. The first step is to familiarize yourself with the steps I just described and experiment with the program by choosing some current problem, other than performance anxiety, to give over to your sleeping brain. It could be a problem you're having being assertive at auditions, a problem with smoking, a problem with your weight. This will give you a chance to see how the program works, and hopefully help solve the problem as well!

ON SLEEP THINKING, PART 2

It's a common experience that a problem difficult at night is resolved in the morning after the committee of sleep has worked on it.

—John Steinbeck

After you've had the experience of using the Sleep Thinking Program on your "experimental" problem, turn your attention to your performance anxiety. If you've been doing the exercises in this book, you've doubtless gained many important insights into your experience of performance anxiety, created and personalized strategies that are already helping you, and are in a great position to pinpoint appropriate sleep-thinking questions. Maybe the problem you would like your sleeping brain to solve is why certain performances scare you more than other performances. For this problem your sleep-thinking prompt might be "I wonder why rehearsal is so much more nerve-racking than the actual performance?" Maybe you'd like your sleeping brain to rehearse some successful performances (it can do that too!). For this problem, your sleep-thinking prompt might be "I wonder what it would feel like to have a really successful performance?"

Generate your list of performance anxiety-related prompts, carefully read through your list, choose one prompt as your sleep-thinking question, and try out the Sleep Thinking Program for a few weeks. Each morning take a few minutes to process the previous night. Some mornings you may write a little and some mornings you may write a lot. Whether you write a lot or a little, you can be sure that your brain is working hard on your performance-anxiety issues. If you stick with this process for several weeks, you'll learn some important new things and feel as if you've been on a real adventure.

> *Much more than recovering from the wear and tear of today, sleep may be an active and dynamic preparation for the challenges of tomorrow.*
>
> —J. ALLAN HOBSON

One client, an actor, used as his sleep-thinking question "I wonder why I panic before auditions?" For the first few nights he had powerful dreams that he couldn't quite remember. What struck him, though, even though he couldn't remember any dream details, was how his brain was suddenly focusing on his acting career and on his performance-anxiety in ways that it had never focused on any issue before. He could tell that his brain was *working* on something. Some of the dreams had a nightmarish quality to them, so the experience was certainly not completely pleasant, but he nevertheless felt proud that he was focusing on an area that he knew he needed to address. After about a week he had a clear insight as he slept. He heard himself say, "Auditions feel like those times when you had to meet your visiting aunts and you would hide behind your mother's skirt."

> *If you tell your unconscious to give you information in your dreams it will oblige you. It's amazing how the unconscious longs for ways to get in touch with us.*
>
> —SUE GRAFTON

The image of hiding behind his mother's skirt was etched crystal-clearly in his mind's eye. It suddenly struck him that he had been treating auditions from a four-year-old place in his being. He had no idea how that had come to pass, but gaining that insight felt breathtaking and eye-opening. The next night he changed his sleep-thinking question to "What would it feel like to approach auditions as the twenty-eight-year-old I am?" That very night he had a vivid dream in which he auditioned

> *A waking man, being under the necessity of having some ideas constantly, is not at liberty to think.*
>
> —JOHN LOCKE

perfectly for a world-famous director and landed a plum role. He could see clearly how, in this dream scenario, he had become a calmer, bolder version of himself. In the morning he found a phrase playing on his lips: "I can do that." It didn't surprise him at all when he nailed his next audition.

> *Night, when man reassembles his fragmentary self and grows with the calm of a tree.*
>
> —ANTOINE ST. EXUPÉRY

Give sleep thinking a try—and a little time. Nothing may happen for several days or even a week or two. You may have the sense that you're not thinking or dreaming about anything special. If that happens, try a different sleep-thinking prompt if you like, but don't abandon the program. Continue going to bed with a specific wonder and spending a few minutes processing the night every morning. It won't cost you much in terms of time or effort, and you may arrive at some powerful insights about your experience of performance anxiety. Who knows—you may even come up with the complete solution!

Chapter Thirteen

STRATEGIES AND TACTICS, PART I

Some readers will have turned to this chapter first, in order to arm themselves immediately with some anxiety-management techniques. Others may have read Chapters 15 and 16 first and already put into practice a long-term anxiety-management program. Both groups, and the rest of you who have just been reading and working along, are confronted now by the challenge of selecting strategies to rehearse and put into practice before and during your performances. These strategies constellate into the following dozen categories:

1. Medication, Diet, and Diet Supplements

2. Relaxation Techniques

3. Breathing and Meditation Techniques

4. Reorienting Techniques

5. Guided Visualizations

6. Affirmations and Prayers

7. Disidentification Techniques

8. Symptom Confrontation Techniques

9. Discharge Techniques

10. Ceremonies and Rituals

11. Preparation Techniques

12. Cognitive Techniques

Some of these strategies will seem very simple. But there's nothing simple about putting a new habit into place. It isn't easy to make use of thought-blocking as the audience filters in, and it isn't easy to make use of it right now, with no particular pressure on you. It isn't easy getting your calming visualization in mind while the orchestra plays the overture, and it isn't easy to get it in mind even in the safety of your living room. Making use of something as simple as an affirmation—just being able to say to yourself "I can do this!" or "I'm glad to be here!" as butterflies dance in your stomach—turns out to be quite a feat. That's why it's so important that you rehearse and practice the techniques you mean to use. They won't be available to you when you need them if you don't learn them, practice them, and make them habitual.

BUILDING AN ARSENAL OF TECHNIQUES

The first step in developing a ready arsenal of useful strategies is this reminder: your central tasks are finding inner peace and strength, on the one hand, and being very well-prepared for your performances, on the other. You want to have arrived at a place—through detachment training, the practice of ten-second centering, your work on handling criticism, and the maintenance of your long-term anxiety-management program—where you are mentally ready to perform without anxiety. At the same time, you want to really prepare for performances so that you know your material, feel comfortable with your material, and feel confident in your preparations. These are tasks, covered in the preceding and following chapters, that can't be completed in the last minutes before you step in front of your audience.

With respect to the following strategies, start with these five steps:

Step 1. Read through all the techniques. Run through them all before settling on any one. Which feel the most congenial? Which seem best-suited to managing your particular symptoms? Mentally give each technique a chance.

Step 2. Select a few and try them out. Practice them. See if you understand them. See if you can make them work. To begin with, they may even increase your anxiety. That's natural. Don't discard a technique because you find it hard, a little strange, or anxiety-provoking. Give even the oddball strategies a chance. Try to be patient.

Step 3. Imagine a performance situation. Use your imagination and visualize yourself about to go on. Try out your favorite techniques in your mind's eye. Do they seem to work? Is some fine-tuning needed? Change and improve the strategies you like according to what you learn from your practice visualizations. Tinker with the words of your affirmation or try another breathing exercise until it feels just right.

Step 4. Create a harmless but real performance situation and try out your techniques. See if the strategy or strategies you plan to use really do reduce your anxiety. Do you seem more present as you perform, less rushed, and generally more capable and confident? Learn from this practice experience and, especially if it didn't go as well as you might have liked, repeat the experience by setting up additional nonthreatening performances.

Step 5. Try out your chosen techniques before and during performances that matter. See if and how they work. If you find that you can't use them and that you're reverting to white-knuckling it, more rehearsal is needed. Continue practicing your techniques between performances and occasionally try out some new ones.

MEDICATION, DIET, AND DIET SUPPLEMENTS

Many professional performers use both prescription and nonprescription drugs to manage their performance anxiety. This is a controversial subject and no easy answers are available. Should a performer take anti-anxiety medication on a regular basis? Should he take it only before his most important performances? Should he make it a point of honor never to use anti-anxiety drugs? It's certainly a fact of life that people take drugs to help them quell their anxieties, to such an extent that the psychiatrist Barry Blackwell predicted, "With the arrival of the millennium the whole of America will be taking tranquilizers."

The most commonly used anti-anxiety prescription drug among performers is propranolol, a beta-blocking drug sold under the trade name Inderal. In the survey of 2,200 classical musicians mentioned previously, twenty-seven percent said that they had used a beta blocker and seventy percent of those said they had used one without a prescription or medical supervision (that is, they borrowed or bought the drug from another performer).

Are beta blockers actually effective? According to Dr. Michael Liebowitz, director of the Anxiety Disorders Clinic at the New York State Psychiatric Institute, they are generally effective if the performer's symptoms are primarily physical ones like sweating, heart palpitations, and tremors. They appear significantly less effective if the symptoms are primarily psychological. In the study of ninety-four musicians referred to previously, ten of the fifteen who suffered from severe performance anxiety and who tried Inderal reported that the drug was not effective in reducing their feelings of anxiety.

Different performers have different experiences with beta blockers. The singer Anna Moffo explained, "My doctor gave me Inderal once for a rehearsal. I was slowed down. I still felt nervous but just weak, with no adrenaline. I thought, 'I couldn't possibly do a performance tonight.' So I never tried the drug for a performance." But Elma Kanefield, coordinator of psychological services at the Juilliard School, noted that Inderal has seductive appeal for many performers: "The problem with Inderal is, it's so appealing. It can quiet the obsessive thinking—'God, I shouldn't be out here,' 'No sound is going to come out' or 'The audience will hate me.' It quells those thoughts by distancing the worries. What people don't realize is that they become psychologically dependent on it."

Klaus Neftel and his fellow authors of *Stage Fright in Musicians: A Model Illustrating the Effect of Beta Blockers* do not believe that psychological dependency is an issue. They concluded:

> *It is our personal belief that beta blockade in stage fright should only be used under medical control and with well-balanced indications, e.g., a serious impairment of public performance in a professional musician. In our experience, psychological dependency on the beneficial effects of single-dose beta blockade in regularly performing musicians is not a relevant problem. In contrast, the sometimes striking results seem able to reinforce self-confidence for future performances. Therefore, a combination of beta blockade and psychological training may be a reasonable answer.*

A different view with regard to singers is presented by Dr. George Gates in a letter to the *New England Journal of Medicine*:

> *We tested the use of nadolol to control performance anxiety in students of singing and found that it did not enhance performance when given in low doses and that it actually detracted from performance in higher doses. In contrast to an instrumentalist, a singer is the musical instrument, and a tension-free performance may be perceived as lacking emotion, dull, or otherwise uninteresting. The control of performance anxiety through maturation and behavior modification is preferable to pharmacologic shortcuts.*

Glenn Wilson sounds a similar note in "Performance Anxiety" (in *The Social Psychology of Music*):

> *Despite the popularity of beta blockers, evidence concerning their efficacy is mixed. Controlled clinical trials show that they do reduce heart-rate and tremor, but they have minimal effect on subjective anxiety and do not consistently improve the quality of musical performance as independently judged. There is also concern about possible side effects, including loss of sexual potency, sleep disturbance, and nausea, and even though these side effects are unlikely at the low doses usually recommended for performance anxiety, they do suggest the need for caution and reinforce arguments in favor of psychological rather than medical solutions.*

Paul Salmon and Robert Meyer argued in *Notes from the Green Room* that if performers found themselves in either one of two presentation situations, they might consider using beta blockers (see box). Given the possible side effects of taking beta blockers, including lowered blood pressure, impaired memory, sleep disturbances, depression, fatigue, and even hallucinations, and considering that the use of drugs does not support your goals of achieving inner calm and emotional strength, you may want to postpone using a beta blocker until you've tried the other anxiety-reducing strategies available to you. The decision is ultimately yours—in consultation with a physician who is aware of the pros and cons of using anti-anxiety medications.

- What is your experience of using drugs (prescription or nonprescription, including alcohol) to help manage performance anxiety?

_____
_____
_____
_____

- What have you learned from these experiences?

_____
_____
_____
_____

- If you are a "pro-drug" sort of person, discuss the downside of employing drugs to handle performance anxiety.

_____
_____
_____
_____

- If you are an "anti-drug" sort of person, discuss the upside of using drugs to manage performance anxiety.

_____
_____
_____
_____

- Do you fear that if drugs worked to quell your anxious feelings, you would become psychologically dependent on them?

_____
_____

USING BETA BLOCKERS IN CERTAIN SITUATIONS

We believe that the use of drugs, such as beta-blockers, may be appropriate under certain conditions. First, when other measures have failed, performers with chronic, disabling anxiety in performance situations may benefit from the use of medications that help control the disturbing symptoms. Performers with histories of chronic anxiety may find that the abrupt cessation of some of the physiological symptoms of anxiety brings a tremendous sense of relief. This may give the performer a glimpse of what it is like to perform without disabling anxiety symptoms. The second situation in which one might consider using beta-blockers would be a performance that is absolutely critical to a performer's development or career. Under such circumstances, it might be argued that a performer should use any therapeutic agent that will result in or contribute to optimal performance.

—PAUL SALMON and ROBERT MEYER, _Notes from the Green Room_

- *Do you see a difference between "relying" on anti-anxiety medication and using such drugs "occasionally"?*

_____

_____

_____

_____

It may also be helpful to hold a written dialogue with yourself about the pros and cons of using prescription and nonprescription medication to reduce your experience of performance anxiety. If you feel that you need more information before entering into a dialogue of this sort, you may want to research the topic and/or chat with your physician.

Being mindful about what and when you eat can help in reducing anxiety before performances. The right kinds of food can have a soothing effect and the wrong kinds can cause upset. Bland food is recommended: a turkey sandwich and a glass of milk is one sort of traditional pre-performance meal. Some people prefer to eat nothing or next to nothing, to scrupulously avoid caffeine and alcohol, and in general to take the path of abstinence. Additionally Dr. Douglas Hunt, who advocates treating all forms of anxiety with nutritional supplements, recommends a specific array of nutrients for quelling performance anxiety (see box).

NUTRITIONAL TREATMENT OF STAGE FRIGHT

Take the following nutritional supplements one hour before the performance:

  Thiamine—500 mg
  Calcium lactate—1,000 mg
  Choline—1,000 mg
  Niacinamide—500 mg
  Vitamin B6—50 mg
  Biotin—2,000 mcg
  Aspirin—5 grains
  Pantothenic acid—1,000 mg
  Folic acid—800 mcg (take four of these tablets)

—DOUGLAS HUNT, *No More Fears*

[Note: Please consult Dr. Hunt's book before beginning this nutritional program and begin it only in consultation with your own physician.]

The relationship between the ingestion of a substance—whether beta blocker, vitamin supplement, nicotine, protein shake, or double espresso—and its increase or reduction of your anxiety is a personal matter. Carefully experiment with various pre-performance regimens, monitor your experiments, and make changes that seem appropriate and necessary.

- *Are you aware of a relationship between what you eat or drink and your experience of performance anxiety?*

_____

_____

• *What is your experience with stimulants (like coffee) and performance anxiety?*

_____

_____

_____

_____

• *What is your experience with depressants (like alcohol) and performance anxiety?*

_____

_____

_____

_____

• *Do particular foods increase your experience of performance anxiety?*

_____

_____

• *Do particular foods help reduce your experience of performance anxiety?*

_____

_____

• *What do you think is an ideal pre-performance meal for you?*

_____

_____

_____

_____

RELAXATION TECHNIQUES

Few of us relax very often or very well, and many of the activities that do manage to relax us—like gardening or bathing—are hardly available to us as we wait in the wings to perform. Those techniques that are available—like progressive relaxation exercises, self-massage, self-hypnosis, the Sarnoff Squeeze, or the Quieting Reflex—must first be learned and practiced. These techniques are not abstract ideas but hands-on procedures that require mastering.

Progressive relaxation exercises are designed to work by relaxing different muscles groups in sequence. Renee Harmon presents a short progressive relaxation exercise in her book *How to Audition for Movies and TV.* The following exercise takes about thirty seconds:

• *Relax your forehead.*

• *Relax the area around your eyes.*

• *Relax the corners of your mouth.*

• *Listen to the sounds surrounding you but do not concentrate on them.*

THE SARNOFF SQUEEZE

The Sarnoff Squeeze is named after the actress Dorothy Sarnoff, who described her technique in Never Be Nervous Again. *She learned this relaxation technique from watching Yul Brynner backstage before performances of* The King and I. *Sarnoff explained:*

Sit down in a straight-backed chair. Carry your rib cage high, but not so high that you're in a ramrod straight military position. Incline slightly forward. Now put your hands together in front of you, your elbows akimbo, your fingertips pointing upward, and push so that you feel an isometric opposing force in the heels of your palms and under your arms. Say sssssssss, like a hiss. As you're exhaling the s, contract those muscles in the vital triangle (below the ribs, where they begin to splay) as though you were rowing a boat against a current, pulling the oars back and up. Relax the muscles at the end of your exhalation, then inhale gently. While you're waiting to go on, sit with your vital triangle contracting, your lips slightly parted, releasing your breath over your lower teeth on a silent ssss.

- *Feel your arms and legs become heavy. At the point of the most intense heaviness, imagine that all your tension flows out of your body. Your fingertips are the exit points.*

- *Feel sunshine warm your stomach.*

- *Lift your chin and smile.*

Take a minute and try out Renee's exercise or, if you feel motivated, create your own progressive relaxation exercise. To create your own, follow the guidelines provided by Edmund Bourne in *The Anxiety and Phobia Workbook:*

Progressive muscle relaxation is a systematic technique for achieving a deep state of relaxation. It was developed by Dr. Edmund Jacobson more than fifty years ago. Dr. Jacobson discovered that a muscle could be relaxed by first tensing it for a few seconds and then releasing it. Tensing and releasing various muscle groups throughout the body produces a deep state of relaxation. The following guidelines will help you make the most of progressive muscle relaxation:

- *Practice at least twenty minutes a day*

- *Find a quiet location where you won't be distracted*

- *Practice at regular times*

- *Practice on an empty stomach*

- *Assume a comfortable position*

- *Loosen any tight garments and take off your shoes, watch, glasses, and so on*

- *Make a decision not to worry about anything*

- *Assume a passive, detached attitude*

Bourne goes on to describe one particular twenty-step progressive muscle relaxation technique. If the idea of progressive muscle relaxation interests you, by all means check out his version or one of the many other versions available to you.

Mental relaxation exercises can be supplemented with physical relaxation exercises like self-massage. Take the time to massage your hands, forearms, upper arms, shoulders, and neck. In doing so, give yourself real pleasure. Make the little sounds that express your satisfaction: Exhale, sigh, groan a little. Find the knot in your shoulder and work it hard. Lose yourself in the process.

Some people who perform find that using self-hypnosis techniques that they learn from a certified or licensed hypnotherapist helps them relax. The concert musician Robert Aitken explained, "It's a very useful thing. I think many of the great musicians always used it, maybe without knowing it. It can even be used for very specific purposes, like speeding up a trill."

Dr. Charles Stroebel, in his book *Quieting Reflex Training for Adults*, advocates that you use the following four-step Quieting Reflex as your primary relaxation technique:

1. *Become aware of the stimulus you are responding to (say, the sounds of the audience arriving or a "what if" thought).*

2. *Give yourself the suggestion, "Alert mind, calm body."*

3. *Smile with your eyes and mouth to reverse their tendency to go into a grim set.*

4. *Inhale slowly and easily to a count of two, three, or four, imagining your breath coming through the pores in your feet. A feeling of "flowing warmth and flowing heaviness coming up through the middle of your legs" may accompany this mental image. As you exhale, let your jaw, tongue, and shoulders go limp, feeling that wave of heaviness and warmth flowing to the toes.*

Part of the work of relaxing before and during a performance is gaining permission from yourself to relax. You may currently believe that you're *supposed* to feel tense at such times, that that is natural or somehow even desirable. But such a thought is worth blocking and replacing with a new one, that you can be as relaxed as you like.

- *Do you have permission from yourself to relax or are you "supposed" to be worried about something all the time?*

_____

_____

_____

- How might you gain permission from yourself to relax? What might you say to yourself or do for yourself to help gain that permission?

_____
_____
_____
_____
_____
_____

- Try to think with a fresh mind about relaxation. What does the word mean to you as you think about it now?

_____
_____
_____
_____

- What sorts of things help you relax?

_____
_____
_____
_____

- Which of these might be well-suited to become part of your pre-performance anxiety-management tool kit?

_____
_____
_____
_____

- Which of these is the very best? Describe how you might use it as your anxiety mounts.

_____
_____
_____
_____

- Learn one progressive relaxation technique and describe how it works for you.

_____
_____
_____

- *Try out the Sarnoff Squeeze. Does it seem potentially effective?*

_____

_____

_____

- *Try out the Quieting Reflex. How does it seem to work?*

_____

_____

_____

- *What relaxation technique or techniques will you add to your collection of anxiety-management tools?*

_____

_____

_____

BREATHING AND MEDITATIVE TECHNIQUES

In *Managing Your Anxiety*, Christopher McCullough describes several breathing exercises. The exercises have names like "Slow, complete breathing," "Slow, deep breathing with shoulder relaxation," "Counting breaths," "Following your breathing," and "Circling your breaths." McCullough describes "Circling your breaths," for instance, as follows: "As you start to inhale, you slowly bring your attention up the ventral centerline of your body from the groin to the navel, chest, throat, and face, until you reach the crown of your head. As you exhale, slowly move your attention down the back of the head, down the neck, and all the way down the spine."

THE VALUE OF BREATH ATTENTION

Zazen practice for the student begins with his counting the inhalations and exhalations of his breath while he is in the motionless . . . posture. This is the first step in the process of stilling the bodily functions, quieting discursive thought, and strengthening concentration. It is given as the first step because in counting the in and out breaths, in natural rhythm and without strain, the mind has, as it were, scaffolding to support it.

—PHILIP KAPLEAU, *The Three Pillars of Zen*

Give McCullough's simple exercise a try. Even simpler is the breathing exercise described by Stephanie Judy in *Making Music for the Joy of It*.

Anxiety disrupts normal breathing patterns, producing either shallow breathing or air gulping in an attempt to conserve the body's supply of oxygen. The simplest immediate control measure is to exhale, blowing slowly and steadily through your lips until your lungs feel completely empty. Don't "breathe deeply." It's too easy to hyperventilate and make yourself dizzy. As long as you make a slow, full exhale, the inhaling will look after itself.

It may seem odd that I repeatedly emphasize something as automatic and everyday as breathing. But both centuries of mindful meditation practice and the experiences of our contemporaries who heed their breathing confirm that breath attention is an anxiety-reduction tool of real value.

- *Spend a little time just paying attention to your breathing. What do you notice?*

_____

_____

_____

_____

- *Learn one breathing exercise, even one as simple as "consciously exhaling." Practice it until it actually serves to reduce your anxiety.*

- *Having practiced your breathing exercise, to what extent does it seem to work to reduce your experience of anxiety?*

_____

_____

_____

_____

- *Imagine yourself about to make a presentation. Picture yourself waiting to go on and using your breathing technique. Get as detailed and visceral a picture as you can. Is your breathing technique working for you?*

_____

_____

_____

_____

- *This is a good time to practice ten-second centering again. If you need to refresh your memory about the details of that centering technique, please revisit Chapter 11.*

Meditation is a discipline that includes breath, body, and mind awareness. Different meditation exercises have different goals. Some help you exercise thought control while others are designed to allow your thoughts free reign. A simple meditative technique is the use of a mantra. As Stephanie Judy explains:

A mantra is one kind of thought pattern you can use to block negative thoughts. Often taught in conjunction with meditative techniques, a mantra is a word or short phrase that is simply repeated quietly, over and over again, aloud or in thought. "Peace" can be a mantra, as well as "one" or "love."

R. Reid Wilson wrote in *Don't Panic*:

Meditation is a form of relaxation training. You learn to sit in a comfortable position and breathe in a calm, effortless way. You learn to quiet your mind, to slow down racing thoughts, and to tune in to more subtle internal cues. You acquire the ability to self-observe. You practice the skill of focusing your attention on one thing at a time and doing so in a relaxed, deliberate fashion. By reducing the number of thoughts and images that enter your mind during a brief period, you are able to think with greater clarity and simplicity about whatever task you wish to accomplish. By spending as little as thirty seconds meditating, you can interrupt your negative thoughts and create a bridge between one mind-set, in which stress predominates, to one in which calmness predominates. In the blink of an eye, you can alter your sense of the situation and dramatically reduce your experience of anxiety.

- *Create several mantras for yourself.*

- *Take a look at your list of mantras and select the most resonant one.*

- *Try it out by practicing it several times and by using it before a performance.*

Bourne suggests the following meditative technique called "Counting Breaths":

1. *As you sit quietly, focus on the inflow and outflow of your breath. Each time you breathe out, count the breath. You can count up to ten and start over again, or keeping counting as high as you like, or you can use Benson's method of repeating "one" on each exhalation.*

2. *Each time your focus wanders, bring it back to your breathing and counting. If you get caught in an internal monologue or fantasy, don't worry about it or judge yourself. Just relax and return to the count again.*

3. *If you lose track of the count, start over again at one or at a round number like fifty or one hundred.*

4. *After practicing breath-counting meditation for a while, you may want to let go of the counting and just focus on the inflow and outflow of your breathing.*

Use the "Counting Breaths" meditation or another meditation that you know, create your own meditation, or take a class in meditation, which will help you keep to a regular practice.

- *Have you tried meditation before?*

_____

_____

- *If not, is that because you have some objections or worries? Can you address those objections or worries and begin a meditation practice?*

_____

_____

_____

_____

- *If you've tried meditation before but abandoned the practice, how might you approach it differently this time so as to incorporate meditation into your anxiety-management routine?*

_____

_____

_____

_____

REORIENTING TECHNIQUES

What we focus on plays a large part in determining how much anxiety we feel. If, before a performance, I focus on how important the performance is for my career, on not feeling prepared, on how small the audience seems, and so on, I'm pretty much bound to grow anxious. On the other hand, if I focus on the cherry bobbing in my Coke, I will have oriented myself away from the impending performance and will reduce my experience of anxiety. Dr. Manuel Smith, in his book *Kicking the Fear Habit*, argues that each of use has a powerful "reorienting reflex" that we can effectively employ to manage our anxiety. He explains that we naturally orient to five kinds of stimuli:

1. *Stimuli with novelty, that is, anything that is unexpected or new.*

2. *Stimuli with biological significance, that is, anything that activates a biological response.*

3. *Stimuli with innate signal value, that is, anything that we instinctually relate to, such as bodily sensations.*

4. *Stimuli with learned or acquired signal value, that is, anything that we have learned to pay attention to.*

5. *Stimuli with instructed signal value, that is, anything that we have been instructed to pay attention to, either by ourselves or by others.*

Thus, while you're waiting backstage to perform, you might orient toward 1) an announcement on the backstage bulletin board; 2) an attractive person across the room; 3) your own breathing; 4) the first line of your presentation; or 5) the entrance routine you've written out on an index card. According to Hunt, reorienting toward that attractive person is the best distracter of all.

The shorthand for what we're talking about here is "where will I focus my attention?" You can focus your attention on the performance and worry about it, you can focus your attention on your fears and doubts and worry about them, or you can choose to reorient your attention and focus on something neutral, positive, and/or distracting. The goal is to get yourself through the period before a performance and into the performance itself, when, typically, your anxiety will abate. Picture yourself getting ready to perform. Then ask yourself, "Where might I reorient my focus to take the attention off the performance and to help me 'slide' into the performance?"

If you discover that you're having trouble orienting away from your impending performance, that will give you a new clue about the nature of performance anxiety. One aspect of performance anxiety is that we feel that we have to remain vigilant. We can't "look away" even for an instant. So you may have to add the following step to your reorienting practice: before you try to orient away from a performance, say to yourself "It's all right if I don't focus on the performance. Nothing bad will happen if I shift my attention away from the performance."

I have study subjects try their hand at reorienting and then report their experiences to me. A doll-maker explained:

I was approaching my sewing table this morning and I asked myself, "Where might I reorient my focus to take the attention off the work and to help me 'slide' into the work on this doll?" I decided that for today I would try thinking about the circus that I went to with my grandchildren last Friday. I found myself lightening up and smiling. I sat right down and worked on the arm that I was worried would be a problem. The arm turned out to be a quite a challenge and I was right to be worried, but by reorienting I got straight to the work rather than procrastinating and avoiding it.

A singer/songwriter related her reorienting experience:

I am sitting at my desk. I am getting ready to call that producer I sent my musical to last month to ask whether he has read it yet and to find out what he thinks about its production possibilities. I am wondering whether it's the right match for him, given some of the other productions he has staged. I'm upset that I have to do this, angry that he's never acknowledged receiving my package, worried that he didn't like the songs on the CD. I am one minute away from becoming immobilized by panic.

But, taking a deep breath, I give myself permission to orient away from all the internal and external aspects of the situation. I remember to do what has always worked for me in the past. I reorient my attention to my Adam's apple and consciously pull it down towards the base of my throat. This, I have discovered, loosens the tension in my throat, opens my vocal cords, makes my voice more mellow and pleasing, and requires some dynamic attention on my breath to hold the position. It's enough of an active physical shift to break the anxiety pattern. I'm not any more eager to make that call, but at least I'm no longer too anxious to make it.

Try adding reorienting to your repertoire of performance anxiety–management strategies.

- *Have you ever reduced your anxiety by reorienting away from an anxiety-provoking stimulus and toward a different stimulus?*

_____

_____

- *What sorts of stimuli grab your attention?*

Stimuli of a sexual nature?

_____

_____

Instructions you create for yourself?

_____

_____

New or interesting visual stimuli (like paint peeling off a wall, the latest model car, etc.)?

_____

_____

Your own breathing?

_____

_____

- *List the different sorts of stimuli that might reorient your mind away from an impending presentation. How would you rank them?*

_____

_____

_____

_____

_____

- *Imagine yourself in a performance situation. Picture yourself reorienting away from the performance and toward some neutral stimulus. Does it seem as if such a technique might work for you?*

_____

_____

_____

We've covered four anxiety-management strategies in this chapter: medication, diet, and diet supplements; relaxation techniques; breathing and meditation techniques; and reorienting techniques. We tackle the remaining eight in Chapter 14.

Chapter Fourteen

STRATEGIES AND TACTICS, PART II

Here are the remaining eight categories of strategies and tactics available to you. Let me repeat my advice from the last chapter. First, read through all of the techniques before settling on those to use. Then select one or two to try out. Next, use them in a performance situation you visualize in your mind's eye, to get a sense of whether the strategy or strategies you've chosen seem effective. Then try your strategy or strategies out in a relatively unimportant performance situation or in one that you put together just for the purpose of practicing. Last, confidently use it or them when it comes time to perform "for real."

GUIDED VISUALIZATIONS

Guided visualizations are mental pictures you create for yourself. You imagine yourself in a tranquil spot—on the beach, in a garden, beside a secluded lake—and spend time there, in your mind's eye, relaxing and letting your worries slip away. For example, the pianist Andrea Bodo created, as part of a five-step routine to help her make her entrance onto the stage, a guided visualization in which she transported herself to a spot beside a pool filled with water lilies. Like meditative and reorienting techniques, guided imagery provides you with a powerful means of "leaving," even when you can't physically leave.

Guided imagery is a versatile technique limited only by your powers of imagination. Providing yourself with verbal cues, you can guide yourself step-by-step through a successful performance, picturing yourself acting or singing with confidence or presenting your message with great flair. You can visualize yourself on a mission or feel yourself protected in a bubble of your own creation. In each case the visualization proceeds similarly:

- *Seat yourself comfortably, placing your feet squarely on the ground. Close your eyes.*

- *Using progressive relaxation and deep-breathing techniques, quiet yourself. Your goal is to drift into the sort of receptive state where images flow.*

- *Slowly, clearly, and calmly, pronounce either silently or out loud the cues you've prepared to produce the desired images in your mind.*

IMAGERY CONTRIBUTES TO BEHAVIOR CHANGE

Meichenbaum uses three main psychological processes to explain why imagery-based therapies contribute to change. The first process is the sense of control that a client develops out of the monitoring and rehearsing of various images. This sense of control over images and inner thoughts in turn helps the client have a greater sense of control over his emotions and overt interpersonal behavior. The second process involves changing for the client the meaning of his maladaptive behavior. This changed meaning will be reflected in altered internal dialogue that is evident before, during, and after instances of the problem behavior. The third process is the mental rehearsal of behavioral alternatives that contribute to the development of coping skills. By engaging in this mental problem-solving the occurrence of the client's own symptoms will become a reminder to use the coping skills he has learned.

—JEROME SINGER, *Imagery in Cognitive-Behavior Therapy: Research and Application*

You will need to practice the visualization cues you mean to use in order to memorize them. If having to memorize a visualization turns out to be an added stress, you can tape record your visualization and play it back before a performance, letting your taped words guide you through the process.

Sometimes there's a person in your life whose presence calms you. It might be a current or former friend or current or former teacher. It might be the one person who always had great confidence in you and would say, "Of course you can do that!" If there has been such a person in your life, you might want to create a visualization that centers around him or her. Picture the person's calm, confident smile, have a little conversation in which you're assured you that everything will proceed splendidly, or in some other way have this person "accompany" you to your performances.

A similar idea is the following one. While for many performers it isn't a good idea to focus on the audience or to imagine what they are thinking, you might, if it works for you, imagine making friends with some member of the audience. You can visualize that new friend smiling, happy to be there, calm and uncritical, entirely on your side.

Think about providing yourself with at least one sturdy visualization, whether it's making a friend in the audience, bringing a friend, picturing an image of tranquility, seeing yourself delivering a masterful performance, or some other visualization of your own creation.

Leslie, a musician, explained:

One of the ways that I coped with giving my doctoral recital for choral conducting was by using positive visualization. Every time I became anxious over a particular piece of music, I simply visualized the piece in every detail being performed beautifully. At the end of my visualization, I would conclude with a statement of gratitude, such as "Thank you (universe, energy source, God, whatever) for how well my piece is going to be performed." By the end of doing this little exercise, I was calmed and ready to move on. I was simply amazed at how well it worked for me during the rehearsal period and then before the actual recital.

- *What natural settings engender a feeling of tranquility in you?*

_____

_____

_____

_____

- *Which of these might you incorporate into a guided visualization?*

_____

_____

_____

_____

- *Generate a list of possible visualizations. Think about them for a while and see if any one feels more resonant than the others. If it does, take the necessary time to turn it into a full-fledged visualization by writing out the complete scenario and all the necessary cues.*

_____

_____

_____

_____

_____

_____

_____

- *Imagine a performance situation. Picture yourself using your guided visualization. See yourself with your eyes closed, listening to your prepared cues, conjuring up a soothing image. Do you have the sense that this technique might work for you?*

_____

_____

_____

_____

AFFIRMATIONS AND PRAYERS

An affirmation is simply a positive statement that you create and repeat as needed, in which you assert that you are capable, confident, and equal to your upcoming performance. To be most effective, affirmations should be short and simple and framed in the present tense. Examples of affirmations are "I'm ready to perform today" or "I know the lyrics." Your affirmation can be as simple as the word "Yes," repeated with conviction.

Any one of the following might make for a useful affirmation:
"I'm equal to this."
"I'm a fine performer."
"I know my job."
"No problem."
"I have no doubt."
"I can do this."
"I love performing."
"I am calm and capable."
"I am prepared."
"I want to do this."

Affirmations are useful tools in the process of cognitive restructuring that I'm advocating. Remember how cognitive restructuring works. First, you fearlessly notice what you're thinking. If it's a negative thought or one of the tricky dodges we discussed in Chapter 2 (dodges that sound like "I'm not ready," "I don't feel like it," I don't feel well," and so on), you then vehemently dispute that thought. You say something like, "The heck with you, thought! Of course I'm ready!" That's the "thought confrontation" step. Then you make use of a thought substitute that really exorcises the previous negative

---

PRAYER

Affirmations are not prayers but prayers can serve as affirmations. If you pray, you might use one of the following biblical passages as your pre-performance prayer:

The Lord himself goes before you and will be with you; He will never leave you nor forsake you. Do not be afraid; do not be discouraged.

Deuteronomy 31:8

The Lord is my light and my salvation; whom shall I fear? The Lord is the stronghold of my life; of whom shall I be afraid?

Psalms 27:1

Strengthen the feeble hands, steady the knees that give way; say to those fearful hearts, Be strong, do not fear.

Isaiah 41:10a

So do not fear, for I am with you; do not be dismayed, for I am your God. I will strengthen you and help you.

Isaiah 35:3–4

---

thought, for instance following up your thought confrontation of "The heck with you, thought!" with the thought substitute "I feel calm and capable."

Affirmations are simply positive thoughts that you substitute for any negative or anxiety-producing language that you may consciously or unconsciously be using. You affirm that you have no need to worry. You acknowledge your strengths, not your weaknesses. You affirm yourself, rather than disparaging yourself. You affirm that the process is working, rather than that the process is derailing. You affirm that the audience is not your enemy. You say "Yes!" and not "No!" You make use of the power of positive suggestion to block negative thoughts, give yourself a boost, and remind yourself of the joy embedded in the moment.

Affirmations serve a dual purpose. First, they positively reframe the moment, calming and encouraging you. Second, they serve to alter your self-image by providing you with new, positive self-talk that actually takes hold over time. One day you'll say "I feel fine" or "I can do this" and discover that you're speaking the literal truth, not uttering a hope or a prayer.

- *Try your hand at creating a variety of affirmations. Create at least a dozen. There are no rules involved: any phrase that feels affirming is a legitimate affirmation.*

_____

_____

_____

_____

_____

_____

_____

_____

- *Take a look at your list. Which affirmation seems to have the most resonance? Why might that be so?*

_____

_____

_____

- *Picture yourself in a performance situation, using your affirmation. Do you have the sense that this is a technique that will work for you?*

_____

_____

_____

_____

DISIDENTIFICATION TECHNIQUES

You'll remember the idea of disidentification from our discussion of detachment training. The Italian psychiatrist Roberto Assagioli argued that people become over-invested in and identified with transitory events (like performances) and transitory states of mind (like the thought "I'm not ready" or "I'm not well") and that the cure for this mistaken identification involves consciously disidentifying. We went on to discuss creating "disidentification affirmations" of the following sort:

"I perform but I am not my performance."
"I am more than the part of me that is anxious."
"I am more than any mistake I might make."
"My body may be acting up but I am all right."
"My emotions may be acting up but I am all right."
"Whatever happens, the essential me will be fine."

Disidentification can prove a powerful technique whose main purpose is not the "negative" one of listing all of the things that you aren't but the positive one of locating your core strength that will carry you through every situation. As Assagioli explained:

> When you have practiced disidentification techniques for a while they can become a swift dynamic leading to a deeper consideration of the stage of self-identification coupled with an inner dialogue along the following lines: "Who am I then? I recognize and affirm myself as a center of pure self-consciousness and I realize that this center not only has a static self-awareness but also a dynamic power. It is capable of observing, mastering, directing and using all the psychological processes and the physical body. I am a center of awareness and of power."

Determine whether you will try to disidentify from your performances as part of your detachment training. If this process makes sense to you, you will need to create your disidentification affirmations, practice and rehearse them in your mind's eye, and use them before and during performance situations.

• *How much do you identify with your performances? Can you put that connection into words?*

_____
_____
_____
_____
_____
_____

• *Try dreaming up ways of disidentifying from your performances. What comes to mind?*

_____
_____
_____
_____
_____
_____

- *Construct a few disidentification affirmations and practice them several times.*

_____

_____

_____

_____

_____

- *Picture yourself about to appear before an audience. Do you have the sense that employing disidentification affirmations and consciously detaching will reduce your experience of performance anxiety without negatively affecting your performance?*

_____

_____

SYMPTOM CONFRONTATION TECHNIQUES

Symptom confrontation is a technique associated with existential psychotherapy and with the therapists Milton Erickson and Viktor Frankl in particular. In therapy of this sort, a client is commanded, apparently paradoxically, to do more of the thing that he came into therapy wanting to do less of. In her book *A Soprano on Her Head*, Eloise Ristad explained how she championed symptom confrontation in her workshops as a way to reduce performance anxiety. Ristad wrote:

> *Take one of your own symptoms—clammy hands, shaky knees, or whatever—and apply the principle of pushing it to the point where it can go no further. Do not try to control it or make it go away; try only to increase the intensity and see how far you can carry this particular symptom. If you are like most people, you will find you can't push your symptom past a certain point, and that when you reach that point the symptom actually reverses. Your saliva begins to flow naturally again, your knees stop shaking, your hands get respectably dry. You may find that almost as soon as you try to intensify a symptom, it begins to disappear. The significance of this information impresses me each time I experience it again.*

Not only can you confront the symptoms you have, you can create symptoms you don't have. Are you only suffering from butterflies in the stomach? Why not have your palms sweat too? Indeed, why not worry about worrying?—an exercise known as the "transcendental metaworry" exercise. As Frankl put it, "A sense of humor is inherent in this technique. Humor helps man rise above his own predicament by allowing him to look at himself in a more detached way." But Frankl is quick to point out that the "paradoxical intention" technique is not a superficial one, even if it employs humor. He added, "I am convinced that paradoxical intention enables the patient to perform on a deeper level a radical change of attitude, and a wholesome one at that."

Trying to increase your symptoms in order to make them disappear is a technique that may or may not appeal to you. More queasiness? More woolly-headedness? More palpitations? What an idea! But if the idea intrigues you, by all means investigate it.

Astounding results are possible for performers who successfully add this technique to their arsenal.

- *Does "confronting your symptoms" seem like a congenial technique to you?*

  _____

  _____

- *In your mind's eye, try confronting a physical symptom like sweaty palms or wobbly knees. Do you see how the technique works with physical symptoms? Do you sense that it might work for you?*

  _____

  _____

  _____

  _____

- *In your mind's eye, try confronting a mental symptom like your inability to concentrate or your sense of impending doom. Do you see how the technique works with mental symptoms? Do you sense that it might work for you?*

  _____

  _____

  _____

  _____

- *Practice "symptom confrontation" a bit. Then give it a try before a real performance.*

DISCHARGE TECHNIQUES

Performers can discharge the tension building up in them by doing something active and dramatic. For instance, they can shake a fist or rail at the audience as they wait in the wings, softly shout a battle cry, or silently scream. These emotional and physical discharge techniques are not quite as dramatic as the actions they stand for, like slaying the audience or really screaming, but can prove effective nonetheless.

A real ear-piercing "primal scream" would certainly discharge a lot of tension. It might feel wonderful but of course it's rather impractical. For one thing, it could do serious damage to your voice. A silent scream, however, can feel almost as cathartic as a real one. Practice a silent scream by noting how wide your mouth opens, how rapidly your head moves, exactly how your neck muscles flex. Practice getting the tension-discharging effects of a real scream without uttering a sound (and without expelling air).

Or imagine yourself preparing for combat and discharge the tension you're feeling by uttering a silent but fiery battle cry. Create your own battle cry and treat the moment as if you were a great hero. Or imagine yourself Don Quixote setting off on a magnificent, foolish quest, jousting with windmills. Shout "Charge!" as wildly and playfully as you dare.

In *Raise Your Right Hand Against Fear*, Sheldon Kopp described the Buddhist symbolic gesture known as a mudra:

Determined to destroy the Buddha, a dark and treacherous demon unleashed an ele-phant charging drunkenly. Just as the raging beast was about to trample him, the Buddha raised his right hand with fingers close together and open palm facing the oncoming animal. The fearless gesture stopped the elephant in its tracks and com-pletely subdued the recklessly dangerous creature. The Sanskrit word for such ritu-ally symbolic gestures is mudra. The Buddha's mudra allowed him to face the fears in his own momentarily uncontrolled imagination.

Try out physical gestures that might be used as mudras. Or just move about. Simply moving about helps reduce anxiety. You can pace, jog in place, skip up and down, stretch, do a little walking meditation or yoga. If you can, go outside and walk around the block. Many performers find that just stepping outside for a few seconds works wonders in reducing their anxiety. This works in part because stepping out gives you a feeling of control. You give yourself permission to leave the scene without actually abandoning the performance. Getting out for a second counteracts that sense of "inhibited flight" that for some performers is the prime source of their performance anxiety.

Emotional discharge techniques come in every shape and size. Dream up some ges-ture or action—a wild dance, an amazing leap, a left jab followed by a right cross—that really works to release tension from your body and your mind. You might make zany faces, laugh, or at least smile a little. Even if you can't smile a lot, try to smile a little. The very act of smiling counteracts the buildup of tension. If you can't find a reason to smile, try telling yourself a good joke. Or imagine that the musicians around you have been transformed into animals out of a Dr. Seuss story. How does your accompanist look now?

- *Try "silent screaming." Practice it a few times and get a good feel for it. Do you have the sense that this technique might work for you?*

  _____

  _____

- *Generate your own list of discharge techniques. Look your list over. Choose one of these techniques to practice. After you've practiced it a bit, evaluate whether you think you might like to add it to your arsenal.*

  _____

  _____

  _____

  _____

  _____

  _____

- *Dream up several mudras (symbolic physical gestures). Do any have real resonance? Can you see your mudra working in a performance situation?*

- *Does the idea of treating performances as battles seem like a congenial idea to you? If so, what discharge techniques might you develop based on the idea of "going into battle"?*

CEREMONIES AND RITUALS

The simplest and no doubt oldest sort of calming ritual involves the use of a good-luck charm. Soprano Lily Pons, for instance, would cut off a piece of the stage curtain to hold onto before each performance. Luciano Pavarotti, plagued by performance anxiety, looked for a bent nail backstage and reputedly would not go on unless he found one. (Bent nails were placed everywhere in order to avoid cancellations!)

Repeated rituals can also have a soothing effect on one's nerves. In her book *The Bright Lights: A Theater Life*, the actress Marian Seldes explained:

> *There is a ritual in the dressing room, private for some, gregarious for others. The look of the room, the temperature, where each article of clothing is set—yours and the character's—mementos from other plays. A different robe for the theater. Special towels, soap, cologne. Brushes and combs. The actual tubes or sticks of makeup.*

Performers can complement their use of good-luck charms and built-in rituals with rituals and ceremonies they consciously devise. A musical ensemble, sales team, or acting troupe can gather for a brief group ceremony. They can shout (or silently shout) a battle cry or they can honor as sacred the event about to begin. Initially such ceremonies may feel forced, false, and embarrassing, but over time they can acquire rich meaning and serve to reduce the group's anxiety level.

- *Do you have a good-luck charm? If you don't, do you want to pick one and use it in performance situations?*

- *Create a list of pre-performance ceremonies or rituals that might work to calm you. Look over the list. Pick out the one that feels most resonant and useful. Try it out in your mind's eye. If it seems as if it might prove effective, give it a try before your next performance.*

_____

_____

_____

_____

_____

_____

GOOD-LUCK CHARMS
The simple faith that a good-luck charm will carry one through is a time-honored way to handle performance anxiety. Often faith in an object actually lowers anxiety and fear, and things consequently go better. Superstitions may seem out of place in modern society, but if not carried to extremes, they can be viable techniques for self-control.

—Douglas Hunt, *No More Fears*

PREPARATION TECHNIQUES

You know by now that you have the job of rehearsing your material, practicing your anxiety-management techniques, rehearsing aspects of your performance that require rehearsing (like your entrances and exits, your answers to post-lecture questions, and so on), and slowly but surely transforming yourself into someone who is prepared and *feels* prepared.

You want to be prepared and feel prepared so that you enter a calm, detached, ready state as you wait to perform. *Being* prepared is not enough. You want to *feel* prepared, which has to do with your actual preparations but also with the way you have built up your confidence and learned to put performance in its place. Right before you go on, you may repeat your entrance line like a mantra, hum the first measures of your piece, or glance again at your note cards, but it will make all the difference in the world if you do these things calmly rather than frantically.

There's a world of difference between frantically glancing at your note cards (and not seeing a word you've written) and glancing at them calmly, even indifferently, your breathing regular and your mind at ease. There's a world of difference between repeating your opening line to yourself over and over again in a panic, because you fear forgetting it, and repeating it to yourself with assurance, repeating it simply to get yourself into the role. No strategy or tactic is a substitute for the profound preparation technique of transforming yourself into a calm, confident person who is armed with certain anxiety-management tools but who doesn't really need them.

That's the most important preparation, transforming yourself. Then come all of the other preparation techniques we've been discussing: using guided imagery to rehearse a successful performance, thinking through how you want to answer certain questions that you suspect you will be asked, crafting your entrance ritual, and so on.

With respect to this last idea, Stephanie Judy recommends the following five-step entrance ritual for musicians:

1. *Acknowledge your audience.*

2. *Make contact with your instrument.*

3. *Make contact with the other musicians.*

4. *Think of a calming image.*

5. *Think about the music.*

- *Create a substantial list of tactics that you might employ in order to feel prepared before a performance. Which of these seem congenial and resonant? Put a few of these tactics into practice as soon as you can.*

- *Which of these tactics belong in your long-term anxiety-management program?*

- *Which of these tactics will you incorporate into your everyday rehearsal and preparation routine?*

- *Which of these tactics are well-suited for use as pre-performance preparations?*

COGNITIVE TECHNIQUES

A wide variety of cognitive techniques are available to you. For instance, the violinist and aikido expert Paul Hirata teaches a technique he calls Half-Half-Half. The idea is to suggest to yourself that you release just half your anxiety, using the word "Half" as a kind of mantra. You exhale, relax, and quietly say, "Half." You inhale again, continuing to relax, and upon the exhalation say "Half," continuing the process as necessary. In this way you never have to get rid of your anxiety—you only have to get rid of half of it!

Another cognitive technique is *reframing.* Rather than believing one thing about a situation, you "change your mind" and resolve to believe something else instead. The objective facts haven't changed but your view of them has changed. For example, rather than feeling trapped as you wait in the wings, you tell yourself that you have the freedom to leave at any time. You reframe the moment as one of freedom rather than entrapment and grow calm as you picture yourself walking out of the hall without a care or a backward glance.

The following is another useful reframing technique. Normally we think of a performance as the climax of long effort and as the reason for the effort. But there's a different way to think of the process. In this "reframed" way of thinking about the process, the exploration phase of rehearsing and practicing is held as the real work. You master the role or the music so as to provide yourself with a joyful, fulfilling experience. Actor Paul Newman explained his version of this idea:

BEFORE THE GIG

The singer and career counselor Reneé Hayes offered the following preparation advice:

- Know your personal ritual. I usually get very nervous the day before the gig and often have a nightmare that night. I'm often terribly nervous before I go on stage and spend time berating myself for choosing this form of torture. Then I go on stage, feel better after the first song, feel worse after the second number, and finally settle into being comfortable.

- Rehearse, rehearse, rehearse, rehearse. There is no such thing as being over-prepared. Give yourself plenty of time! Don't rush to the gig. Make sure you know how to get there and leave in plenty of time.

- Come to the venue early and take the time to stand on the stage (or the place you'll stand when you sing). Take a look around. Take in where the audience will be. "Own the joint." Tell yourself that it's yours and that when people come in the door they will be walking into your territory.

- Recognize that that awful feeling of "butterflies in the stomach" is just adrenaline. Adrenaline is energy. Terror is your friend. In other words, "reframe it."

- Minimize the goal. Remember that just getting there and opening your mouth is a triumph.

- Feel the fear and do it anyway.

- Concentrate on the song instead of the fact that you are the one performing; focus on the words you are singing, the message you are giving.

- Have fun!

- Please your own self.

My fantasy is that you get a marvelously inventive director and you cast the play the way it ought to be cast, not because you have to cast it a certain way. You get together and you have four incredible weeks of rehearsal, and then you shut it down. No one ever sees it.

The main cognitive technique you want to master is learning to replace negative self-talk with positive self-talk. As we've already discussed, performers commonly talk to themselves in ways that are anything but encouraging and that provoke rather than lessen anxiety. They'll exaggerate potential problems, magnify small threats, and engage in other "mind tricks" that increase anxiety. Sometimes the negative thought is easy to recognize ("I'm not very talented!") and sometimes it's harder to spot ("I wish a bigger audience had turned up!"), but whether overt or covert it does the job of raising the performer's anxiety level.

The way you alter this self-sabotaging pattern is by actively stopping the negative thought and substituting a new, positive one. For example, the negative thought "Gosh, I'm about to be scrutinized!" may pop into your head. If you've mastered thought substitution, you know to dispute that thought the instant it arises and replace it with a thought like, "Hey, I enjoy being watched!" "I'm worth watching!" or "Of course the audience will watch me! What else would they be doing?"

Here are some more examples of successful thought substitutions:

- *Negative thought: I know they're going to judge me.*

Substitutes:

No one can judge me.

I expect I'll do a fine job.

Judging is their business, my job is performing.

- *Negative thought: I know I'm going to bore them.*

Substitutes:

If I bore someone, that's life.

If I really make music, no one will be bored.

I get bored myself sometimes.

- *Negative thought: What if I suddenly have to scream?*

Substitutes:

I expect to have a good evening.

If I feel like screaming, I'll silently scream.

After the performance I'll enjoy a good scream.

• *Negative thought: What if I goof up and look stupid?*

Substitutes:

I'll survive whatever happens.

I can live with a little embarrassment.

I'm prepared, and everything will go smoothly.

• *Negative thought: I won't perform as well as I did last time.*

Substitutes:

Each performance is unique.

Why shouldn't this time be better?

I don't compare my performances one to another.

• *Negative thought: What if I begin too fast?*

Substitutes:

I have my entrance routine down pat.

I know exactly how fast to start.

Everything's under control.

• *Negative thought: What if I disappoint myself?*

Substitutes:

I'll learn from whatever happens.

I'm allowed to disappoint myself sometimes.

I expect to do just fine!

Try out some of the cognitive techniques I've just described. Bring up a negative thought and then stop the thought by actually shouting "Stop!" Create some thought-stopping techniques that range from the not-so-dramatic to the very dramatic. Practice Hirata's Half-Half-Half technique, create a list of all-purpose thought substitutes, or work on visualizing performance situations and framing them in their most positive light. Through patient practice, get in the habit of personal mind control.

- *Do you find that you can successfully stop your own negative thoughts? If you can't, what might you try as your own personal "thought-stopping" technique?*

_____

_____

_____

_____

- *Are you practiced at reframing situations in an affirmative way? If you aren't, are you willing to test out and practice some reframing techniques?*

_____

_____

- *Can you readily substitute positive thoughts for negative ones? If not, are you willing to practice mastering thought substitution?*

_____

_____

Chapter Fifteen

LONG-TERM ANXIETY MANAGEMENT, PART I

It's time for you to put together a long-term anxiety-management program that makes use of the strategies and tactics outlined in the last several chapters. This chapter and the next describe such a program.

BECOMING NEW AND WHOLE

I recently watched a TV documentary about a stand-up comic. For years this young man had worked the comedy clubs. Then, one day, the phone call that all comics pray for arrived, from a *Tonight Show* producer. The documentary follows the comic as he prepares for his debut. At the last minute his appearance is rescheduled—or has it been canceled? Neither he nor we feel anything but high anxiety as he realizes that his big chance may have gone up in smoke. But it turns out that his appearance has only been postponed. Now the performance is on again—and, with it, more anxiety.

He discusses his palpable fear with the comic Jerry Seinfeld, who replies matter-of-factly, "First time on *The Tonight Show*? Terrified? Of course!" We watch the young comic as his big day arrives, as his makeup is applied, as he waits to go on. To live in his shoes is to be convinced that performance anxiety can't entirely be eliminated. It can't be eliminated even from the lives of those fortunate few who feel good about themselves and it especially can't be eliminated if we have dreams that require that we perform beautifully in crucial situations. Since it can't be eliminated entirely, it had better get managed!

Performers evolve complicated methods of binding their anxiety but their contortions do not necessarily add up to a successful plan. One client of mine, a highly anxious stand-up comic, attempted to reduce his feelings of anxiety by using alcohol, marijuana, food, and prescription drugs. He also contrived to create a super-nervous stage character, so as to make "good use" of the anxiety he believed he couldn't eliminate or disguise. He argued that by using this character he could provoke laughter—albeit nervous laughter—just by walking on stage.

But of course this approach failed him in several ways. First, at really important performances, and especially at competitions, he could not deliver his act. He forgot bits, missed on the timing, even dramatically shortened the set. Second, a great deal of the material that he wanted to deliver this nervous persona of his could not deliver, as it would have been out of character. This shaking, sweating onstage character turned out to have a very limited range. Third, maintaining this stage character exacerbated, rather than lessened, his general feelings of anxiety, which played themselves out in alcoholic binges and sudden flights from his day job and his everyday responsibilities.

My client was *already* managing his anxiety—but reflexively and poorly, not in ways that either reduced his experience of anxiety or served him as a human being and artist. These reflexive methods of handling anxiety necessarily begin early in life. If, as a child, we don't feel safe, if we're criticized or abused, if we experience our parents as absent, untrustworthy, or dangerous, then reflexively managing anxiety becomes our primary mission. Our personality forms around the job of handling anxiety, and that formed personality is who we are and who we remain, unless and until we remake ourselves.

RESPECTING YOUR EFFORTS

Stop everything for a few minutes. Get up and take this book with you to a new location, perhaps to a seat by a window or to a garden spot. As you move to this new location, allow yourself to feel the many ways you are not pleased with yourself. Allow yourself to suffer. But even as you honorably experience those feelings, remind yourself that in a core place you are worthy. You are worthy of your own attention, worthy of respect, worthy of love. You are important; you count; and thus you will seriously and adamantly respect the attempt you are about to make to reconstruct your personality and make yourself into a calmer, stronger, more confident person. Not only will you make such an effort, but you will make it lovingly, with an attitude of self-regard and self-respect. Try saying out loud, "I will respect my own efforts." Do you feel that it is possible to care about yourself? Do you feel that it is possible to take yourself seriously? Sit in this new location awhile and enjoy the sensation of being alone with yourself and kind to yourself. Revel in the prospect of becoming your own best friend and advocate.

The psychologist Karen Horney explained, "Although the range of manifest forms of anxiety, or the protection against it, is infinite and varies with each individual, the basic anxiety is more or less the same everywhere, varying only in extent and intensity. It may be roughly described as a feeling of being small, insignificant, helpless, and endangered, in a world that is out to abuse, cheat, attack, humiliate, and betray." Horney argued that personality forms in one of three ways as a response to threats and dangers experienced in childhood: A person withdraws, learns to be compliant, or attempts to look powerful. These responses "work" insofar as the experience of anxiety is made bearable in the moment. But there is a cost to the person in a lack of inner security and in an inability to effectively cope with reality.

Thus the factors that contribute to the experience of anxiety, all the factors that we've discussed in earlier chapters, take root in the formation of our personality. They become built right into the structure, as it were. So, too, do our reflexive anxiety-management strategies: the way we avoid performance situations, the way our defenses rise up to prevent us from admitting that we're anxious, the way we experience confusion or psychogenic pain before we go onstage. Therefore, the goal of a long-term anxiety-management program is not the management of anxiety per se but the remaking of personality. This is a formidable task but also a beautiful one: to become new, to become a person so confident and strong that you experience anxiety much less often and know how to effectively manage the anxiety that remains.

The following ten elements constitute a long-term plan that will help you transform yourself into a less anxious person. The first five elements are discussed in this chapter and the second five in Chapter 16.

1. Awareness training

2. Experiential learning

3. Awareness of creativity issues

4. Cognitive restructuring

5. Stress reduction

6. Interpersonal analysis

7. Counseling, therapy, and coaching

8. Discipline practice

9. Discipline understanding

10. Preparation

AWARENESS TRAINING

Very little in the typical school curriculum helps a child with the task of self-examination, and very little in the typical home does either. Even in homes where children are financially advantaged and sent to weekly piano or dance lessons, it is unlikely that children will be invited to get to know themselves. Instead children are taught to do certain things, like get good grades, and not do other things, like use drugs, but they are not encouraged to reflect on their thoughts and feelings or on the world's complex realities.

Thus it becomes hard for people to know what their thoughts and feelings really are, to manifest their creativity, to choose values different from society's values, and to air and release their fears and anxieties. These tasks require a willingness to look at oneself and listen to oneself and real practice in doing exactly that. As a consequence of growing up in a home and a society where self-awareness is not valued, the child, and later the adult, becomes relatively unequal to meeting inner challenges like anxiety management. A clarinetist may meet every challenge her music conservatory places before her, she may even graduate and join a good orchestra, and still not possess the skills she needs to be able to examine psychological issues like performance anxiety.

You need presence of mind, the kind of centeredness that we discussed in Chapter 10 when we examined detachment and in Chapter 11 when we examined ten-second centering, and genuine access to your thoughts and feelings. Presence of mind is related to genuine self-esteem and self-confidence, which, if not fostered in youth, may still be fostered by the self-caring adult. The person who feels inwardly secure, who looks out for himself, who is unafraid of the opinions of others, who maintains personal integrity and affirms his right to be, can manifest this presence of mind.

Understanding of mind is based on certain habits and practices, including introspection, reflection, self-analysis, self-evaluation, and the working through of denial and other ego defenses. Self-awareness is the practice of identifying and understanding your thoughts, feelings, and behaviors. Learning "mindful meditation" is one possible starting point. Every style of meditation has its own premises and rituals; some traditions stress point-focus concentration and have the subject focus on a flame, part of the body, or an iconic object. Others stress openness and the freeing of attention. All teach breath observation, which is an excellent beginning tool for gaining self-awareness (see box).

BREATH OBSERVATION

As the patient attempts to concentrate on his own inhaling and exhaling, activities of mind become very apparent. This exercise, if carried out faithfully for several minutes, will serve to make a patient aware of his own mental preoccupations, for some patients notice a predominance of thoughts about past events (memories) interrupting their breath observation, while others notice that they are most frequently interrupted in breath observation by thoughts pertaining to the future. The patient will quickly discover a rather complicated, but comforting, situation: one aspect of his mental "self" is calm and psychologically strong, and can watch, label, and see the melodramas of the other "selves," selves which get so involved in painful memories or beautiful and escapist fantasies of the future.
—GARY DEATHERAGE, *The Clinical Use of Mindfulness Meditation Techniques in Short-Term Psychotherapy*

A person who meditates learns to discriminate between what is inside and what is outside the self (see box). This ability to discriminate is of vital importance to the performance-anxiety sufferer, whose pain is in large measure a product of her own thoughts. Gaining self-awareness is no easy matter, because to gain it one must volitionally produce uncomfortable feelings (see box). Most of us prefer to deny, ignore, or ward off feelings we don't like, rather than let them into consciousness and experience them. If the number of people willing to let them in is small, the number of people willing to produce them for the sake of examining them is even smaller. No matter how intelligent or sensitive a person may be, and no matter how great a performer, this task may feel beyond her capabilities.

DISCRIMINATING STIMULI

The phrase discrimination training is used to describe the process by which an organism acquires the ability to discriminate one stimulus from another. In one hour of meditation, a practitioner may have hundreds of experiences of being identified with thought, then returning to a more attentive state. The process can be regarded as discrimination training, since the meditator is learning to discriminate thought from other stimuli. Being skilled at discriminating thought from other events puts the meditator in a particularly strong position of mental health. In fact, it could be argued that since nearly everyone has a certain number of neurotic thoughts, mental health is dependent upon the ability to recognize that they are "just thoughts." The author has found that clients who learn to discriminate thought from other kinds of stimuli characteristically regard the discovery as a revelation.

—C. G. HENDRICKS, *Meditation as Discrimination Training:*
A Theoretical Note

At different points throughout this book we've talked about the consequences of a lack of self-awareness. To take one example, the person who is upset by an experience of mild performance anxiety is in a real sense simply unaware that the experience is a mild one. That he or she has "butterflies" or feels the need to urinate means nothing beyond its obvious meaning: a mild anxiety is present. Mild performance anxiety is a normal, natural, and perhaps inevitable byproduct of exposing our abilities and our being to public scrutiny. Neither the arousal nor the anxiety need frighten us.

To internally label this state as "dreadful" or "unnatural" is to make an awareness mistake. The pianist Glenn Gould, for instance, once explained: "I used to take my pulse rate just before a concert out of scientific curiosity, and it was always very fast. So there was obviously a kind of unnatural excitement." That he called this excitement unnatural is interesting and may help explain his preference for the recording studio over the concert hall. By framing his modest anxiety as unnatural, he may have lent it greater weight than he realized.

Similarly, a person with a social phobia (as stage fright is often conceptualized) is typically unaware of the grounds for that fear. This, again, is an awareness problem. To put the matter in a different context, if you panic on a wilderness walk and, when questioned, reply "I saw a snake, and I'm afraid of snakes," your fellow trekkers will tend to accept your answer. But they could legitimately continue, "Why? Was it poisonous? Was it near you and ready to strike?" If you replied, "I just have an irrational fear of snakes," or "I'm just very anxious, and snakes are one of the things that make me anxious," you might satisfy your companions. But your answer does not amount to an explanation. Seeing the snake produced anxiety symptoms. The snake is clearly a "source" of anxiety for you. But why? The question is not so much "What are you afraid of?" as "Why are you afraid of what you're afraid of?" To find the answer, you will have to analyze yourself. Until you do, you remain at the mercy of snakes—or heights, elevators, mice, or public speaking engagements.

Take the case of Wynn, an actor who regularly sabotages himself at auditions. What is so striking is the obviousness of his attitude—everyone concerned can't help but recognize his cynicism and flippancy. And Wynn, too, is aware that he is bringing an "attitude" with him, but he is not aware *enough*. He is not able to ascertain his real motives. If he could, he might understand that his attitude is the result of the following piece of self-protective logic: "If I am ironic and casual about the whole thing, I can't experience failure. I may fail to get the role, I may look like a jerk, I may alienate the casting director, but I won't experience failure, because I won't have stooped to playing their stupid little games."

The performer who magnifies her experience of anxiety, the person who has never examined his phobia, the self-sabotaging actor are all insufficiently self-aware. To become more aware, they must agree to become more aware. They can't simultaneously grow aware and fight off self-understanding. They must contract with themselves to experience the anxiety of learning about themselves. If they can leap that hurdle and make that contract with themselves, they can begin to gain self-awareness.

- *What prevents you from understanding yourself?*

_____

_____

_____

_____

- *What do you fear you would learn if you were to gain self-awareness?*

_____

_____

_____

_____

- *Is that an old fear, no longer relevant today? Are you perhaps better equipped to look at yourself and deal with whatever you find than you used to be?*

_____

_____

_____

_____

- *Is there a single aspect of your inner life about which you would like to grow more aware?*

  _____

  _____

  _____

  _____

- *Why do you suppose that we are slaves to our thoughts, even though we ourselves produce them?*

  _____

  _____

  _____

  _____

- *How will you work to gain self-awareness? Please spell out your plan.*

  _____

  _____

  _____

  _____

  _____

  _____

EXPERIENTIAL LEARNING

The most useful and powerful way to gain self-awareness is to learn from your own experiences. It isn't enough to have experiences; a person has to stop and actually *learn from them.*

PRACTICING SUFFERING

Why do people keep suffering even when they "know they are the ones who are doing it"? It seems that people are unconscious or ignorant of what they are habitually doing. They do not know how they "make" pain, discomfort, sadness, etc. The purpose of practicing suffering, then, is to bring the method of making discomfort into awareness. The focus is on how discomfort is made, rather than on the external attributes (i.e., content) of a situation. Patients who are unable or unwilling to shift their focus from the content of suffering to its process are not successful in this therapy. The therapeutic task is to change the direction of attention and interest toward the discomfort rather than toward avoiding it.

—EDWARD WORTZ,
Application of Awareness Methods in Psychotherapy

I regularly taught a college course called "Personal and Professional Assessment" to adults returning to college after a long absence from school. In it, students had to write five experiential-learning essays in which they demonstrated that they had learned something from their experiences. Having had experiences was not enough to gain them credit. They had to demonstrate, by reflecting on their lives and analyzing and evaluating their experiences, that they could think and write intelligently about a given field of inquiry. They had permission to write about alcoholism, divorce, office management, cancer, personal finance, or a hundred other topics, but in each case they were obliged to do more than anecdotally recite their personal experiences. They had to make use of their personal experiences to illuminate the concepts involved. This is exactly what a performer ought to do with respect to performance anxiety.

- *Ask yourself: What have I learned from my firsthand experiences of performance anxiety? Write your answer freely and at length, for several pages at least, with an eye to answering this specific question: that is, with an eye to fathoming what you've learned from your experiences and not just recounting your experiences.*

The idea of learning from experience is at the heart of any long-term anxiety-management program. You already have enough performance situations behind you from which to learn. You already have a wealth of data and the skills of mind to analyze that data. What you need is the courage to look at experiences that are likely to feel painful and embarrassing. If you can manifest that courage, you will come to

AN ACTOR LEARNS FROM EXPERIENCE

Suddenly, as the camera began to roll, I realized that I didn't have a reason in the world for speaking, no objectives, no purpose other than to say the words and collect a check. I then seemed to mentally disconnect from my own self, sort of standing aside and watching myself as I grew pale under the makeup. I began to sweat profusely and my heart raced. Thoughts raced through my brain. "What if I can't say the words?" "What will the producers think of me?" "What if they can't finish the show because of me?" It was a moment of sheer terror. For several months after that, I was afraid that it would happen again. I went into auditions trying to avoid negatives rather than pursuing positives, and I'm sure I lost some good jobs that way.

Finally, I realized that I needed to reconnect with my roots as an actor, needed to get back in touch with what it is to play a pure action, to have a strong intention. I had become too accustomed to playing supporting TV roles that were frequently poorly written and merely relied on my personality to make them work. So, with my heart in my throat, I went out and got cast in a stage play. Knowing that I would be in front of an audience for prolonged periods of time each night and knowing that, if I was going to self-destruct there, it would be the end of acting for me altogether, I was nervous big-time. Fortunately, I stood toe-to-toe with the demon and won. The play was a success, I didn't fall apart, and I learned a valuable lesson. Now, no matter how trivial the role or acting challenge seems to be, I treat it like it is Hamlet, preparing myself fully, identifying my objectives and intentions as an actor. The terror has not happened since then.

—ED HOOKS, in personal correspondence

understand that experience is the best teacher. An excellent example of learning from experience is the excerpt (see box) from actor Ed Hooks, who describes filming a scene of a TV episode. Take a peek at it to see how insight gained from experience points you in the direction of the work you need to do next.

Stopping to learn from your own experiences is the best awareness-training tool available to you. Toward that end, I recommend that you keep a performance notebook in which you record what you learn from your experiences of performing. Remember that we're using "performance" in the broadest sense, so that a visit to a casting agent, a call on a customer, an appearance at a conference, or a post-concert reception might all get recorded in your journal. Record the following:

1. Specific details about the performance: the nature of the audience, the circumstances of the performance, and so on.

2. Whether you experienced performance anxiety and, if so, details about the experience. The richer and more detailed your observations are, the better.

3. Your thoughts and feelings about what transpired. Focus here on the internal "whys"—more on why you reacted in a certain way than on what the circumstances were that provoked the reaction.

4. Your thoughts about what you might have done differently or might do differently in the future.

5. Your thoughts about what strategies you might incorporate into your long-term anxiety-management program. Did this particular experience tell you something about what you might do on a daily basis to reduce anxiety and feel stronger and calmer?

Begin this notebook as soon as possible. After a performance, find a private place and write in your notebook so that you can begin the process of learning from your experiences.

- *Describe one experience in detail that reveals something about your anxious nature.*

_____

_____

_____

_____

_____

_____

_____

_____

- *What have you learned from your life experiences that you can put to use in rebuilding yourself as a less anxious person?*

_____

_____

_____

_____

- *What specifically prevents you from learning from experience?*

_____

_____

_____

_____

- *How can you better train yourself to learn from experience? What techniques (like keeping a performance journal) might you employ?*

_____

_____

_____

_____

_____

_____

AWARENESS OF CREATIVITY ISSUES

Many performers, especially professional ones, are also "creative people" who must come to grips with what being a creative person means. This entails understanding their personality makeup, the nature of creative work, and how their art discipline functions.

I've written more than a dozen books in this broad area. One focused on the relationship between creativity and depression (*The Van Gogh Blues*). Another looked at the place of anxiety in the creative process (*Fearless Creating*). A third presented self-coaching techniques for creative people (*Coaching the Artist Within*). A fourth examined the affirmation process (*Affirmations for Artists*). I can't do justice to this vast area in this brief section; suffice it to say that you will face many challenges as a result of your creative nature and your decision to manifest that nature, challenges almost certain to exacerbate your experience of performance anxiety.

You may, for instance, be prone to existential depression, which affects how you view your performances and which may cause them to matter "too much" or "too little," producing anxiety in either case. You may feel alienated from the prevailing culture, which may distance you from your audience and lend your performances an oppositional air, raising your anxiety level. You may be more intelligent than average and "see through" the material you're obliged to present, increasing your anxiety on that score. You may be introspective, desire solitude, and spend so much time alone that facing an audience becomes an unusual—and hence strange-feeling and anxiety-provoking—event.

How, for instance, is an actress to make use of her intelligence and creativity if the roles she garners are silly and insipid? Isn't an inner conflict of that sort a recipe for the production of anxiety? Indeed, how is she to "locate" herself in her culture? Is she essentially an entertainer? Is she looking for artistic success or commercial success? Does she mean to be popular and attract a large audience, which essentially means working in television or film, or to act in an area of performance that she loves, like live theater, which neither pays well nor attracts many fans? How does she feel about commercials and industrials? All of these issues affect how anxious she feels.

It's imperative that you understand the nature of the challenges that you face as a creative person and learn how to best meet those challenges. It's equally vital that you appreciate the ways in which your experience of anxiety—generally, and specifically with respect to performance—are affected by the contours of your journey as a creative person attempting creative work within the confines of a particular culture. I hope that you'll make use of the resources available to you, including many of my other books (see Appendix), to better understand these issues.

- *Can you describe the special challenges you face as a creative person?*

_____

_____

_____

_____

_____

_____

- *How do these challenges affect your experience of performance anxiety?*

_____

_____

_____

_____

- *What techniques or strategies can you incorporate into your anxiety-management program that address the issues you've just described?*

_____

_____

_____

_____

_____

_____

COGNITIVE RESTRUCTURING

The literature on performance-anxiety treatment suggests that cognitive-behavioral therapy is the best way to treat performance anxiety. It's therefore vital to understand the principles of cognitive-behavioral therapy and to implement cognitive techniques as part of your long-term anxiety-management program. Simply put, cognitive-behavioral therapists believe that people can alter their experience of a situation by changing the way they think about themselves and about the situation. They further believe that this cognitive restructuring is not only theoretically appropriate but also eminently doable.

I worked with a client, a painter, in just this fashion. She wanted to attend a certain gallery opening because she admired the work of the painter exhibiting there. But she was afraid that the visit would depress her because she'd be reminded that she hadn't produced many paintings recently. She was positive that going to the opening would trigger the thoughts that regularly plagued her, namely: "I'm not good enough" and "I don't work hard enough."

We worked on stopping and blocking the thought "I'm not good enough" and substituting new thoughts for it. This work required that she try out various thoughts in a hunt for ones that, when substituted for the negative thought, would not only replace it but serve to defuse it. There appeared to be two directions to take. First, she truly believed that attending the opening was a necessary part of her process as a painter and that the experience would have value and meaning for her. The thought substitutes that she created in session included the following three: "It's important that I be here," "I want to be here," and "This is part of my process."

She also felt that attending the opening would help her rekindle her love of art and, more broadly, serve to bring a measure of love into her life. While involved in an intimate relationship and progressing nicely in a second career, she nevertheless felt that too little in her life had a real loving feel to it. Visiting with art, like visiting with friends, had always helped take the chill out of life, and she wanted that experience again. She therefore tried out in session various thoughts that she might use at the opening to capture this idea, including the following four: "I love this," "This makes me happy," "It feels good to be here," and "I feel warm here."

As she worked to find thoughts that might effectively be substituted for "I'm not good enough," she realized that the process of thought substitution involved one single, simple principle. It struck her that mental health was largely a matter of training herself—that is, training her thoughts—to dwell on the positive and the present. She realized that the words "positive" and "present" could themselves be used to block out unwanted thoughts or substitute for unwanted thoughts and could even be used to inoculate herself beforehand so that unwanted thoughts wouldn't intrude. "Positive and present" became her mantra and her all-purpose thought substitute.

According to Aaron Beck and other cognitive therapists, the negative self-talk that plagues people constellates into a certain number of characteristic "cognitive distortions" (see box). Please take a minute to consider these cognitive distortions.

- *Do your thoughts tend to pattern themselves in any of these ways?*

_____

_____

_____

_____

- *Do you have a sense how these cognitive distortions may have arisen?*

_____

_____

_____

_____

- As part of your long-term anxiety-management program, what techniques will you use to alter these distorted ways of thinking?

_____

_____

_____

_____

COMMON TYPES OF COGNITIVE DISTORTIONS

1. *Selective abstraction: focusing on a detail out of context.*

2. *Arbitrary inference: making conclusions on the basis of inadequate or improper information.*

3. *Overgeneralization: making blanket judgments or predictions based upon a single incident.*

4. *Personalization: overestimating the extent to which particular events are self-related.*

5. *Polarized thinking: sorting information into one of two dichotomous categories.*

6. *Magnification and exaggeration: overemphasizing the most unpleasant, negative consequences that can arise in any situation.*

7. *Assuming excessive responsibility: attributing negative events to one's supposed personal deficiencies.*

8. *Incorrect assessment regarding danger versus safety: overestimating the risk involved in situations.*

9. *Dysfunctional attitudes about pleasure versus pain: setting up prerequisites for true happiness or success—for example, "My value as a person depends on what others think of me."*

10. *Automatic self-injunctions, or "tyranny of the shoulds": unrealistically high standards for human conduct—for example, "I should know, understand, and foresee everything."*

—RICHARD BEDROSIAN and AARON BECK, *Principles of Cognitive Therapy*

THOUGHT-STOPPING IN THERAPY

In this first phase of thought-stopping, the counselor assumes the responsibility for interrupting the thoughts. The interruption is overt, consisting of a loud Stop! that can be accompanied by a noise such as a hand clap, a ruler hitting a desk, or a whistle.

1. *The counselor instructs the client to sit back and let any thoughts come to mind.*

2. *The counselor instructs the client to verbalize aloud these thoughts or images as they occur.*

3. *At the point where the client verbalizes a self-defeating thought or image, the counselor interrupts with a loud Stop! Sometimes, in addition, a loud noise stimulus such as a hand clap, a whistle, or a ruler hitting the desk is used.*

4. *The counselor determines whether the unexpected interruption was effective in terminating the client's negative thoughts or images.*

—WILLIAM CORMIER and SHERILYN CORMIER, *Interviewing Strategies for Helpers*

Cognitive therapists employ various techniques designed to change faulty thinking patterns and encourage cognitive restructuring. These techniques include questioning the validity of a client's hypotheses; decentering ("the process," according to Beck, "of prying the patient loose from the belief that he or she is the focal point of all events"); and decatastrophizing (presenting "normal" alternatives to a client's persistent worst-case scenarios). These various techniques aim at helping a client acquire and practice "rational responses to dysfunctional thoughts." Other techniques include cognitive modeling, thought-stopping (see box), and stress inoculation.

The application of cognitive therapy to the treatment of performance anxiety has received considerable attention. In one study, fifty-three pianists were treated for performance anxiety either with special rehearsal techniques (that is, they were trained to rehearse in a certain way) or with cognitive techniques. While the rehearsal techniques proved successful in many instances, the cognitive techniques proved significantly more successful. Another study investigated the relative merits of treating performance anxiety with cognitive methods versus using the anti-anxiety medication buspirone. Again the results demonstrated the greater effectiveness of cognitive therapy.

Cognitive work is a vital component of a performer's long-term anxiety-management program. You should make a real effort to identify and record your negative self-statements and practice cognitive techniques like thought-stopping and thought substitution. Many books on this subject are available to you, as are therapists who use this treatment option. There is magic in this method for those who master it.

STRESS REDUCTION NOW

Take at least one active step now toward reducing the stress in your life. You might:

- *Check with your health plan to see if it offers stress reduction workshops, biofeedback classes, or yoga or meditation classes.*

- *Locate books on stress reduction. Look through them and select one that makes sense to you. Begin to put into effect some of the stress-management strategies offered in that book.*

- *Begin to do the one thing you know helps to reduce your experience of stress. Is it walking three miles a day? Getting to the beach on the weekend? Talking with a certain friend?*

- *Learn one meditation technique and begin to use it.*

- *Learn one self-massage technique and begin to use it.*

- *Change one thing in your life that you know you need to change to reduce stress. Is it talking to your mother less often (and then not feeling guilty about it)? Is it finding different day care, changing your day job, making a new friend, somehow getting out of debt?*

Start by doing just one thing that supports your intention of reducing the stress in your life.

- *How would you define "cognitive restructuring"?*

_____

_____

_____

Which techniques will you employ to alter your thought patterns and reduce your negative self-talk?

_____

_____

_____

Describe how you'll incorporate these techniques into your long-term anxiety-management program.

_____

_____

_____

_____

_____

_____

STRESS REDUCTION

It's an open question how well cognitive restructuring or any other anxiety-management technique can work if you can't reduce the stress in your life. Please incorporate several of the following stress-reduction strategies into your life: that is, really make use of them. These twenty-five techniques, some of which we've discussed already, are culled from a variety of sources, among them the University of Illinois at Urbana-Champaign McKinley Health Center, the University of South Florida Counseling Center for Human Development, Aetna InteliHealth, and mindtools.com.

Progressive Relaxation

Tense individual muscle groups for several seconds and then release the tension, allowing muscles gradually to relax.

Biofeedback

Biofeedback uses electronic sensors to measure stress. This feedback may take the form of movement of a pen on a graph plotter or the pitch of sound coming through earphones. You learn how to relax and reduce stress by using an informational feedback loop system.

Deep Breathing

Sit in a comfortable position and take deep, measured breaths, e.g., inhaling while counting up from 1 to 5, exhaling while counting down from 5 to 1. Do this twenty to thirty times. One way that deep breathing assists in stress reduction is by increasing the amount of oxygen in the body.

The "Relaxation Response"

Harvard University physician Herbert Benson devised this simple technique. Sit comfortably, close your eyes and relax your muscles. Focus on your breathing and continuously repeat one word aloud or in your mind. It can be a word like "relax" or "easy" or a word like "om" used in transcendental meditation.

Visualization

Get into a comfortable position, close your eyes and visualize a scene or place that you associate with safety and relaxation. It doesn't matter what you visualize, as long as it's calming to you. As you relax your mind, your body also relaxes.

Remove Stressors

Determine what you can realistically do and stop promising more than you can reasonably handle. Learn how to say "no" to added duties and responsibilities, even those that have some payoff.

Thought-Stopping

Thought-stopping helps you overcome excessive worry, repetitive thoughts, and negative thinking. Thought-stopping involves concentrating on the unwanted thoughts and, after a short time, suddenly stopping and emptying your mind, by using the mental command "stop" or a loud noise to interrupt negative thinking.

Assertiveness Skills

Being assertive can reduce stress as you express personal thoughts and feelings. You are behaving assertively when you stand up for yourself, express your true feelings, and refuse to let others take advantage of you. Being assertive increases self-satisfaction, respect from others, self-esteem, and confidence.

Write About Your Stress

Research reported in The Journal of the American Medical Association *revealed that writing about stressful experiences can not only reduce stress but can even help reduce the symptoms of common diseases such as asthma and rheumatoid arthritis. A growing body of research indicates that writing about thoughts and feelings can lead to improvements in immune functioning, fewer visits to the doctor, and an increased sense of well-being.*

Manage Your Time

The more you think ahead about how to manage activities or control your time, the less stress you will experience. Some practical ways to take control of your situation are to write a list of items that need to be addressed, schedule time to work on the items you've listed, and organize the list and schedule by priority or necessity.

Maintain a Healthy Diet

Studies suggest that maintaining a good diet may help reduce the stress you feel. It may be terribly difficult to give up a comforting treat, but the treat may backfire, making you feel worse. A balanced nutritious diet and a reduced amount of comfort food may result in you feeling more—not less—comfortable.

Exercise

After more than 1,000 studies, experts agree that exercise can reduce your stress. For maximum effect, try an aerobic exercise (such as running, swimming or brisk walking) that increases your heart rate for twenty minutes or more. If you can't do that, even a ten-minute walk can help. Yoga and non-aerobic movement such as stretching can also reduce stress by inducing a calmer, meditation-like state.

Socialize

Because we are social creatures by nature, we need other people, particularly during stressful times. Having supportive friends, family members, and colleagues is a great way to reduce stress. Discussing your difficulties with someone you trust can relieve tension and may also help you begin to solve your problems.

Seek Therapy

If you've tried numerous stress-reduction techniques but continue to feel more stress than is comfortable, you might want to talk with a therapist about how to cope with stressful conditions, how to better handle conflicts, and how to resolve some of the problems that are causing you stress.

Sixty-Second Break

Just close your eyes and take a few deep breaths. Visualize yourself lounging on a sunny beach or watching the sunset or relaxing in the shower or sauna.

Five-Minute Vacation

Spend a little more time breathing, visualizing, and relaxing. Let your imagination carry you away to a special spot that's calming and refreshing.

Chest Massage

Relax your chest muscles and open up your breathing with a vigorous massage along the midline and across the chest below your collarbone.

Bother List

Write down a list of all the worries, pressures, and concerns that are crowding your mind and clamoring for attention. Then burn the list or tuck it into your wallet for later attention.

Stretch and Move

Stand up and stretch. Arch your back and stretch your arms and fingers out to the side. Hold that posture for a while and then let go. Now move your body all around to get the blood pumping. Clap your hands. Jump up and down. MOVE!

Exhilaration Break

Imagine yourself doing something exciting, exhilarating or awe-inspiring (e.g., standing on a cliff above the ocean, cheering at an exciting football game, crossing the finish line at a race, or laughing uproariously with friends). Let the vividness of that vision charge your batteries.

Pep Talk

Give yourself a pep talk. Use your best persuasive powers to motivate, encourage, cajole, support, cheer, or challenge yourself. Ask somebody else to join in!

Stirring Music

Turn on some lively music like a march or a mazurka. Start moving. Dance. Bounce. March. Sing along. Get involved. Let the music pump you up and pull you along.

Body Bracer

Gently pat or tap all over your body in an energizing rhythm. Keep it up until you tingle all over and are charged up.

Pretzel

Imagine that your body is all tied up in knots and only you know how to untie them. Beginning with your toes and gradually moving up the body, tense and relax each set of muscles. Visualize that you are tightening the knots as you tense the muscles and picture yourself undoing the knots as you relax the muscles and let go.

Self-Massage

Reach across your body and massage the muscles of your neck and shoulder with long, firm strokes. Firmly knead any especially tight areas with circular or back-and-forth motions. Then repeat the process on the other side. With both hands, massage the base of your skull with firm, circular strokes. Continue over the scalp and face, stopping to give special attention wherever you notice tension. Don't forget the jaw!

Each of us needs to manage stress on an ongoing basis. Some stressors can be eliminated; others can only be marginally reduced. Even if we can't make our stresses go away, we have the opportunity to employ the simple but effective stress-reduction techniques that are available to us. Whether it's a hot shower, a stroll by the ocean, an evening with a mystery novel, or the regular and formal use of biofeedback, yoga, or meditation, stress reduction practices need to become a real and integrated part of our life.

- *Identify some of the stressors in your life and spend a little time brainstorming how you might eliminate or minimize them.*

_____

_____

_____

_____

_____

_____

_____

- *Which simple stress-reduction techniques will you employ in an ongoing way as part of your long-term anxiety-management program?*

_____

_____

_____

_____

Chapter Sixteen

LONG-TERM ANXIETY MANAGEMENT, PART II

In this, our last chapter, we turn our attention to the last five elements of your long-term anxiety-management program.

INTERPERSONAL ANALYSIS

Performance anxiety is a problem embedded in a social context. Whether you're performing before an audience of millions or just one, an imagined audience or a real audience, a live audience or one at the other end of the airways, it is because you feel observed by other human beings that you feel anxious. Therefore it will help you tremendously if you better understand your relationship to other people and make any changes that will help you to feel less nervous and self-conscious among people.

To begin with, please answer the following questions.

- *What exactly do you have to be nervous about in the company of others?*

_____

_____

_____

_____

- *Has it become a habit of mind to frame social situations as threatening and anxiety-provoking?*

_____

_____

_____

- Is there any chance that you could let go of that habit of mind just by "snapping your fingers?"

PERFORMANCE-ANXIETY SUPPORT GROUPS

The process begins with a support team of three to six who want to be more effective in front of groups.

1. *Each person in turn takes three minutes in front of the group to take in total support and to see what comes up to say, or not to say.*

2. *The person maintains eye contact with the audience one at a time rather than scanning the group.*

3. *Dare to be boring rather than chattering to cover anxiety. Be willing to feel the anxiety.*

4. *Try to let the speech come from the relationship with the audience at that moment rather than from memory or ideas.*

5. *In the second round each person gets up for five minutes.*

6. *After each five-minute talk, the group gives the speakers the opportunity to quickly report on their experiences. The rest of the group gives brief, rapid-fire and supportive feedback.*

—LEE GLICKSTEIN, *Group Work and Stage Fright Recovery*

It may be that a natural pressure to perform well and to hold up your end of social interactions has grown into something like a phobia. Even if your anxiety about your relationship to others hasn't reached phobic proportions, it will still pay real dividends for you to obtain a clear understanding of what pressures you feel in social situations, what style you adopt, and, especially, how threatening such situations seem to you. Your goal is to be able to walk into any social situation anxiety-free, just as it's your goal to be able to perform anxiety-free, and in order to reach these goals it makes sense that you engage in some thoughtful interpersonal analysis.

A good way to study the exact nature of your relationship to others is in formal group work. The group can be a psychotherapy group formed for that purpose; a group formed by an acting, music, dance, or speech teacher (see box); groups like AA or Toastmasters; or a leaderless group formed by peers who are willing to work together to support and learn from each other. Not all such groups are successful and not all such learning experiences are positive ones, but when they do work, they provide information that is hard to obtain in any other way.

As you're working to gain confidence in interpersonal and group situations, you'll want to identify those interactions that increase your performance anxiety. For instance, do you and your department manager need to iron something out that you've been afraid to talk about? Is something going on between you and other members of the cast that needs airing? Your goal of anxiety management is served by your ability to engage in direct talk when direct talk is required and to weather social interactions, even conflictual ones, without undue psychic distress. To reach these goals, you'll want to learn effective communication skills and to think through how you intend to conceptualize and handle social interactions.

- *Can you evaluate which aspects of your interpersonal relationships provoke the most performance anxiety?*

_____

_____

_____

_____

PSYCHOANALYTIC TREATMENT OF A CELLIST'S ANXIETY

In therapy, the patient, a talented cellist with severe performance anxiety issues, quickly developed a dependent transference on me, yearning for my approval and not wanting to leave my office after sessions were over. He longed for my words of approval. He recalled experiences of childhood where he felt especially close to his mother, since his father frequently traveled out of town on business trips. During the early stages of his therapy he took several auditions, always experiencing such severe stage fright that he knew his chances were eliminated before he left the audition. Also, his tendonitis often flared after lengthy hours of intense practice prior to these auditions. It became evident during his therapy that each time he traveled to a new city to audition, he became angry at me for "allowing" him to leave. It felt as though I was sending him away (just as it felt that his teacher was sending him away when therapy was suggested). The only way he could express this anger (and guilt for feeling angry) was indirectly, by unconsciously sabotaging his audition.

As we worked through unconscious issues and the feelings they engendered, the patient gradually began to realize how he was re-experiencing and reenacting his past in the present. Conductors and I had become parent substitutes and authority figures whom he had to please in order to be nurtured and loved. His failure at auditions had an unconscious protective meaning for him—he could stay at "home." Also, by not winning auditions, he was punished for his perceived transgressions, such as his rivalry with his father for the favor of his mother. Before treatment, his conflict sabotaged his quest for independence and adult autonomy. After treatment, he was successful in winning a chair in a good orchestra and currently is enjoying his life without debilitating anxiety and self-doubts.

—JULIE NAGEL, *When Good Teaching Isn't Enough*

- *Do you tend to feel that your audience is sitting in judgment of you, or do you consider them friendly or at least neutral?*

_____

_____

- *Are you overly concerned about the opinions of others?*

_____

_____

- *Do people in authority—directors, gallery owners, conductors, and supervisors— tend to make you nervous?*

_____

_____

- *Do your peers tend to make you anxious?*

_____

_____

- *What one thing would you like to change about your interpersonal relationships?*

_____

_____

- *What activities or strategies would you like to incorporate into your anxiety-management program to help you feel less anxious about your interpersonal relationships?*

_____

_____

_____

_____

COUNSELING, THERAPY, AND COACHING

That a person experiences occasional butterflies before giving a speech or going onstage is not a reason to begin counseling or therapy. Even a severe case of performance anxiety may occur as a "perfectly normal" event in a performer's life, because a great deal is riding on the performance or because the performance task is more difficult than anything you've undertaken before. These are circumstances where hiring a coach who specializes in performance situations may be useful, but that's a different matter from visiting a mental health professional whose training and way of operating point him in the direction of transforming your natural anxiety into a clinically defined mental illness.

An actress with many roles under her belt may suddenly experience severe anxiety before auditioning for the lead in a TV sitcom. She can't help but realize that a hit series, one that is picked up by the networks and eventually syndicated, will lead to her full financial independence. Most members of the Screen Actors Guild earn less than $1,000 a year from their acting, but some earn millions—and on the basis of successfully handling this one audition, she may become one of those few. No wonder she feels dizzy and experiences trouble breathing! To repeat, this is not a situation that cries out for mental health counseling. If anything, it cries out for specialist help from someone who knows how to deal with performance anxiety.

That person might conceivably be a therapist who specializes in performance anxiety issues but is just as likely to be a coach, teacher, "body worker," "energy worker," or some other "alternative" therapist. It might be your family doctor, if anti-anxiety medication is part of the picture. Or you might just take care of the matter yourself. Regular bouts of mild performance anxiety and occasional bouts of severe performance anxiety can be handled in ways suggested in this book, by practicing long-term anxiety-management strategies and by having an arsenal of techniques available that you use before and during performances.

When painful past experiences still live in the present, airing that pain with a therapist can prove tremendously cathartic. For instance, a client of mine who played the trumpet still felt, in his early fifties, the sting of his high school band conductor's withering criticisms, and finally released that pain after several therapy sessions. Served up by parents, friends, peers, teachers, critics, agents, directors, or conductors, critical remarks may so profoundly get under a performer's skin that they kill his ability to perform without high anxiety. The detective work of therapy can help resolve those painful issues.

A particular experience of failure may likewise prove difficult to forget. Did you give a poor presentation at work or bomb in a college play? Did you massacre an important audition or string of auditions? Have you failed to prepare adequately for tests, recitals, and other important performances? The knowledge of our own failures can prove to be powerful secrets that we carry around with us and that manage to wound us over and over again. Letting them out in therapy may remove their sting for all time.

But what if your performance anxiety is rooted more in your formed personality than in any criticism you received or mistake you made? Is it possible to gain insight into the system when you are the system, when you are the observer and the observed? Psychotherapists argue that, with their help, people can do just that. Formerly blind to the characteristic ways that they hurt or hinder themselves, clients learn in therapy to become more psychologically minded and keenly aware of their motivations and behaviors. Even though their defenses remain intact, protecting them from their therapist's comments (which can feel accusatory), clients can, in a good therapeutic relationship, let down their guard enough to learn a great deal about themselves.

What sort of treatment might occur? From our earlier discussion of cognitive restructuring you have an idea how a cognitive-behavioral therapist might work, by identifying negative self-talk, teaching thought-stopping and thought substitution techniques, and focusing on helping you "get a grip on your mind." A psychodynamic approach (see box) can work equally well. A given therapist may specialize in working with phobias, panic attacks, and other anxiety disorders or may pursue anxiety-reduction from some specific theoretical orientation, say an existential, gestalt, humanistic, transpersonal, or self-psychological one. While all therapists are trained to diagnose according to guidelines set forth by the American Psychiatric Association, how they treat—that is, what they actually do—varies tremendously from practitioner to practitioner.

Sometimes even a single session with the right practitioner can produce important and remarkable results. Stephanie Judy writes in *Making Music For the Joy of It*: "I was treated for stage fright on a stage in front of fifty people. The therapist was a Neurolinguistic Programming (NLP) practitioner, doing a demonstration for a group of students. The improvement was immediate and it has lasted. On a scale of 10, my nervousness has gone from a paralyzing 9.9 to an acceptably anxious 3, though I still have to work at it."

Under what circumstances should a person include psychotherapy or counseling as part of her long-term anxiety-management program? Among good reasons to do so are any of the following:

1. If your symptoms or experience of distress are recurrent and severe.

2. If a family history of disturbance is burdensome to you or suggests that there may be hereditary links to your present state of distress. If you are the child of an alcoholic parent, if one of your parents committed suicide, or if there is a history of severe depression in your family, you may be more susceptible to these problems than the next person.

3. If you've identified specific issues you want to work on with a therapist. One study concluded that while there were no gender differences with regard to the amount of performance anxiety experienced by subjects, males and females differed in their self-reports about the causes of their performance anxiety. Males and females listed "loss of control" as their chief anxiety but fear of failure ranked second with males and fourth with females, while fear of rejection ranked second among females and fourth among males. Thus a woman might come into therapy with a clear idea that she wanted to work on "rejection issues" while a man might come in wanting to work on "fear of failure" issues.

4. If you use anti-anxiety medication. It is possible to use such medications without also engaging in psychotherapy but it's generally wiser to use medications in conjunction with "talk" therapy.

5. If you have the desire to work on performance-anxiety issues with someone who specializes in that sort of work. You might get a word-of-mouth recommendation from someone who performs on a regular basis; ask a voice, music, or acting teacher for suggestions; or contact a local university's counseling clinic for a referral.

Counseling can prove valuable to you as long as you actively take part in the process, bring up the issues that concern you, and work to make changes in your life. Although counseling, therapy, or coaching may not be a necessary component of your long-term anxiety-management program, it's a possibility worth considering.

- If you've previously engaged in counseling, what did you find to be its strong points?

_____

_____

_____

- What were its weak points?

_____

_____

_____

- What would you look for in a counselor or psychotherapist?

_____

_____

_____

- If you haven't engaged in psychotherapy before, have you felt the need or desire to do so but found yourself resistant?

_____

_____

_____

- If so, can you identify the reasons for that resistance?

_____

_____

_____

- What do you suppose would constitute a good therapeutic relationship?

_____

_____

_____

- Name some symptoms or warning signs that might lead you to seek out counseling or therapy.

_____

_____

_____

FEAR OF MEMORY LAPSE

Many players memorize only through their fingertips. This works—while playing at home. But the moment the player is exposed to any stresses and strains, i.e., an examination, audition or public performance, the fingertips do not have the necessary physiologic authority to carry him through. Cures:

1. A release from physical blockages.

2. The division of each piece into sections.

3. The identification of the notes within each section through singing, and miming with the rhythmic pulse before playing it on the violin.

4. The alive lead of the left-hand control with the bowing arm responding.

5. The elimination of the "self" through a systematic training of the mind.

The learning of a piece through the total coordination of mind and body not only helps the player release physical tensions when on stage, but also enables him to give full vent to his musical imagination.

*—*KATO HAVAS, *Stage Fright: Its Causes and Cures*

DISCIPLINE PRACTICE

Pianist and conductor Vladimir Ashkenazy reflected on how musicians can effectively manage performance anxiety: "Working hard at practice is also the best defense I know against pre-concert nervousness. That nervousness can never be entirely eliminated but it can be psychologically prepared for by convincing yourself that you have done all the homework necessary for a solid performance and that everything will work out all right." Or as Spencer Tracy succinctly put it, "First of all, learn your lines." Practice and rehearsal can be great anxiety reducers.

Practice means considerably more than the repetitive playing of your repertoire or the repetitive rehearsing of responses to interview questions. It also means practicing techniques and strategies that help you present yourself more confidently and fearlessly. Kato Havas in *Stage Fright: Its Causes and Cures*, for instance, analyzed the fears that violinists typically encounter. Among them are a fear of dropping the violin, of a trembling bowing arm, of being out of tune, of high positions and shifts, of not being loud enough, and of not being fast enough. To combat each fear, Havas suggests certain exercises and "cures," as for instance with respect to the fear of a memory lapse (see box). The procedures that Havas describes help performers deeply learn their music deeply, because deep learning breeds confidence and reduces anxiety.

Similar procedures can help actors learn a script (see box), speechmakers learn a speech, or test-takers learn test material. Why is this deep learning so important? Think back to Suzuki's definition of anxiety as essentially an incomplete knowledge of a given situation. The more we know about the material we're going to present, the deeper our connection to that material, and the more complete our knowledge, the less anxious we feel. If we take the time to read about the history of the period in which our play is set, for instance, we will create a reservoir of information that may manifest itself in some gesture we adopt but, more importantly, in the confidence we feel as we inhabit our role.

It also helps to identify anything that you fear about your material, discipline, or instrument. For instance, if you make oral presentations, do you fear that the quality of your speaking voice or something about your posture is reducing the effectiveness of your speeches? If you are an actor, do you fear that your accent is losing you roles? If you are a singer, do you fear your ability to act opera? Each of these challenges can be met if you include meeting them as part of your practice regimen. You will want to take measures to actually correct the problem—by taking an acting class if you doubt the strength of your acting, by working with a dialect coach if you want to get rid of your accent, and so on—and create exercises to dispel the fears themselves, so that residual fears don't linger and unconsciously provoke anxiety.

ABSORBING A SCRIPT

I opened the workshop by saying, "I think I have found a way to learn a script in one reading." Then I gave these instructions: "Read the script through slowly on as deep a level as possible, seeing and feeling everything that takes place. If it is in a restaurant, be in that restaurant. See and feel and hear and smell what it is like. Create your own version of the restaurant. If you are aware that you're thinking, 'That's a long speech,' or if you find yourself wondering what happens next, then you have stopped feeling and started thinking. Stop reading, breathe deeply, and go back to feeling the script again." By the end of the scene everyone was joining in and even correcting small details. There was tremendous certainty and enthusiasm, and I began to get excited about our success.

—ANN BREBNER, Setting Free the Actor

• *What is your current practice and rehearsal routine?*

_____

_____

_____

_____

• *Is it below average, adequate, or excellent?*

_____

_____

- *Have you noticed a relationship between a lack of practice and an increase in performance anxiety? Can you describe that relationship?*

_____

_____

_____

_____

- *What sort of ideal practice routine would you like to set up for yourself?*

_____

_____

_____

_____

- *How will you go about learning your material in a deeper way? Can you map out a plan?*

_____

_____

_____

_____

_____

- *What about your discipline, material, or instrument scares you? What measures do you need to take to rid yourself of these specific fears?*

_____

_____

_____

_____

_____

DISCIPLINE UNDERSTANDING

In addition to learning your material deeply, you will also want to gain a thorough understanding of your particular discipline. If you delve deeply into the history, theories, and techniques of your discipline, if you work long and hard to gain mastery of technique and material, you will enrich your performance experience while simultaneously reducing your experience of anxiety. You will begin to understand the music you're performing in multiple ways, not just as notes in a score but as a piece that connects to a history and a tradition. You will begin to understand the role you're playing not just in terms of the character's words and behaviors but as the character connects to similar characters in a long theater tradition. This deepened learning is both exciting and calming.

Prodigious and even amazing feats of mind and memory are the fruits of a richer relationship with the discipline in which you work. Like a novelist who carries around in his mind everything he needs to know about his characters and who never worries about losing track of them, or like Mozart, composing different pieces simultaneously, you can, if you get deeply connected to your discipline and your material, produce miracles of memory. Michael Raucheisen, piano accompanist to the violin virtuoso Fritz Kreisler, told the following story:

> When we arrived in Tokyo we found that the Japanese attached special importance to sonatas. During the eight performances at the Imperial Theatre of Tokyo, Kreisler was expected to perform virtually the entire existing sonata literature. Kreisler had, of course, not prepared for such an unusual situation. Imagine, eight different programs! And yet, one—I repeat—one rehearsal sufficed and Kreisler played the sonatas which he had not had on his repertoire for many years by heart, without a single flaw of memory, before this select international public. "I never have any trouble remembering," Kreisler said. "I know the music so well that I do not even keep the violin part. I get it into my head with its accompaniment."

To really fathom your discipline and to learn by heart are excellent goals. An understanding this deep has a tremendously calming influence on you and produces performance situations very different from the anxiety-filled situations you experience when you know your discipline and material shallowly and superficially.

• *Describe what "deepening your relationship" with your discipline might mean.*

_____

_____

_____

_____

• *Does your description suggest concrete actions you might take to foster that deepening?*

_____

_____

_____

_____

• *Is your relationship to your discipline a loving one? Describe the ways in which it is and/or is not.*

_____

_____

_____

_____

• *How can you enter into a more loving relationship with your discipline?*

_____

_____

_____

_____

PREPARATION

Everything we've discussed so far may fairly be thought of as preparation. Even taking it in its narrowest sense, "preparation" should include more than getting your clothes pressed, thinking about your character one last time, or organizing the note cards for your speech. It should include all of the following:

- Taking care of the business end of the event, which includes such things as mailing out announcements to people on your mailing list, creating interview opportunities, personally inviting the people you want to attend, and so on, insofar as these tasks fall on your shoulders.

- Arriving at the point of feeling satisfied about the nature and quality of the material you will perform; or else coming to terms with the ways in which the material falls short and detaching enough that its problems don't make you anxious.

- Arriving, through practice and rehearsal, at feeling confident about your readiness to perform; or, if you aren't ready, detaching enough that your lack of readiness doesn't add to your feelings of anxiety.

- Walking yourself mentally through the performance. Part of the process of effectively preparing for a performance is picturing it in your mind's eye. Try rehearsing, detail by detail, the whole event, beginning prior to your arrival and including the time after you leave the venue.

Apart from the other benefits that mental rehearsing affords, it serves to desensitize you to the performance environment. As Ann Seagrave explains in *Free from Fears*:

> *Imagery desensitization gives us an opportunity to think or imagine a situation the way we would like it to occur. Instead of imagining that a catastrophe befalls you, imagine that you will feel comfortable and secure in the situation, filled with confidence about your skills. If, as you are doing this, anxiety creeps into your conscious thoughts, stop the imaginary event, use your relaxation technique, and then begin again. Depending on the event, it may take days to go all the way through the exercise free of anxiety, but rest assured that you will reach the point of being able to think through or imagine a feared situation without having an anxiety reaction.*

Research conducted by Donald Meichenbaum has shown how the use of mental imaging can become a technique of great power and versatility. When you mentally rehearse, you provide yourself with the chance to practice your coping skills and anxiety-management techniques. You bring the performance to mind, notice your own negative thoughts or anxiety reactions, and stop everything in order to try a technique out right then and there. Mental imaging provides you with the miraculous opportunity to work through performances in the privacy of your own mind.

Each performer will naturally create her own idiosyncratic preparation plan. To take one example, Stephanie Judy recommends that musicians play their whole program at least once a day; arrange some dry runs that simulate the concert hall experience, maybe in front of an audience of their friends; rehearse in the hall where they will be performing, if that's possible; and practice until they are really satisfied with their program. These rehearsal preparations, including mental imaging of the performance situation and the disciplined practice of anxiety-management techniques, reduce anxiety in the days and weeks leading up to the event and help ensure your readiness at curtain time.

- *Try using mental imaging for an upcoming performance. When you've completed the process, describe what you learned from the experience.*

_____

_____

_____

_____

_____

_____

- *Describe your complete preparation plan, including the anxiety-management strategies you mean to acquire, how and when you'll practice them, how you mean to prepare for each performance, how you intend to deepen your understanding of your material and discipline, and so on.*

_____

_____

_____

_____

_____

_____

_____

_____

_____

WORKING STEP BY STEP

We've covered a lot of ground. To put together a long-term anxiety-management program that addresses all of the issues we've discussed will prove quite a prodigious feat. But you can accomplish this feat by working step-by-step. Certain things you'll want to do on a daily basis, like practicing your favorite stress-reduction techniques or using mental imaging for your next performance. Some things may occur regularly but not on a daily basis, like visiting with a therapist or coach. Other things, like writing "dear critic" letters, will occur only as needed. Construct a program that takes these various elements into account and seriously begin your work.

Let me end by quoting the concert pianist and career counselor Peggy Salkind. Her words help remind us why we prefer to accept some measure of anxiety and bravely perform rather than free ourselves of anxiety by abandoning performance. She writes:

> _Musical performance is a celebration of aliveness. Each time I sit down and play the piano I relive the most poignant emotions and experiences of my life. They are always present in the music. During those moments I also explore new avenues of feeling and deepen my philosophical perceptions. I know now that music is a reservoir of feelings containing the ultimate distillation of love. That awareness has guided my life. Music enables me to open my heart to my mortal brothers and sisters and to assimilate the beauty and terror of existence._
>
> _Piano performance is not without nervousness and anxiety. Those aspects reflect the existential dilemma of being an artist and of being human. The player no sooner chooses how to execute a particular passage than he or she is faced with the decision of how to follow up on that choice. And so it continues from second to second and phrase to phrase. The sense of risk-taking is tremendous. But so is the exhilarating sensation of aliveness. In confluence with the score, I create and recreate myself in each succeeding moment. I learn that to be human is not to be perfect but to persevere in giving myself over and over again to the dynamic energy of the universe of which music is an integral vibration. My humanity is reborn with every breath and every note._

That you've finished reading this book is an excellent sign of your readiness and willingness to deal with the performance anxiety in your life. The next step is doing the work: learning anxiety-management techniques, practicing them, trying them out in the world, slowly but surely transforming yourself into a less anxious person, and presenting fearlessly. If you do the work, the payoffs will be tremendous: richer experiences in front of audiences, renewed joy in performing, and a career unhampered by performance anxiety. I wish you great luck!—and may all of your frights be little ones.

EPILOGUE

We've covered a lot of ground. It makes sense, here at the end, to tease out the most important points about handling performance anxiety. If you make an effort in the following four areas, you will significantly decrease the performance anxiety in your life.

• Get a grip on your mind

We spent many chapters looking at the way that the mind makes anxiety, by turning shadows into major threats and by trying to hide from reality through linguistic dodges. Your mind does these things insofar as you let it. You must take charge of what you think. If you do not get a grip on your mind, it will do what it is built to do—scan for threats and make anxiety.

You get a grip on your mind by being honest about what you're thinking and honest about why you're thinking those thoughts. You can't resolve an inner conflict, exorcise old ghosts of shame and guilt, let go of an inchoate fear about a poor performance leading to your annihilation, or otherwise clean mental house until you will yourself to look in the attic. You don't have to do this in a formal way, by adhering to some program or by keeping a certain kind of journal. You do this by entering into a permanent relationship with yourself, characterized by the demand that you know what you're thinking and why you're thinking it.

• Learn to detach

Just as you want to get a grip on your mind, you want to get a grip on your life. Your goal is to be fully present in the moment while detaching from the pressure to do anything but walk your own path and live by your own principles. Your upcoming performance is not a test, not a hurdle, not a threat, and not a marker of who you are; it is simply something you do on the path you have chosen to walk. The integrity of your path is the larger matter, your upcoming performance the much smaller matter.

You learn to detach by feeling compassion for human folly and by articulating your convictions. You adopt a general attitude at once fierce, because you have confidence about what you're doing, and philosophical, because you understand about mortality, human nature, and the gods of whimsy. When you perform, you are *right there*, because you value presence, but you are also *calm and free*, because you know the place of your performance in the bigger picture.

• Be prepared

You want to be prepared on many levels. You want to be prepared with respect to particular material, on the order of knowing your lines or knowing your fingering. You want to be prepared as a performer, that is, as someone who understands that performance is part of your life and that you need to stand ready to perform "at the drop of a hat." You want to be prepared on the level of personality, as someone who has grown wise, confident, compassionate, self-directing, and otherwise "all that you can be."

You prepare your material by taking whatever time is required to learn your material deeply. You prepare yourself as a performer by looking for performance opportunities, rather than ducking them; by thinking through how you want to present yourself when you perform; and by holding yourself ready to perform as a doctor holds himself ready to administer medical assistance. You prepare your personality by doing whatever work is required, perhaps including seeking a therapist, counselor, or coach, to move yourself in the direction that you have consciously mapped out for yourself.

• Come armed

Even if you manage to become the confident, detached, philosophical, self-trusting person that I hope you'll become, you'll still want to acquire an arsenal of self-help strategies that you know have a good chance of reducing your experience of anxiety. At a minimum you'll want to learn and practice one deep-breathing technique, to physically release anxiety, and one cognitive restructuring technique, to mentally release anxiety. As ten-second centering combines both elements, that might prove the best arrow in your quiver.

You own these techniques only through practice and use. You can't lose weight or gain muscle tone by thinking about dieting or thinking about exercising. It's time to make a commitment to acquiring some simple, solid anxiety-management techniques by learning them, practicing them, and using them. All of the strategies and techniques described in Chapters 13 and 14 are available to you, as is the long-term plan for managing anxiety outlined in Chapters 15 and 16. The ball is now in your court. Good luck!

APPENDIX

Eric Maisel Resources

The following books of mine supplement the ideas and strategies provided in this book.

Coaching the Artist Within: Advice for Writers, Actors, Visual Artists & Musicians From America's Foremost Creativity Coach (New World Library)

Self-coaching lessons, exercises, and anecdotes about creativity-coaching work with clients. Offers a complete program for developing the habits that make creating an everyday practice, and teaches you how to become your own creativity coach and transform your relationship with the creative process.

The Ten-Second Pause: Transform Stress, Tension and Anxiety with One Breath, Anywhere, Anytime (Sourcebooks)

Teaches—through lessons, exercises, and anecdotes—the centering technique devised by the author called ten-second centering.

Everyday Creative: 30 Ways to Wake Up Your Inner Artist (Red Wheel)

A set of easy-to-use daily reminders in deck form.

Everyday Smart: 30 Ways to Spark Your Inner Genius (Red Wheel)

A set of easy-to-use daily reminders in deck form.

Everyday Calm: 30 Ways to Soothe Your Inner Beast (Red Wheel)
  A set of easy-to-use daily reminders in deck form.

A Writer's Paris: 60 Lessons from the City of Light (Writer's Digest Books)
  Lessons about the creative life set against a Parisian background.

The Van Gogh Blues: The Creative Person's Path Through Depression (Rodale)
  An investigation of the existential depression and meaning crises that regularly afflict creative people, and strategies for handling these pernicious problems. Emphasis is on the idea of creating as a meaning-making activity and what happens when a creative person can't make or maintain sufficient meaning.

Fearless Creating: A Step-By-Step Guide to Starting and Completing Your Work of Art (Tarcher/Penguin)
  An examination of the stages of the creative process—nurturing the wish to create, choosing creative projects, starting a project, working to completion, and showing and selling the work—with a focus on handling the particular anxieties associated with each stage. Many tips and exercises provided.

A Life in the Arts: Practical Guidance and Inspiration for Creative and Performing Artists (Tarcher/Penguin)
  An examination of the practical and emotional challenges that working artists face, organized into three interrelated areas: personality challenges, creative work challenges, and marketplace challenges ("personality, work, and world"). Many tips and exercises provided.

The Creativity Book: A Year's Worth of Inspiration and Guidance (Tarcher/Penguin)
  Designed as a year-long program of weekly lessons and exercises, *The Creativity Book* explores such vital issues as forgiveness and self-forgiveness, mindfulness, creative exploration, truthfulness, ambitiousness, discipline, risk-taking, resiliency, and planning and scheduling.

Write Mind: 299 Things Writers Should Never Say to Themselves (and What They Should Say Instead) (Tarcher/Penguin)
  A cognitive approach to overcoming writing blocks is presented in Write Mind. Using the device of paired sentences, one a "wrong thing" that a writer might say to himself and the second the "right thing" he might prefer to say, writers are helped to understand how to identify and overcome negative and limiting self-talk.

Deep Writing: Seven Principles That Bring Ideas to Life (Tarcher/Penguin)
  Seven principles of importance to all creators are presented: hushing the mind, holding the intention to create, making creative choices, honoring the creative process, befriending one's creative work, evaluating one's creative work, and doing whatever is necessary to achieve and sustain a creative life.

Affirmations for Artists (Tarcher/Penguin)

The affirmation process is taught, 200 issues of importance to creative individuals are identified and described, and an affirmation is provided for each issue. Issues examined include achieving balance, cultivating an audience, finding community, building confidence, honing craft, surviving criticism, and maintaining discipline.

Living the Writer's Life: A Complete Self-Help Guide (Watson-Guptill)

Subjects covered include a writer's work, a writer's education, a writer's craft, a writer's personality, a writer's challenges, a writer's strengths, a writer's relationships, a writer's world, and a writer's career. Provocative questions and solicited pieces from writers and editors (for instance, on the psychological relationship between editor and writer) highlight each chapter.

Sleep Thinking: The Revolutionary Program That Helps You Solve Problems, Reduce Stress, and Increase Creativity While You Sleep (Adams Media)

Presents an eighteen-step program for using deep (NREM) sleep as a time to solve problems, including creative problems, and argues that if creative people will go to bed wondering about their work, they will wake up each morning ready to create. Supported by recent scientific evidence, the Sleep Thinking Program helps creative people hold the intention to create, increase their creative output, and deepen their work.

The Art of the Book Proposal: From Focused Idea to Finished Proposal (Tarcher/Penguin)

Explores the main elements of the nonfiction book proposal, the nonfiction writer's primary selling tool, and talks writers through the process of moving from vague idea through the many changes that naturally occur until a focused book idea finally takes shape.

About the Author

Eric Maisel, Ph.D., is the author of more than twenty-five works of fiction and nonfiction. His nonfiction titles include *Coaching the Artist Within*, *Fearless Creating*, *The Van Gogh Blues*, *The Creativity Book*, *Performance Anxiety*, and *A Writer's Paris*. A columnist for *Art Calendar* magazine and a regular contributor to *Artist's Sketchbook* magazine, *Writer's Digest* magazine, and *The Writer* magazine, Maisel is a San Francisco–based creativity coach and creativity coach trainer who presents keynote addresses and workshops nationally and internationally.

Maisel holds undergraduate degrees in philosophy and psychology, master's degrees in counseling and creative writing, and a doctorate in counseling psychology; is a California licensed marriage and family therapist; and founded and wrote *Callboard* magazine's "Staying Sane in the Theater" column. Maisel has presented at venues as diverse as The American Psychological Association annual conference, the Romance Writers of America annual conference, the San Francisco Conservatory of Music, the American Conservatory Theater, the North Carolina School of the Arts, and the Paris Writers Workshop.

Visit www.ericmaisel.com to learn more about Dr. Maisel; or write the author at ericmaisel@hotmail.com.

JOURNAL